WHAT EVERY WOMAN NEEDS TO KNOW BEFORE (AND AFTER) SHE GETS INVOLVED WITH MEN & MONEY

WHAT EVERY WOMAN NEEDS TO KNOW BEFORE (AND AFTER) SHE GETS INVOLVED WITH MEN & MONEY

Lois G. Forer

RAWSON ASSOCIATES
New York
MAXWELL MACMILLAN CANADA
Toronto
MAXWELL MACMILLAN INTERNATIONAL
New York   Oxford   Singapore   Sydney

Lyrics from "Mommy Number Four," by Mae Richard, from the off-Broadway musical *Cut the Ribbons* reprinted by permission of Mae Richard.

Rawson Associates
Macmillan Publishing Company
866 Third Avenue
New York, NY 10022

Maxwell Macmillan Canada, Inc.
1200 Eglinton Avenue East
Suite 200
Don Mills, Ontario M3C 3N1

Macmillan Publishing Company is part of the Maxwell Communication Group of Companies.

Macmillan books are available at special discounts for bulk purchases for sales promotions, premiums, fund-raising, or educational use. For details, contact:

Special Sales Director
Macmillan Publishing Company
866 Third Avenue
New York, NY 10022

Packaged by March Tenth, Inc.

Designed by Stanley S. Drate / Folio Graphics Co. Inc.

Library of Congress Cataloging-in-Publication Data

Forer, Lois G., 1914–
    What every woman needs to know before (and after) she gets involved with men & money / by Lois G. Forer.
        p.   cm.
    Includes index.
    ISBN 0-89256-360-5
        1. Women—Legal status, laws, etc.—United States—Popular works.
    I. Title.
    KF478.Z9F67   1993
    346.7301'34—dc20
    [347.306134]   93-36188
                                                                 CIP
10 9 8 7 6 5 4 3 2 1

Printed in the United States of America

ACKNOWLEDGMENTS

Many authors are fortunate enough to have the benefit of advice and counsel from their colleagues. A trial judge, however, has a lonely life. Trial judges rarely have the time or opportunity to discuss the problems they encounter in litigants' lives with fellow judges, or with many other people—thus this book. It is the product of my experiences and my concerns for the women who came before me for so many years.

I am most grateful to my friend and agent Emilie Jacobson for her faith in this undertaking, and to my publisher, Eleanor Rawson, whose advice and suggestions have been of inestimable value. I am deeply indebted to my husband Morris L. Forer for his unfailing encouragement.

I thank Mae Richard for permission to reprint her lyric from *Cut the Ribbons*.

CONTENTS

PART 1: TO YOU, THE READER OF THIS BOOK

1 Why I Wrote This Book   3

2 Why You Need This Book   14

3 The Five Commandments Every Woman
Needs to Know   21

PART 2: LOVE AND FAMILY

4 Before You Decide to have a Relationship   29

5 Before You Decide to Change Your Name   54

6 Before You Decide to Marry   64

7 Before You Decide to Become a Mother   87

8 Before You Decide to Divorce   112

9   Before You Settle the Divorce   *136*

10   Before You Decide to Marry Again   *157*

11   Before You Go to Court   *177*

PART 3: WORK AND MONEY

12   Before You Take a Job   *205*

13   Before You Reach a Dead End at Work   *224*

14   Before You Join an Organization: Stop, Look, and Listen!   *243*

15   Before You Buy a Home   *259*

PART 4: THE SECOND HALF

16   Before You Make a Will   *275*

17   Before the Autumn Years   *298*

PART 5: FOR EVERY WOMAN

18   Final Words   *319*

Notes   *324*

Appendix   *330*

Index   *333*

PART I

TO YOU, THE READER OF THIS BOOK

1
WHY I WROTE THIS BOOK

"Why didn't I know this before?" was the constant complaint of my female clients during the many years I practiced law. It was also an anguished cry I frequently heard from women litigants who appeared before me during the sixteen years I was a trial judge in Philadelphia. There, I saw all kinds of women: white; black; Hispanic; Asian; and Native American. They were young and old, rich and poor, educated and underprivileged. What they had in common was greater than their differences. All were in distress. All looked to the law for justice. Most were disappointed. Most received neither justice nor fair treatment.

They were not a select group. Their cases were randomly assigned to me. They constituted a fair, representative picture of American women today: all races; all economic and social conditions; all family situations—married, divorced, single mothers, grandmothers, employed, unemployed, welfare recipients, retirees, healthy, and ill. Their problems were also representative of the problems of injustice for which American women vainly seek redress in the courts.

All believed, with much justification, that if they had known how the law really operates they would not have found themselves in such unfair and disastrous predicaments.

My clients were not stupid, impulsive people. Many were

highly educated professional women. They used their good common sense and their training in most business and social activities. They acted with wisdom and forethought. But in their most critical relationships with men, as lovers, husbands, fathers, sons, employers, and partners, they proceeded under false assumptions because they were unaware of the practical legal consequences of their actions.

My clients and the litigants who appeared in court before me as civil plaintiffs and defendants, and as defendants in criminal court, assumed that the law would provide them with the same protections and rights it provides for men. It does not.

Despite gender-neutral statutes, affirmative action programs, and the Constitution, the law in action, as it operates in courts throughout the land, on a day-to-day basis, in civil, criminal, and family courts, does not give women the fair treatment they seek. With the feminization of poverty, women are doubly disadvantaged before the law, not only because they are females, but because they usually are less well off economically than most of the men they come up against.

When I was a practicing lawyer I tried to help my clients use the law to their benefit, and when the law was against them, I showed them how to avoid the legal process. I would try to work out some kind of solution, even though it often was far from satisfactory.

But during the long, frustrating years when I was a judge all too frequently there was nothing I could do to help the women litigants who appeared before me in civil, family, and criminal court. All too often the law compelled *unjust* decisions. By following the law, I was required to enter verdicts that were manifestly unfair. The law impelled me to preside over injustice. I felt betrayed by my calling.

All rational people act on certain tacit assumptions. They make sensible calculations about what society considers acceptable behavior and the remedies they believe will be available when those expectations are not met. In the United States the ultimate arbiter of conduct and the force that provides both punishment *and* redress is not the family, the community, or the church, but the law. And it is the law that fails most women in their personal, commercial, and family problems.

Law and the legal system have a preeminent position in American government. Authority is not based on a hereditary monarchy or military might, but on the rule of law. It is the underlying basis of our social order.

The administration of this sacred law is entrusted to a special group of people—lawyers and judges. They spend years studying to be admitted to the bar. They must pass examinations and be certified as having good characters before they are licensed to practice law and represent clients. A judge is a lawyer who has been appointed or elected to be a public official. Judges take a solemn oath to obey the law and provide equal justice to all litigants. Many times these mandates are mutually inconsistent. Adhering to the strict code of the law denies equal justice to many litigants, particularly women. Judges are invested with awesome powers: to deprive people of their lives, their liberty, their property, their spouses, their children.

After I left the bench, I examined those cases in which everything was done properly but the results were tragically wrong. The lawyers were competent and well prepared; they presented the evidence properly, I believe; the witnesses testified truthfully; and I, the judge, faithfully followed the law. But the verdicts were wrong. The litigants who had been unjustly treated were women, children, and the very elderly. It was not the fault of the lawyers, the litigant, the juries, or the judge, but the law itself. I discovered the endemic bias against women in our law that is supposed to provide equal justice for all.

Many times—as I mentioned—I saw women litigants worsted in the courts, despite my best efforts, because of their inferior economic position.

◆ The men and corporations opposing them had vastly more money. They could retain top-flight lawyers; they could pay for expensive expert witnesses; they could engage in protracted discovery; and they could appeal indefinitely.

◆ All too often the women litigants had very limited finances or were at, or near, the poverty level. Their lawyers were no match for the counsel of their opponents.

◆ The women could not endure the lengthy procedures either financially or emotionally. The race in the courts is not to the swift but to the litigant with the greater staying power.

◆ But even in the unusual instances when female litigants had resources equal to those of their male adversaries and had emotional stamina, they lost because the legal system is based on *male perceptions of what law and justice should be, and how a "reasonable man" would act in the various conflicts of life.*

This legal test, on which the entire common law is based, is predicated on the perceptions and responses of men. This test is now often phrased as the "reasonable person" test. But this new, benign, gender-neutral phraseology is simply a camouflage for the old male standard.

The standard of fault in negligence cases is what a reasonable man would or would not do under the circumstances. Whether the phrase reasonable man or reasonable person is used makes little difference when all the legal precedents are based on what *a man's reactions would be.* Most women confronted by an oncoming car freeze rather than jump to safety. Most women seeing a child in danger leap from the safety of the curb and rush into the path of a speeding truck to rescue that child.

In criminal cases the issue of self-defense, or in rape cases, consent to intercourse, is based on what a reasonable *person* would do under those circumstances. The response of a *woman*, physically smaller than her assailant and terrified, is very different from the response of a *man.*

These differences in response can result in a woman's failure to recover for injuries and a man's acquittal in a criminal case.

The myth that American law provides equal protection for women is dangerous. Myth is not fact. On the contrary it is a fictional presentation of history designed to promote a particular view of society. Equal protection of the laws, a phrase enshrined in the Fourteenth Amendment to the U.S. Constitution, is a myth that persists in the face of blatant discrimination against women.

When individuals base their actions on myths rather than facts they are bound to be disappointed. For many American women there is now widespread disillusionment and the plaintive cry, "If only I had known *before* . . . I would have acted differently."

The myth our mothers and grandmothers lived by was that if they were good, sweet, and faithful they would get married and live happily ever after. Most of them did get married and lived ever after with the same spouse. But no one knows how happy they were or how many women would have made other choices if they had not been under the spell of this popular mythology.

In the 1990s women of all ages have relegated this myth to the attic with their outgrown teddy bears and dolls. Today, many women believe that at long last they can have marriage, children, and a career for which they are qualified. They believe that they will be compensated and advanced at the same rate as their male colleagues. And they expect to be treated with dignity by their mates, employers, and fellow workers.

What most women want in the 1990s is *what women have always wanted and what most men have considered to be the natural expectations and rights of every man:* love, marriage, children, satisfying and adequately compensated work, and respect. In the past women did not dare to hope that all these wishes could be fulfilled. They settled for what they could obtain.

Men have always considered these desires among the inalienable rights of Americans. The fundamental difference between the expectations of men and women was that men did not have to choose between marriage and career or between fatherhood and work. They demanded both. And they expected to be compensated at the going wage rate and to be treated with respect and dignity by their fellow workers.

Today, despite many changes to their advantage, women are

under the spell of a dangerous myth: the myth that the law will provide them with the same remedies and protections it offers to men. When they turn to the law for redress in actions concerning men and money, they often learn that equal protection is not a fact, but an illusion.

It has long been my belief that women can come to protect themselves in such situations only as they are helped to understand fully where the law malfunctions for them. *Thus—this book!*

I believe that women and men can live together in happiness when there are mutual respect and fair treatment of each other and without domination or deceit by either party. I believe that love and marriage is possible and desirable for all those who choose it.

This is not another male-bashing volume. It does not view heterosexual relations as male dominance, but as an equal and normal part of life. Nor is this book another antifeminist tract. I believe the women's movement has had a beneficent, although limited, effect on both women and men. Nor do I subscribe to the cryptoantifeminism of those like the writer Doris Lessing who blame the women's movement for women's ills.

This book is not concerned with male psyches, nor with the purported emotional differences between the sexes. I do not admire the mythic Iron John, seeking some atavistic world of male violence, nor his counterpart, a fictional silken Susan who seeks a never-never land of gentle submissiveness and a cocoon of infantilized protection.

Many sociologists and psychologists argue about whether women are psychically the same as men, or whether society has created differences between them. This debate makes interesting dinner table conversation but is really irrelevant to *your* problems. Either view can be used to prejudice you. In the early nineteenth century the French philosopher known as Le Père Enfant presented the idea of a *couple-pape*. The male pope would stand for reflection and the female pope for sentiment. This was supposed to empower women. It did not. Similarly, the gender-neutral jurisprudence of the past half century was intended to liberate women. It did not.

Rather than seeing hostility and mistrust between men and women, I prefer the Eastern concept of yin and yang, the complementary and necessary existence of two equal genders to create a whole society. As the Chinese say, "Women hold up half the sky." In the United States we hold up more than half of the sky and the land.

Economists are just beginning to discover that in many communities, especially in sub-Saharan Africa, women provide most of the food and commerce as well as child bearing, child rearing, and care of the sick and elderly. Studies by the Rockefeller Foundation reveal that the quickest and cheapest way to improve underdeveloped countries is to educate the women. Educators know that when one educates a man, one has educated a single individual. When a woman is educated, a whole family is educated.

Despite these proven facts, women are still ignored in medical and social research. Housework, child care, and care of sick family members are not counted in the gross national product or the national wealth. Women are still given less treatment for heart ailments than men. Although AIDS is one of the five leading causes of death in American women, women are not included in many treatment programs. The litany of inequalities of treatment of women in the United States is endless.

One book cannot begin to correct these overwhelming problems. Massive political, economic, and social changes in America will be required. It will take time, effort, education, and money.

This book has a less ambitious but achievable goal. It is intended to show *you*, the reader, how to avoid the most common kinds of discrimination against women that occur in our daily lives and in our courts in every city and every county in this country every day.

This book does not, like so many books, blame the female victim by telling her to raise her self-esteem, to love herself, to remake her psyche or her body. Injustices befall women who have self-esteem, who are physically beautiful, and psychically sound.

They occur not because of what the woman does but because of the legal system.

Nor does this book rail against backlash or assume that there is a war against women. Instead, it tells you how to deal with the problems of everyday life so that you will not be shortchanged in your dealings with men.

Although this is a guide to living for American women, it does not simply deal in generalities. Like a legal casebook, the kind of text that law students study in every American law school, or a psychiatry textbook, it teaches by giving real life examples of average women. It also provides a simple set of rules—*Five Commandments*—*that any woman can follow.* It shows you how average women have successfully coped with common problems when they obeyed these commandments and how average women were the losers because they did not follow these commandments before they entered into the ordinary trans-actions of daily life.

Although each woman is unique and every case is different from all others, there are common situations that most women experience. The common law itself is built on the principle that similar situations will be treated in like fashion. I detail the expe-riences of these women because you will probably encounter not precisely the same but very similar situations throughout your life. And as Aesop observed almost three millenia ago, "Example is the best precept."

These stories of women are not hypothetical cases dreamed up by an academic, but real life cases involving women I have known, women whom I represented when I was a practicing attorney, and women who appeared in court before me when I was a judge. In order to preserve their privacy I have changed their names and some immaterial facts. If a woman was an engi-neer, I call her an accountant. If she had two children, I give her three. All these real women who are essentially private persons are given only first names. When I refer to women who are public figures such as Eleanor Roosevelt, Gloria Steinem, or Simone de Beauvoir I use their full names.

Sociologists often scorn evidence based on real life stories as "anecdotal." They prefer statistics. They count the *number* of orgasms for example. They do not ask how *satisfying* they are.

When our remote ancestors sat by a fire in a cave, they undoubtedly told stories. We can only surmise what these stories were. They were probably tales of brave and clever women and men who outwitted the predatory beasts lurking in the forests. We do know that they illustrated the world they saw in the remarkable cave paintings in the South of France and in Spain, and even in remote Australia.

I, too, illustrate the rules with stories of both wise and foolish women from whom you can learn how to outwit your adversaries and how to overcome the inequities in American society. Some of the women you will meet in this book achieved their goals because they acted wisely and with forethought. Many of the other women in this book suffered crushing disappointments and personal and financial losses.

They were not ignorant or naive. They knew that one in every two marriages will end in divorce. But what many women did not know was that after divorce they would be left with the care of their children and very little, if any, money.

They knew that they had the right to attend all institutions of learning. They did not know of the invisible glass ceiling that would prevent them, regardless of their qualifications, from rising to positions of authority and commensurate pay, nor did they know that if they tried to cope with both career and children they might be relegated to the "mommy track."

They knew that they had the right to be paid the same wages as men for the same work. But they did not know that women earn 68 cents for every dollar earned by a man.

Many of these women were employed and paid their taxes. But they did not know that fewer than 40 percent of working women have benefits that would cover them on a six-week unpaid family leave.

Their Social Security payments were deducted from their earnings every week, but they did not know that the Social Security system provides less protection for them than for their colleagues because they, like most women, had to interrupt their employment to bear children, to care for them, and/or for elderly relatives, and thus accumulated fewer quarters of earnings.

They paid their income taxes like their male fellow workers but were given a tax credit of only $2,400 a year for care of one child, and $4,800 a year for care of two or more children. The average cost of child care is $4,500 a year per child. However, business executives can deduct half the cost of their often lavish business meals and business entertaining expenses. Are meals and entertainment more important to civilization than bringing up children? Apparently! Nor did women know that in their quest for fair treatment, they would in most instances be thwarted by the law to which they turned for justice.

Even though every college, university, and law school has courses on women's studies, and many have esoteric courses such as women in Scripture and anger in women, they do not provide female students with the facts they need to know in their everyday lives. Like most academic programs, these courses review the past; they analyze and psychoanalyze historical personages and characters in novels. They discuss decisions of the appellate courts. But they do not explain the ordinary problems that most women encounter and the legal and practical consequences of the decisions most women make.

This book is the fulfillment of a promise I made to my female clients and the women litigants who appeared in court before me when I was a judge. I told them that I could not change the educational programs in American schools and universities. I could not change the law, even when I was on the bench. But I promised them that I would write a book setting forth in clear and unmistakable language what every woman needs to know before she:

- ◆ Enters into a relationship with a man
- ◆ Changes her name for his
- ◆ Marries
- ◆ Becomes a mother
- ◆ Divorces
- ◆ Seeks custody of her children

- ◆ Remarries
- ◆ Goes to court
- ◆ Takes a job
- ◆ Faces a dead end at work
- ◆ Joins an organization
- ◆ Buys property
- ◆ Makes a will
- ◆ Arrives at the autumn season

This book is addressed to every female from the age of fifteen to seventy-something and beyond. It tells her of the likely legal results of her various choices and how to avoid outcomes in which she will be the loser.

This book will help every woman, no matter what her race, religion, economic status, or sexual preference. It does not give legal advice; for that, you must consult an attorney. Rather, it tells her how to protect herself and how to achieve life goals.

It is about a new frontier of freedom. It shows women how to use the law to be winners, not losers in their personal, business, and professional lives.

It is every woman's survival manual for the rest of this decade—and beyond!

2

WHY YOU NEED THIS BOOK

A life I did not choose chose me.

ADRIENNE RICH

The end of the twentieth century is the best of times for American women. It is also the worst of times. Whether you will be one of the fortunate females who has the benefits of the good times or whether you will be one of the unfortunate females who lives in the worst of times depends to a great extent upon you and the choices you make.

Powerful forces in politics, the economy, and the family are working to deny women the benefits that should be freely available to every person. Some women are working to assure that all women will move into the twenty-first century as free persons with personal, social, economic, and political rights. Others, through fear, ignorance, or because they have been co-opted by misogynistic males, are working equally hard to deny what should be every person's freedoms and rights.

To know where you are and what choices you have, let us look at both aspects of our times: the good and the bad.

The good news is that 1992 was called "The Year of the Woman."

The bad news is that nothing changed for the vast majority of nonpolitical women.

The good news is that the 1990s were declared "The Decade of the Child."

The bad news is that the U.S. Supreme Court has denied children the right to sue the state agencies that fail to protect them.

The good news is that the law now prohibits sexual harassment.

The bad news is that such harassment continues in the military, the civilian workplace, and in the home.

The good news is that the law now prohibits institutions of learning from excluding you because you are female.

The bad news is that many institutions and the individuals employed there, both male and female, are part of an old boys' network and attempt to deny you access by subtle, devious, or coercive means.

The good news is that the law now requires that women receive equal pay for equal work.

The bad news is that American women now earn barely 70 percent of the wages of American men. A greater percentage of women of all ages than men lives below the poverty level.

The good news is that women are legally entitled to advancement equal with men. The bad news is that women who choose to have children are relegated to the lower-paying "mommy track."

The good news is that no woman has to remain in a loveless or unhappy marriage. The bad news is that when a woman divorces, her income drops by 74 percent and when a man divorces his income increases by 42 percent.

The good news is that you have a legal right to the custody of your children after divorce. The bad news is that you will have to wage a legal battle to obtain custody.

The good news is that your ex-husband is obligated to support his children.

The bad news is that more than 50 percent of divorced men do not pay support.

The good news is that the law prohibits employers from discriminating against women in promotions.

The bad news is that only 3 percent of women in the United States hold top jobs.

The good news is that there are more women lawyers, doctors, engineers, and other professionals than ever before.

The bad news is that women's lives are harder, more pressured, and unhappy than those of their male professional counterparts.

The good news is that more women are gainfully employed than ever before.

The bad news is that the majority of women have low-paid jobs with little hope of advancement or security.

The good news is that the United States still is one of the wealthiest nations in the world.

The bad news is that an increasing number of women and children live in poverty.

The good news is that science and technology have removed the lifelong dread of unwanted pregnancy for women. There are reasonably reliable forms of contraceptives that are not dangerous to health. And if the contraceptive fails or if you fail to use it, or if you are raped, abortion when done in a qualified clinic or hospital is actually safer than bearing a child.

The bad news is that the U.S. Supreme Court has upheld laws restricting a woman's right to an abortion, requiring parental consent for minors, denying poor women public funding for abortions, and prohibiting the importation of contraceptive pills.

The good news is that American women have a life expectancy of 78.6 years.

The bad news is that most elderly women live in poverty, either alone or in wretched nursing homes.

The good news is that all political positions are now legally open to women.

The bad news is that only 14 percent of public officials are women. Few women hold policy-making positions in the political parties.

The good news is that there is more awareness among both men and women of the persistent bias against women in all walks of life.

The bad news is that so little has been done to remedy this situation.

What Can You Do?

◆ In your own life, whatever your political beliefs and social orientation, you can make intelligent choices so that you will be among those fortunate females who live in the best of times rather than the majority of females who live in the worst of times.

◆ You can be an activist for women's rights if that suits your philosophy and temperament. There are countless organizations in every community devoted to improving the economic, political, educational, and social status of women. Join with other women to improve life for all women.

◆ Whenever you encounter a situation in which a woman is being unfairly treated, speak up. Make others aware. All too often both women and men do not even notice the most outrageous discrimination because they are accustomed to it. You can make women and men aware. This rarely requires action, only understanding and the courage to speak.

Whether you are one of the winners in life or one of the many losers depends upon the choices you make at critical moments throughout your lifetime. These turning points are challenges, opportunities for you to move from the losing track to the winning track, or if you are on the winning track to stay there. These turning points in every woman's life begin at a very early age. And the possibilities for change continue to be available well into old age.

Your choices begin in high school. Will you finish high school or will you be a dropout, a teenage mother, who is relegated to welfare and the most menial, worst-paying jobs? Or will you finish school and go on to get higher education or advanced job training so that you can lead a satisfying and comfortable life?

When you leave school, will you take a position with possibilities of advancement or will you settle for a paycheck?

In your sex life, no matter what your age, will you have an affair with a man simply because he wants it? Or will you choose the kind of man you want?

Will you marry just because your family and society think marriage is the lot of every women? Or will you decide whether marriage with this particular man is right for you, not only for today but in the foreseeable future?

Will you make a decision to marry before either of you is old enough to have explored your potential—or wait until you learn more about your life goals, and seek someone truly attuned to them?

Will you have a baby just because that is what young women are expected to do or because some man thinks that inseminating you is a proof of his masculinity? Or will you examine the man carefully and coolly and decide whether he will be a good father to your child and whether you will make a good and happy mother at *this* time in your life?

If your marriage is not what you expected, or your husband decides he "wants out," will you simply say, "That's it!" and get a divorce or acquiesce in his decision to divorce you? Or will you consider rationally whether the marriage is worth saving and, if so, how you should save it? If after carefully weighing the arguments on both sides you determine to proceed with a divorce, will you go ahead blindly or will you see that your future is protected both financially and with respect to your family?

If you are lonely and feel that life is passing you by, will you rush into a relationship or a second marriage just for the supposed comfort of having a man in the house? Or will you weigh the benefits and burdens, the pleasures and obligations, the advantages and disadvantages—both economic and social—of marriage versus a relationship?

Will you choose the career, the life work, that you really want or will you be coerced into taking the job that your parents, husband, or teachers think is right for you?

If you are a victim of crime, will you rush to the prosecutor demanding justice? Or will you consult victim counselors to learn the costs—emotional and financial—of prosecution and then make an informed decision?

If you are a victim of civil wrongdoing—medical malpractice, sex discrimination, age discrimination, or simple negligence—will you rush to court to vindicate your rights? Or will you get a second opinion as to the likely costs of such an action, monetary, emotional, and careerwise, and weigh them against the likely recovery and then decide what is in your best interests?

Will you remain stuck in a rut in a job or profession you do not like or will you carefully decide whether or not to make a change?

Will you buy a home because it is supposed to be "good for the children" or will you consider whether or not this choice of home is good for *you* as well as your family?

Will you join an organization just because a friend asks you to and the name sounds benign, or will you investigate and find out what the organization really does before you give it your name and your time or money?

When your parents or your children or other relatives seek your help, will you open your home and your purse to them because you love them and don't want to be thought ungenerous? Or will you sit down with the family and discuss frankly their situations and yours before you embark on a rescue mission?

In old age will you move to a retirement community because that is what is convenient for your children, or will you decide what will make you happy?

At some stage in every woman's life, you or your daughter or sister or your mother will be confronted with such questions. The way you answer them, the choices you make, can have a liberating or a devastating effect on your entire future.

Now is the first time in the long story of human beings in their journey from the precarious existence of cave dwellers to the high-technology world of today that women have ever had the opportunity to shape their own destinies.

Only a few centuries ago in the Western world, daughters were married off by their fathers to promote familial interests or they were immured in convents for the same reasons. Only a few decades ago, women's choices were limited to marriage or unpaid or miserably underpaid "suitable female jobs." Only a generation ago divorce carried a social stigma. And only within this generation has family planning been theoretically, at least, available to all women. Only today do women have equal legal rights to education, jobs, and pay.

But before you rely on these rights, find out whether they are actually enforceable. Will a protective order really prevent an abusive man from attacking you or should you take other means to protect yourself?

Because the law provides for an equitable distribution of marital assets, will the courts construe equity as meaning half, or only 40 percent, or less for you?

Because you have a right to file a complaint for gender discrimination, will you find out the likelihood of winning?

Will you investigate and find out whether the rights declared in the statute are actually the rights you will receive in court? These are all decisions you must make before . . .

Every Woman Is a Pioneer Today

Because all these choices and opportunities are so new, society has not developed behavior patterns that are generally accepted by men, women, and children. Each woman today is in a real sense a pioneer. Each of you is embarking on an uncharted voyage of life in which you will encounter dangerous shoals, hidden reefs, and cloudy skies where even the North Star pointing the way to survival is obscured.

To help you navigate this dangerous and exciting life journey I am giving you five rules, a modern Pentalogue of Five Commandments that will help you make the decisions that are right for you.

Memorize them. Remember them at each turning point in your life when you have the opportunity to choose. And act on this advice *before* . . .

3

THE FIVE COMMANDMENTS EVERY WOMAN NEEDS TO KNOW

A few strong instincts and a few plain rules.
WILLIAM WORDSWORTH

Moses brought the Ten Commandments down from Mount Sinai. These holy laws have been guidelines for the Western world for several millenia, although they have been observed in the breach as often as they have been obeyed.

I offer you a new Pentalogue, the Five Commandments that should be every woman's guide to successful living. I did not go up a lonely mountain or out into the desert to commune with a deity to formulate them. No God gave me these laws on graven tablets. No deity whispered in my ear or thundered to me from on high. I learned these survival laws in sordid courtrooms where I saw the sad results that befell good, decent, intelligent women who had been caught up by legal myths and ideals and did not know these five commandments.

Many of these women had obeyed the Ten Commandments and had lived by the Golden Rule. Others had not. But regardless of their virtue and obedience to moral law, women lost in life and in the law courts because they had not learned these five simple commandments.

These commandments do not prohibit sin, but stupidity and lack of foresight. They do not replace the Ten Commandments, but add five more rules that every woman can follow even though she may at times succumb to feelings of lust or envy, and may

21

sometimes lie, cheat, commit adultery, and fail in filial and pious duties.

They do not demand moral purity or goodness. Any woman can obey them. Memorize these commandments and use them in all situations in which you must make decisions with respect to men in all aspects of life. They are also helpful in making decisions with respect to women.

COMMANDMENT I
Thou shalt protect thyself.

COMMANDMENT II
Thou shalt anticipate disaster.

COMMANDMENT III
Thou shalt act on thy best judgment based on the facts.

COMMANDMENT IV
Thou shalt wear a velvet glove over an iron hand.

COMMANDMENT V
Money is not a dirty word. Thou shalt use it.

Whether you are always virtuous and pure or occasionally stray from the paths of virtue, you like all women will assuredly have to make decisions. These five rules will help you to make your decisions wisely and in your own best interests.

This book is not based on principles of looking out for number one or narcissism. It does not advocate being selfish, uncaring, or egotistical. Every woman can be kind, caring, and generous without being a patsy. Every woman can and should command respect. Every woman should be able to fulfill her expectations for a life of love, marriage, children, career, financial security, honor, and happiness if she acts with foresight in her own best interest.

COMMANDMENT I
Thou shalt protect thyself. Don't rely on someone else. Remember that love and friendship may not last forever. No one

knows how long she or anyone else will live. The person you rely on may not be there when you need him. And even if he is alive and geographically available, he may no longer be your lover, friend, or spouse.

Knighthood is no longer in flower or in fashion. A fragile, helpless maiden will wait in vain for someone to rescue her from physical or financial peril.

A self-reliant female is more likely to attract friends and lovers than one in distress. Justice Benjamin N. Cardozo wrote in 1921, "Danger invites rescue." In the 1990s most people don't want to get involved. They decline the invitation to be a volunteer rescue squad. Don't expect someone else to take care of your problems. Do it yourself. The best way to do so is to avoid problems by *protecting* yourself in each of your encounters with a man, whether they are sexual, emotional, social, or business.

COMMANDMENT II

Thou shalt anticipate disaster. Prepare for the worst scenario you can imagine. If it occurs, you will be able to deal with it. If it does not occur, you will have lost nothing and you will not be prejudiced.

No one expects her house to burn, her car to be stolen, or that she will be in an accident. But all sensible people take out insurance to protect themselves from these possible disasters. No one has much sympathy for a person whose home is burglarized and who doesn't have insurance.

"It's too bad you lost all your furniture, your computer, your TV set, and your jewelry. But, at least, if you had insurance you could replace most of these items," your friends will say. And you will feel like a fool if you have to go into debt to repurchase household necessities.

You can't replace heirlooms and items of sentimental value, but insurance will pay for replacement of most household goods.

Similarly, you can't prevent heartbreak and disappointment when love is stolen or lost. But you can prevent financial disasters by the exercise of common sense and foresight.

COMMANDMENT III

Thou shalt act on thy best judgment. It is sensible to seek advice from friends and knowledgeable persons. But remember that you, not your advisors, will have to bear the consequences of your actions.

Cassandra knew that the Trojans would be defeated by the Greeks. The rulers of Troy refused to believe her and confidently anticipated victory. If Cassandra had acted on her own good judgment, she would not have been captured, enslaved, and then murdered. She would have left Troy and gone to a safe place.

Persons in positions of power and authority are not always wise. Their advice may be good in general but it may not be beneficial to *you*. You are the person best situated to know what is in your own best interests.

COMMANDMENT IV

Thou shalt wear a velvet glove over an iron hand. This was the advice of Charles V of France who is known as Charles the Wise. Learn from history and have both a velvet glove *and* an iron hand.

All too often women resemble the Israeli fruit called sabra. It is prickly on the outside and soft on the inside. The wise woman is the opposite—soft on the outside and steely hard on the inside. When a woman raises her voice in argument, she is considered a termagant. A man is called commanding. When she uses the same forceful language as her male opposite number, she is called shrewish. He is deemed manly. For the same attitudes she is described as aggressive, he as forceful.

The Bible admonishes that a "soft answer turneth away wrath." If you use a gentle voice it probably won't change an opponent's views. But a soft answer will blunt hostility and facilitate negotiations.

On matters of principle be gentle but adamant. A velvet glove will protect your iron hand from scratches! If you are firm but not abrasive, you, like Charles V, will be wise.

COMMANDMENT V

Money is not a dirty word. Thou shalt use it. Money is not the root of all evil. In our society no one can live without money. Money may not bring happiness. The lack of it will surely cause unhappiness. Independence and self-empowerment are not possible unless a woman has some money of her own.

Discuss all financial arrangements in advance of any transaction involving money. You are not living in the Garden of Eden. You must wear clothes. Food cannot be picked freely from trees. You must have shelter. All these necessities of life cost money.

In every transaction involving more than one person, whether it is eating a meal in a restaurant, going to the movies, or buying a house, one or the other party must pay or both must share the cost. Find out in advance what the arrangement is to be. This will avoid friction, disappointment, and embarrassment later.

In grandma's day, the rules of conduct between men and women were clear, although never discussed. The man was expected to take the initiative and pay the bills. A woman was not expected to have sexual relations prior to marriage. And after marriage she was supposed to acquiesce meekly and gratefully to all his demands. Many women did submit to brutality, cruelty, indifference, stinginess, and degradation.

Today women do not have to wait for him to make all the moves. They can enjoy sex outside of marriage without ignominy or shame. They can make their own decisions. They do not have to accept unfair and demeaning situations. Women can get divorces. If they are abused there are shelters to which they can go.

These new rights and freedoms are not cost-free. They entail responsibilities. You have to make decisions for yourself. You have to know before what you expect of him and what he expects of you. Unless you do, you may find yourself in a precarious financial and emotional situation that could have been avoided by having a frank discussion *before* . . .

Many of the most common difficulties between men and women do not arise out of sex or misunderstandings. These difficulties occur not because men and women don't speak the same language but because they don't talk about money *before* . . .

Some women still have grandma's expectations: namely, that he will pay for everything. Some men also expect to pay but many do not. Other women are financially independent and prefer to pay their own way. Let him know your views and find out his expectations *before* . . .

There are no universally accepted rules of behavior between men and women in the 1990s. Some people follow the old practices; others the new. Unless both the man and the woman understand clearly which mores prevail there can be tragic misunderstandings.

Some men believe that if a woman has sex with them it is not an expression of her love but evidence of her promiscuity.

Some men still assume that marriage entitles them to domination and control of all decisions.

Other men assume that they have no financial or other obligations to the women they make love to and the women they marry.

You should know which rules the man observes *before* . . . Is he playing by grandpa's rules? Does he believe that there are two kinds of women: the one he marries and all the others? Does he believe that by giving a woman a ring and a marriage license he has acquired a docile, obedient slave?

Or does he give lip service to the new-style male? Some men pick and choose which female rights they recognize. Does he believe that she should pay half the bills and do *all* the housework? Child care? Laundry? Cooking?

Does this new-style man believe that his female friend is entitled to work and contribute to their joint support but that he is free to end the relationship at his pleasure? That he has the right to make all the decisions as to their home, lifestyle, and friends?

Or is he a truly new-style man who believes in mutuality and sharing of obligations, benefits, and decision making? Is he sufficiently secure in his masculinity to cherish your femininity? Or does he complain, "Why can't a woman be like a man?" like Henry Higgins did in the show *My Fair Lady?*

PART II

LOVE
AND
FAMILY

4

BEFORE YOU DECIDE TO
HAVE A RELATIONSHIP

Come live with me and be my love
And we will all the pleasures prove . . .
CHRISTOPHER MARLOWE

Love, courtship, marriage; These have been the accepted stages in the pattern of intimacy between a woman and a man for many years. Today there is another common pattern: love-relationship. This may or may not be followed by marriage. The relationship may also exist openly between two women or two men. In this chapter we explore the pitfalls to be avoided when women and men decide to live together. This lifestyle is today a common and accepted alternative to marriage. The U.S. Census Bureau reports that in 1990 22.6 percent of Americans over the age of eighteen had never married. The number of weddings decreases each year. The relationship in lieu of marriage is so frequent that it is even recognized by the Census Bureau under the quaint caption "persons of opposite sex sharing living quarters."

A relationship may be intended to be temporary, or one or both parties may contemplate that it will be permanent. Such a relationship is much like a marriage in that it is open and recognized, although not sanctioned by either state or church. It is not a furtive arrangement in which the woman is a mistress or kept woman paid for sexual favors. Today women of all ages and conditions of life live with a man openly without being married and without stigma or embarrassment. What few of these women realize, however, is that they are without legal protections.

There is a lag between contemporary mores and the law. Except for a few cases in California involving aspiring, beautiful young movie starlets and their elderly, wealthy male companions, women's claims arising out of relationships have not been recognized by the courts. When couples separate, the woman rarely has any valid legal claims for support or alimony. And if she has a child by her partner, she will have even more difficulties than a married mother who is divorcing.

Women enter into this kind of arrangement for many reasons. Usually there is love or affection between the parties. They do not want to enter a marriage for many reasons. Young people often simply are not ready for long-term commitment. Older couples may not be able to marry because one of them has not obtained a divorce or for financial, religious, or other reasons, cannot do so. Other couples find that a marriage will create problems with Social Security, pension rights, and family obligations. In this situation, some women believe that they can find the love, companionship, and home life they desire without those entanglements. Many do find happiness and fulfillment; others are sorely disappointed.

This chapter points out many of the pitfalls to be avoided. You must bear in mind that a relationship has both emotional and financial aspects. It is more like a marriage than like choosing a roommate or a business partner. Therefore, a woman must consider carefully her personal needs and desires and the character, lifestyle, and finances of her partner.

Ask yourself these questions before you enter into the relationship:

◆ What does he do for a living?
◆ Who are his friends?
◆ What do they think of him?
◆ What are his hobbies and favorite recreations?
◆ What is his lifestyle?
◆ What are his future goals?

If you don't know the answers to these questions, find out *before . . .*

Women are conditioned by literature—much of it written by men—to treat a relationship between a woman and a man as a romance, a beautiful, otherworldly confluence of eclectic affinities and sexual attraction. We speak of a good marriage as one "made in heaven," as if it did not involve the practicalities of daily living. And so, many intelligent women are reluctant to let the daylight of common sense obtrude upon the moonbeams of romance.

However, a relationship, like a marriage, involves both sunlight and moonlight, work and play, affection and obligations. In other words, it is a coming together of two complete human beings with all their attributes—their strengths and *all their weaknesses*.

Women no longer wear veils that conceal their faces and obscure their vision. When you enter into a relationship with a man, he sees you clearly. *It is most unlikely that he pictures you as a fairy princess, angelic and pristine. You should not construct a fantastic image of him as a romantic prince. You can see both the moonbeams and the man in his totality if only you will look.* I hope this book will help you to achieve this clarity!

You would not hire a secretary, a domestic worker, or a babysitter without checking references. You should know at least as much about the man with whom you intend to have a relationship as you know about an employee.

Although it is easier to terminate a relationship than to obtain a divorce, the consequences are often similar. Usually it is the man who ends the relationship, just as it usually is the man who wants a divorce.

Some relationships are like a stage of courtship that culminates in marriage. More often *relationships do not lead to marriage.* Therefore, it is sensible not to expect the relationship to endure until death do you part. When it ends, the woman will probably feel a sense of loss. She may have to begin a new lifestyle. And she may be severely disadvantaged economically. What follows tells you why she doesn't have to be.

You can protect yourself by bearing in mind the five new commandments before entering into a relationship. The women you will meet in this chapter were not stupid. They believed that the men with whom they became involved were honest, upright, good individuals who truly cared for them. But they failed to find out facts about these men that they subsequently learned to their sorrow and disadvantage.

Young Love Founders on the Shoals of Daily Life

Like a marriage, a relationship usually begins with some variant of this familiar dialogue.

Michael said, "I love you."

Samantha said, "I love you, too."

Michael said, "Why don't we live together? We're together all the time. And think how much money we'd save on rent."

Samantha did think about it for several days. After a particularly wretched meal in a restaurant and an uncomfortable night with Michael on her narrow bed she agreed.

They were in their mid-twenties. Both were graduate students working on their doctorates. They planned to get married in the spring when both expected to receive their degrees and obtain teaching jobs. He was a music major; she an economics major.

They looked for an apartment for several weeks without success. Then Samantha learned that there was a vacancy in the graduate student housing of her university, a lovely one-bedroom apartment with a modern kitchen. They saw it and were entranced. However, the apartment was available only to students enrolled in that university. Michael was a student at a different university. They decided that Samantha would lease the apartment. She paid the security deposit and the first month's rent. He would buy the furniture. They would share living expenses equally.

Samantha knew that Michael had more expensive tastes than she. He also had a wealthy father who indulged him. Samantha's parents were having a difficult time paying for her younger sister's college education. Samantha was accustomed to economizing. Michael was not.

She knew that her budget was stretched to the limit. But she was a self-sufficient young woman who treasured her independence. She wanted to pay her own way. When Michael suggested dividing the expenses it sounded fair. She thought that if she asked him what his budget was she would appear miserly or grasping. In her home, money was an omnipresent worry but it was never discussed. That was considered vulgar. And so she never inquired. Besides, she really loved the apartment. And living with Michael was wonderful for the first few weeks.

"When we get married we can continue to live here," they said contentedly. And so they moved in. Michael put his piano in the living room. Samantha's computer went into the bedroom. They loved shopping, cooking, even cleaning. They felt like children playing house and also like a happily married old couple. The meals were delicious. Their love life had never been better.

But they soon realized that they were not getting much work done. Michael couldn't compose while Samantha was working on the computer. She couldn't study while he was composing. Each day they were falling behind in their schedules for completion of their dissertations.

Samantha also discovered that instead of saving money the new arrangement was far more expensive for her. Her breakfast was a half a grapefruit, a piece of toast, and a cup of coffee. His breakfast was juice, bacon and eggs; sometimes waffles and coffee. Wine with dinner each night was another expense. She drank half a glass; he drank two glasses. Cleaning the kitchen was an unexpected and unwelcome chore that consumed precious time.

After a miserable day when his new composition was rejected and the first draft of her dissertation returned for extensive revisions and a stormy night of recriminations, Michael announced that he was leaving.

He went back to his rented room. A mover came and took away his piano. When Samantha asked Michael for his half of the rent he told her that he had not signed the lease; it was her responsibility. The university would not permit a sublet. She was responsible for the rent for the remainder of the year. In order to make the payments Samantha had to take a part-time job as a waitress and also obtain a second student loan. She could not complete her dissertation on time. With some difficulty she was granted an extension for another semester.

Michael received his degree in June and soon got a teaching

job. He also acquired a wife. Samantha acquired several thousand dollars of debt.

How did Samantha, a bright, attractive young woman become a loser?

◆ **She violated the Fifth Commandment: She failed to discuss money with Michael.** Had she done so she would have known *before* how much it would cost her to share the apartment with him. She would also have pointed out to him her obligation on the lease and had a clear understanding that he, too, should be obligated.

◆ **When they separated, Samantha violated the Fourth Commandment. She cried; she yelled; she called Michael a selfish boor.** And then she permitted him to walk out of her life, leaving her with the debts. Had she wisely worn an iron hand in a velvet glove, she would have spoken to him softly but firmly. She would have barred his moving his piano without his agreeing to be responsible for half the rent.

◆ **Samantha violated the First Commandment. She did not protect herself.** Since the apartment was technically hers, she should have refused to let the movers enter. Samantha briefly thought of doing that, but decided it would not be ladylike. And she didn't want Michael to hate her. Despite their problems in living together she still loved him.

◆ **And she also violated the Second Commandment. She did not anticipate disaster.** Every relationship, like every marriage, has the potential for failure. But partners, unlike some wives, rarely have legal rights.

Probably their relationship could not have been saved. Samantha would undoubtedly have lost Michael. *But she need not have lost money or suffered a major setback in her career.*

Had Samantha obeyed the Five Commandments she would not have been the loser. And Michael probably would have respected her for her firmness rather than hating her for his guilt feelings.

The Reluctant Father

After Philippa's divorce, she was sure that she never wanted to marry again. Craig had been a spoiled, selfish young man who expected his wife to wait on him as his doting mother had done. Philippa was an intelligent competent woman, thirty-four years old. She was a computer expert and had a responsible job. In fact, she earned more money than Craig. But he had expected her to be cook, housekeeper, and laundress, as well as breadwinner.

For several years after the divorce Philippa reveled in her freedom. She indulged herself in all the luxuries Craig had denied her. She traveled; she played tennis regularly; she bought her dream house on a hillside and decorated it to suit herself. She began to buy modern art. She thought she was happy living alone until she met Burton.

He was tall and handsome, a good tennis player, and a bon vivant. He was a successful lawyer. He, too, had been divorced for several years. He had three children who lived with their mother, whom he seldom saw, although he regularly paid support and alimony. Burton thought Philippa was just the woman for him, a free and independent spirit who, unlike his ex-wife, made no demands on him. She supported herself. She was available to go to the theater, to go scuba diving or skiing. There was never a question about finding baby-sitters or staying home with a sick child, helping with homework, or having a pack of noisy youngsters disturbing him when he wanted to read.

Gradually Burton spent more and more time at Philippa's house. It was much more attractive than his bachelor digs. After a few months he moved in.

"This is civilized living," he exclaimed happily. "No kids to interfere with us, just you and me. I do love you, Philippa."

And she murmured, "I love you, too."

The seasons came and went filled with hedonistic pleasures and free of discord.

"It's wonderful living with you," Burton said. "We have nothing to fight about."

Philippa knew that was true. But they also had nothing to bind them together. Her thirty-seventh birthday was approaching and she realized that if she was ever going to have a child, she should do so now. So Philippa surreptitiously threw her diaphragm away and waited hopefully for nature to take its course.

Several months later she happily announced to Burton that she was pregnant. She had rehearsed the scene in her mind for weeks while she waited and hoped. She expected him to take her in his arms and murmur, "Darling, I'm so happy."

What he actually said was, "No. That's not possible."

"I'm afraid it is not only possible, it is a fact," Philippa replied.

"I have three children! I don't want another! Get an abortion."

Philippa was shocked. She knew Burton wasn't fond of children but she had confidently expected that he would love *their* child.

"You have three children. I don't have any. I want this child," she told him.

"You don't know what parenthood means. You've never had morning sickness, backaches. You've always been slim and beautiful. You won't be when you're pregnant. And you haven't experienced labor—hours of pain and screaming until the baby is finally born. Then the diapers, the breast-feeding, up all night with a crying child, trying to find decent help. Believe me, it's not worth it."

"But I want a child," Philippa declared.

"If you have it, you'll have it without me. I think you deliberately planned this. You deceived me," Burton said angrily. "Either you get an abortion or I leave," he told her as he abruptly left the house.

Philippa waited a week, two weeks, and then she called him.

"Have you arranged for an abortion?" he asked.

"No," she replied. "I'm not going to."

"If that's your decision, we'll just say good-bye now. I'll send a messenger to pick up my things."

Philippa consulted a lawyer. He bluntly told her that she had no claim on Burton. "Even if you could prove that he had promised to marry you, breach of promise suits are out of fashion. No court would compel a man to get married. And no court will order him to pay you support. After the baby is born you can sue him for child support."

Philippa had not planned to be an unwed mother. She didn't know what to tell her business associates—who were mostly married people—or her conventional parents. By this time she was in her second trimester. She knew an abortion would be more difficult and she still wanted a child. After discussing her problem with her best friend, a divorcee, Philippa bought herself a wedding ring and announced to her business associates that she was married.

When the baby was born she put Burton's name on the birth certificate as the father. Then she went back to the lawyer and told him to sue for child support.

Burton contested her claim. He asserted that she had breached their implied contract that they would not have a child and that he was already paying more child support than he could afford.

The male judge was sympathetic to Burton. But, as he explained, the law requires a father, willing or not, to support his children. Burton earned more than $200,000 a year reported income, and probably a great deal more, as Philippa pointed out to the court. He paid $50.00 a week support for each of his legitimate children and $15,000 a year alimony to his ex-wife. The judge decided that $25.00 a week would be sufficient support for Philippa's baby until it reached the age of eighteen.

After a few weeks, Burton simply stopped paying. Philippa went to court four times during the first year to enforce the meager support order and then she simply gave up. It wasn't worth the effort.

When I saw Philippa on the baby's second birthday she told me that Burton had never seen the child.

"I love my daughter dearly. I'm glad I had her. But, what will I tell her when she is old enough to ask for her father?"

A year later Philippa told me she had married a man she did

not love because he agreed to adopt her daughter. "I think I owe my child a father," she explained. "I didn't know the law would let a man walk away from his child."

The days of *The Scarlet Letter* are long past. A woman who has a child out of wedlock is not a pariah. But the unwed father's only legal responsibility is a minimal support payment for the child. He owes nothing to the mother of his child.

"Are you happy?" I asked Philippa.

"No," she replied. "But this is the best arrangement I could make. Time was running out. She starts nursery school next month and I want her to have a father."

A few years later Philippa divorced her husband. She is bringing up her daughter alone. And she wonders what she will tell her when the child asks why the man she thinks is her father never comes to see her.

Philippa, like many intelligent women who feel that their biological clock is running down, acted impulsively. She ignored the First Commandment. She did not protect herself. She disregarded the Second Commandment. She did not anticipate disaster. And she ignored the Fifth Commandment. She never discussed money with Burton.

If she had told Burton she wanted to have a child by him, perhaps she could have persuaded him to agree. If not, she could then have made a decision to leave him and find a man who wanted to have a child. When she knew she was pregnant, she should certainly have discussed money with Burton and made him aware of his legal responsibilities to the child.

Philippa is another woman who wishes she had known that the law would afford her no protection *before . . .*

Ignorance of the Facts Is Not a Legal Excuse

"Ignorance of the law is no excuse" is a well known and true adage. It is equally true that ignorance of the facts will not excuse you from legal responsibility.

Velma and Booker

Booker said: "I love you."

Velma said: "I love you, too."

Booker said: "Live with me. We'll be so happy."

Velma said: "Yes."

Velma was twenty, a strikingly pretty girl. She was intelligent and determined not to be trapped in a life of poverty as her mother had been. She saw her classmates getting pregnant, dropping out of school, living difficult, hopeless lives of poverty and she resolved that this would not happen to her. She kept her many boyfriends at arms' length. She graduated from high school. And she got a job as receptionist in a doctor's office.

When Booker saw Velma in her crisp white uniform greeting patients he was enchanted. Her smooth brown skin, her shining black hair, and dark melting eyes were irresistible. Booker gave his name in a dignified voice. Velma looked up and saw an impeccably dressed man she thought was middle-aged, wearing a Rolex watch. He spoke softly and correctly. This was the kind of man she wanted: intelligent and clearly middle class.

Surreptitiously Velma looked up Booker's file. She learned that he was only forty-five, married, with two children. He lived in a nice section of town. The file did not contain information about his business.

Booker came to the doctor's office the following week.

"You don't have an appointment today, sir," Velma told him.

"I didn't come to see the doctor," he replied. "I came to see you."

And so the friendship began. Booker told Velma that he was separated from his wife, that he could not get a divorce at this time but that he loved her and wanted her to live with him.

Velma went to Booker's home. It was the most elegant house she had ever been in. Seeing herself in this setting was like a dream come true. She told Booker that she helped support her mother and two younger sisters. Booker immediately agreed to pay the rent for them. He gave Velma lovely presents, including jewelry and an automobile. He gave her a credit card. And then he suggested that she quit her job so she could travel with him and run his household.

Velma told the doctor for whom she worked what she intended to do.

"What do you know about Booker?" he asked her.

"He loves me."

"There's more than love to be considered," the doctor warned.

"He's good and kind and generous. That's all I care about," she replied.

In due course, Velma had a daughter Tiffany. Booker and she were very happy. On the day of Tiffany's third birthday when Velma was busy getting the balloons and favors ready for the party, she received a call from Booker. He told her to go to a certain address, pick up a package, and deliver it to another address. Throughout the years Velma had done this many times. The first time she asked Booker what was in the package.

"Don't bother your pretty head about business affairs," he replied. "I'm making enough money for us."

And since Booker rarely asked anything of her, she was happy to do as he requested, deliver the package and leave money matters to him.

On this day, she got into her Mercedes and drove to the address Booker had given her. She had picked up other packages there and knew the way. Velma was in a hurry to get back home for the birthday party and did not notice a small black car waiting in front of her house. She did not see it follow her and park across the street from where she went. When she came out of that house carrying a small package wrapped in brown paper, two men jumped out of the car and announced, "You're under arrest!"

"Me? There must be some mistake. I have to get home to my daughter."

"You're coming to the police station with us," she was told. Then she was warned of her rights and told that she might call a lawyer.

"I don't know any lawyer," Velma protested. "May I call Booker?"

When she reached Booker he told her not to say anything, to keep the package, and he would send a lawyer over immediately. A lawyer arrived within half an hour and posted bail for Velma. It was only at the bail hearing that she learned that the package contained heroin and that she was charged with possession of drugs with intent to deliver. The drugs were worth $50,000 and were clearly not for Velma's use.

Booker was arrested a few days later and also posted substantial bail. About six months later their cases came up for trial. Booker's lawyer was able to work out a deal for him. Booker, who was a dealer, promised to tell the police the names of the drug lords who were his suppliers. He was put in a witness protection program, given a new identity in another city, and supplied with ample funds.

When Velma came to trial she testified that she knew nothing about the drug trade, nothing about how Booker earned a living. Because she was not married to Booker she was required to testify against him and to tell the number of packages she had delivered and describe his lifestyle. Booker was furious.

Velma was between a rock and a hard place. If she didn't testify, she would have little chance of proving her innocence. But when she did take the stand she had to answer all questions. A wife cannot be questioned about her husband's allegedly criminal activities. The jury did not believe Velma.

Velma, who knew nothing at all about the drug business, had no information to trade. Under the law she was required to be sentenced to five years in the penitentiary. Once a year her mother manages to take a seven-hour bus trip with Tiffany to see Velma. Tiffany does not recognize her as her mother.

It was only after the arrest that Velma learned that Booker was in the drug business. Like countless poor ghetto boys he wanted money and all the good things it buys. So he became a drug pusher. He was smart and personable and soon became a dealer. Like many men engaged in illicit enterprises who use their innocent wives and girlfriends as "mules" to deliver the illegal goods, Booker had involved Velma in crime. She paid the penalty. He did not.

When she appeared in court seeking a new trial, Velma said to me, "If only I had known *before* . . ."

When a man says, "Don't bother your pretty head about business or money," *he is not protecting you. He is protecting himself* by concealing facts he does not want you to know. If Velma had persisted in her inquiries, Booker probably would have become angry. She would then have realized that he was concealing something of importance to her. Because she did not know of Booker's illegal activities, there was nothing she could do to protect herself.

Had she known she would have had options:

◆ She could leave him.
◆ She could inform herself about his illegal business so that if he were caught she would have information to trade for her freedom.
◆ She could have insisted on having money of her own in the event of disaster.

Being ignorant of the facts, she was helpless.

◆ **Velma violated the First Commandment. She did not protect herself.**

◆ **She violated the Second Commandment. She did not anticipate disaster.**

◆ **And she violated the Fifth Commandment. She did not discuss money with Booker.**

Velma's troubles could have been avoided if she had obeyed these three commandments.

Purchase of Property Is a Legal Transaction, Not an Act of Love

Sidney and Ruth repeated the well-worn dialogue.
He said, "I love you."

She said, "I love you, too."

They were in their fifties and both were divorcées. He was a college professor who earned more than $70,000 a year in salary, royalties, and lecture fees. He also had investments. She earned $50,000 a year in an advertising firm. Her only asset was her cooperative apartment.

Both were lonely. Each had been divorced for a number of years. They were tired of the singles life. Although neither desired a second marriage they wanted companionship.

Ruth enjoyed being with Sidney. It was a welcome change from her close group of women friends—widows and divorcées—who went to dinner, theater, and concerts together.

But when Sidney suggested that they live together, Ruth was hesitant. She cherished her hard-won independence. Her marriage that had begun with such hope and promise had ended in bitterness. It had not been easy to go back to work after twenty years as a housewife. She had started work again as a secretary and had by much toil become a vice president of the company. She did not want to jeopardize her position.

Ruth discussed Sidney's suggestion with her friends.

"What do you have to lose? Introduce us to his friends," they urged enviously.

And so with some misgivings Ruth agreed to live with Sidney. They found a condominium, an apartment far more beautiful and spacious than her cooperative or his rental apartment. The price was $150,000 but if each paid half it would not be too costly.

Ruth sold her cooperative and used the proceeds to pay for her share of the apartment. Sidney sold some securities to pay for his share. They agreed that if they came to the parting of the ways each could buy out the other for $75,000.

For five years both enjoyed their life together. Sidney and Ruth entertained their friends; they traveled extensively; they lived well. Ruth thought she had the best of all possible worlds until—Sidney fell in love with a beautiful young graduate student. Although his waistline was expanding and his hairline receding, Sidney suddenly felt youthful and virile.

Ruth kept a slim figure through careful dieting, exercise, and her expensively tinted hair and cosmetic embellishments. But she looked and felt middle-aged. She worked much harder than Sidney and she was tired.

When Sidney announced that he wanted to leave, Ruth told him in her quiet dignified way, "If you don't want me, then I don't want you."

"Do you want to buy the apartment?" Sidney asked.

"Of course, I do" she replied. "But you know I don't have $75,000. I spent all my capital to buy half of this place. And I've spent every cent of my income and savings helping to maintain it in the lifestyle *you* insisted on."

"Don't be bitter, dear" he rejoined. "I'll pay you $75,000 for your half and you can buy another place."

During the five years Ruth and Sidney had lived together real estate had escalated. Their condominium was now worth $400,000. There was nothing acceptable on the market that Ruth could buy for $75,000.

She consulted an attorney who told her,

"You should have seen me *before*."

Ruth is now one of the army of the newly poor, older women without a man. She is also without a home.

◆ Her assets are $75,000.
◆ His assets are a home worth $400,000, and his savings and securities.
◆ She is alone.
◆ He has a wife.

Purchase of property, whether it is a home, an automobile, or a picture is a legal transaction. It is a contract. It involves one or more sellers and one or more buyers who have rights and obligations. When you enter into a contract you are bound by the terms of the agreement, even though it subsequently turns out to be unfair unless there was fraud or deceit.

When a married couple buy a home together they own it jointly (either as joint tenants or tenants by the entireties) even though one of the couple pays 100 percent of the purchase price. If they separate, the law protects the wife's interest. When two unmarried people buy property their rights depend on *the contract*, the bargain they made.

Before a relationship was generally accepted, a woman who lived with a man out of wedlock knew that she was at a disadvantage both socially and legally. Most women in that position took steps to protect themselves financially. Today few women want to be beholden to a man, to trade sex for money. They believe that sharing financial obligations protects their dignity and independence. Ruth, like many women, confused love and dignity with money. She did not view the purchase of an apartment as a purely legal transaction and so she failed to examine the economic consequences of the contract.

◆ **Ruth violated the First Commandment. She did not protect herself.**

◆ **She violated the Second Commandment. She did not anticipate disaster,** although she should have foreseen that a professor like Sidney would find an adoring young student attractive. It is not farfetched to anticipate that an older man who is in daily contact with young women will be attracted to one of them and be tempted to leave the older woman with whom he shares both the pleasures and irritations of daily living. *Ruth could not ensure Sidney's fidelity but she could have ensured her own financial security.*

◆ **Ruth violated the Third Commandment. Instead of acting on her own best judgment, she took the advice of her friends.**

◆ **And she violated the Fifth Commandment.** Like Samantha, the young graduate student, she did not have a full and frank discussion of money *before* they lived together. If she had openly discussed her financial situation with Sidney when he was eager to have her live with him she probably would have made a more equitable arrangement. Surely they should have shared any appreciation or depreciation in the value of their apartment.

They should have discussed the cost of living. If his lifestyle and entertainment were more expensive than hers, then the costs should have been shared on a proportionate basis. With $200,000 instead of $75,000, she could have bought a suitable apartment. If her savings were intact, she would have been able to maintain her standard of living. And she would not have had to face the ignominy of knowing that her stupidity had financed Sidney's marriage.

When a man makes a declaration of love, he usually means it at that time. Most women can spot obvious phonies. When Sidney said, "I love you," he meant it. It was not a failure of communication about their feelings that caused trouble. It was a failure to discuss the practicalities of their respective financial situations and her unwillingness to face the possibility that changes would take place in their relationship as she became an older woman and he became an older man, *with the advantage always tilting in the older man's favor in the mating game.*

The Five Commandments Can Protect a Relationship

David and Lisa met at a book party. The author was a college classmate of David. His editor was Lisa's boss. Both David and Lisa were in their mid-thirties and divorced.

"David, this is Lisa," the author said.

"David and Lisa, my favorite movie," Lisa murmured and looked into the limpid brown eyes of a thin, tired-looking man.

"Mine, too," he said. "I must have seen it three times. So Lisa grew up to be this attractive woman. What a success for her psychiatrist."

"Don't blame my shrink, I don't have one."

"Neither do I."

After a few minutes David said, "We've done our duty by our friends. Let's go out to dinner."

"I'll call the baby-sitter and see if she can stay later."

They began dating casually. Soon they were dining together every night. When Lisa wanted to be home with Jason, David would bring in take-out food and the three would eat at Lisa's apartment. On weekends they would take Jason to the zoo or just to play in the park. When it was Jason's weekend to be with his father, Lisa would go to David's apartment.

David was a successful stockbroker. He lived in a posh three-bedroom co-op on the swanky East Side of New York City. Lisa lived in a one-bedroom apartment on the less upscale West Side. Jason had the bedroom. She slept in the living room. Although Lisa had a job that she loved, it was not very lucrative. Her former husband was casual about paying child support. Day care was expensive.

"Why don't you and Jason live with me?" David suggested. "You'll be much more comfotable. With what you save on rent you can hire an au pair to help take care of Jason. There's plenty of room in my place and I won't have to go across town in the middle of the night."

Lisa was tempted. David was a pleasant man, the nicest one she had met since her divorce. Jason adored him. But Lisa was also an aspiring author as well as an editor. She lived in a literary world. David was bored by her friends. His friends were big spenders. They liked fancy restaurants, tickets to Broadway shows, weekends at ski lodges—things she could not afford. Also, his firm was establishing branch offices in other cities. Lisa knew that if he were tapped to move to one, she would not want to leave New York, where she had the publishing world, her friends, her sister, her support system.

"I can't afford your lifestyle," she told him.

"It won't cost you anything. You won't have to pay rent, food, cleaning woman, anything except Jason's day care."

Lisa's friends thought David was manna from heaven.

"Life will be so much easier. Think of the fun you'll have going to parties, fancy weekends. And, if you break up, you can always go back to the West Side. What can you lose?" they said.

It sounded so easy. David was a nice man, but she was not in love with him. Mike, her ex-husband, had also seemed to be nice and gentle until they were married. Then she discovered he had a terrible temper; he expected to be "the boss." It had taken her two years to muster up the courage to get a divorce. She had had to scrimp and save and do extra free-lance editing to make ends meet. She was just beginning to hold her own. If David moved away, where would she find another apartment? What about her job?

"We'll try it for a year," Lisa told David. "I'll sublet my apartment so that I have a home if it doesn't work out. And no matter what happens to your job, you agree not to sell your co-op until the end of my sublet."

David was delighted with the arrangement. He showered Lisa and Jason with presents. He hired a full-time maid. Everything was perfect except that Lisa had a book contract. She was working on it nights after Jason went to sleep. Now she had no time for herself except when David went away on a business trip. She found that she looked forward to his absences as much as to his returns.

After six months David was transferred to Houston. He asked Lisa if she and Jason would go with him. She said, "No." They would still be friends and be together whenever he came to New York.

"I guess I'll have to sell the co-op," he said.

"Not until the end of the year," she reminded him.

The purchaser agreed to wait to take possession until the end of Lisa's sublease when she and Jason moved back to their old home. Jason was not happy. He missed David and Nina, the au pair; he missed the big apartment and all the goodies life with David had brought. But after a few weeks he was back playing with his old friends. Lisa finished her book.

David comes to New York frequently and sees Lisa. He is thinking about returning.

"A fancy house and swimming pool and big stock options are very nice but maybe not everything. What would you say if I came back to New York? Would you make it permanent?"

"Wait and see," she said. "I like our friendship."

"So do I," David said.

Lisa and David may or may not get married. Whatever they decide in the future, they will be good, loving friends.

Lisa obeyed the commandments.

◆ She protected herself. She anticipated that David might move and saw to it that she and Jason would not be without a home.

- She did not follow the advice of friends but acted on her own good judgment.
- She wore a velvet glove over an iron hand. She did not fight with David but she insisted that he live up to his promise.
- And she discussed money problems with him *before* . . .
- Because Lisa maintained her independence, assured herself of a place to live and keep her job, she could not be victimized if David had changed his mind or if, as happened, he moved out of town. Neither David nor Lisa had any reason for resentment or hostility. Because she did not feel financially dependent on David, Lisa was not obliged to do everything David wanted. She did not have to try to convince herself that she loved him simply because she needed him.
- By carefully considering her own desires and needs *before* making a decision, Lisa avoided recriminations and regrets. Whatever happens, she and David will think of their relationship with pleasure.

What You Should Do Before

A useful device to help you decide whether to embark on a relationship is the old-fashioned balance sheet. Take a long piece of paper and draw a line lengthwise through the middle. On the left side list the significant facts of your present life situation. On the right side opposite each fact list the changes that will occur if you enter into the relationship. When you compare the pluses and minuses you will be in a better position to make a wise decision. You may find out that there are many things you don't know. Find out before . . .

Present Situation	Future Situation
Housing—my apartment	Housing . . . his or mine?
Finances—savings, salary	What are his finances?
Companionship—am I lonely? have I good friends?	Do I feel happy with him and with his friends?
Leisure activities—music, hiking, art exhibits	Does he like these activities?

Present Situation	Future Situation
Reputation—What do people think of me?	What do people think of him?
Career—Is mine promising?	Is his career promising?
Personality—warm/ aloof?	What is his personality?
Vacation ideals—travel, the beach, skiing	His vacation ideals
Five years from now—my vision: family; career; home; finances?	What is his vision of life five years from now?

If you and he have the same interests and the same goals, if he likes your friends and you like his, if you have a realistic understanding of finances, then your prospects for a happy relationship are good.

But if he likes the city and you like the country, if he wants to roam the world and you want to establish a home, think carefully before you say yes.

If you don't know about his work, his friends, his life dreams, then find out before . . .

In the old days of arranged marriages, match makers, and debut parties, families vetted a woman's prospective suitors. Today no one will do this job for you. You must do it yourself. Although your friends may think they know what is best for you, it is you, not they, who is establishing a relationship. It is your happiness and well-being that is at stake.

Before getting married many couples enter into prenuptial agreements. Each party consults his and her lawyer. They iron out financial arrangements so that both parties are protected in the event of death or divorce. Young couples who do not have much money or family obligations rarely think of future problems. They believe their love will last. As we shall see in succeeding chapters, many women are cruelly disappointed.

Ethologists tell us that some species of birds mate for life. This is not a biological trait of human beings. It is wise to follow the Second Commandment *and anticipate disaster.*

- All sensible married couples get legal advice before buying a home, signing a lease, taking out a loan, or any major financial obligation. The law has some limited protections for a wife. *There are almost none for an unmarried woman.*
- You and the man you contemplate living with will have to make some decisions that involve money.
- Where are you going to live?
- Who will sign the lease if you rent?
- Who will be the owner if you buy?
- What rights will the other party have if the relationship ends? Remember the Fifth Commandment and discuss these matters *before* . . .
- When he says, "I love you," that is romance. When you sign documents you are entering into the domain of the law. The old maxim, "Ignorance of the law is no excuse," still prevails.
- If you are ignorant of the legal rights you have and those you do not have when you enter into a relationship, you have no one to blame but yourself when you discover that the law does not protect you.

You do not have to choose between romance and common sense. You can have both: sweet words; music, and moonlight and also a fair arrangement of all the important aspects of daily life together.

You can have a happy and satisfying relationship with a man if you observe the Five new Commandments. Like many women of all ages, educational backgrounds, and economic conditions, you can find love and companionship in a temporary or permanent relationship. It can be a wise option to marriage or loneliness. Whether it brings you happiness or regret depends in large part on what you do *before* . . .

BEFORE YOU GET INVOLVED IN A RELATIONSHIP

5 Things He May Say or Do That Could Be a Warning Signal	5 Ways to Protect Yourself Against These Warning Signals
1 As he prepares to move in when before you planned it he says, "We'll save money by living together; two can live as cheaply as one." He may well mean that it will be cheaper for him to live with you.	Tell him you live by a budget. Sit down and make a *joint* budget. Decide *before* you live together what each will pay for.
2 It may sound fair and equal when he says, "Let's go fifty-fifty on everything." But equal contributions from people with unequal incomes is *not* equal sharing. If he has more income than you, fifty-fifty is *not* a fair arrangement.	Tell him you want to divide up the expenses in a ratio equal to your respective incomes; each will pay the same percentage of expenses as the ration of your assets and incomes.
3 If he resents the time your job takes and urges you to quit, saying, "I'll take care of your expenses," beware! What will happen to you if the relationship ends?	Tell him that this isn't fair to him and you want to pull your own weight.
4 If he is not forthcoming about his business affairs and dodges your inquiries, he probably doesn't want you to know what he is doing. (But if you live with someone *you are legally involved* in his activities.)	Tell him you don't want to set up an arrangement unless you can share *all* his life, and that you *want* to understand exactly what he does.

5 Things He May Say or Do That Could Be a Warning Signal	5 Ways to Protect Yourself Against These Warning Signals
5 When he says, "I love you, I want to live with you," but indicates he doesn't intend to change his lifestyle, beware. Living together means sharing and compromising.	Write a list of the values and activities that are truly important to you, and without being obvious, question him about each of them; if they don't add up positively—be warned.

5

BEFORE YOU DECIDE TO CHANGE YOUR NAME

The magic of a name . . .

THOMAS CAMPBELL

Most of us accept the names our parents gave us, whether we like them or not. In our presumably rational and scientific world, we tend to overlook the emotional and subliminal effects of one's name. Today you do not have to keep a name you do not like. You can legally change your first name, your surname, or both names. You can choose any name you like unless you are doing it for a fraudulent purpose. Changing your name may in some circumstances save you discomfort, embarrassment, and legal complications. It can also cause personal and legal problems.

Names have many functions. They identify an individual. They place her within a family. Before the widespread use of Ms. as a term of address, a woman's marital status was declared by the inevitable Miss or Mrs. Often a name indicates ethnicity or nationality. A given name usually signifies gender.

Among many primitive peoples, the name of the individual is so important that the real name is never used, lest it become a tool in the mouth of an enemy. A pseudonym is accordingly employed in daily life.

For countless generations in our patriarchal and patronymic culture a child was given the surname of the father. On marriage, a woman was expected to assume her husband's name. She was no longer Mary Smith but Mrs. Edward Jones. Assuming one's husband's name was a common custom for generations. Such erasure of one's identity and assumption of another is no longer legally required. Today a woman has many options. She can retain her maiden or birth name; she can assume her husband's name; she can hyphenate her name with her husband's name, use her maiden name as her middle name, or she can adopt another name.

In a multicultural nation like the United States a family name often geographically and ethnically identifies an individual. A person named Murphy is Irish; a person named Rizzo is Italian. Any one named Ching or Wong is Chinese. Many new immigrants have abandoned their birth names and acquired "American" surnames. Often this name change took place at the port of entry, perhaps in the post at Ellis Island, where an immigration officer simply wrote on the precious entry card a familiar name that sounded somewhat like the name mumbled by the frightened immigrant.

Name change is a common practice in the process of assimilation of new Americans. Many have done so in order to evade anti-Semitism, anti-Italian, and other xenophobic prejudices that have prevented women and men from obtaining jobs and admission to universities and professional schools. Recent legislation prohibiting discrimination in employment, education, and housing has eliminated much of the impetus for name changes.

Film stars and people in the entertainment world formerly were frequently given professional names that producers and public relations persons considered glamorous. Marilyn Monroe, for example, had as her birth name Norma Jeane Baker.

People in other occupations chose names they thought would help them advance. Hattie Carnegie, the great designer, simply took the name Carnegie because of the importance of Andrew Carnegie, a famous millionaire philanthropist. She thought the name connoted wealth, a desirable attribute for one in the fashion world.

Names affect how others see us, not only in commercial transactions but in all the social and ordinary interchanges of life.

A name can be an advantage or a disadvantage. An enterprising poor young man discovered that there was a scholarship at

Harvard for anyone with the name Peabody. He went to court and legally changed his name to Peabody and received the scholarship.

Some names are melodiously beautiful, like Annabel Lee; others sharply brusque, like Kurt. A multimillionaire Texas woman went through life with the name Ima Hogg. If you have such an unfortunate combination of names, you can change one or both.

There is usually a triggering event that causes us to think about our names and the desirability of change. The most common events are:

1. going to college
2. obtaining a professional degree or position
3. marriage
4. divorce
5. remarriage

But, you need not wait for such an occasion to consider changing your name.

Styles in names, as in all other aspects of life, do change. Ethnicity in nomenclature is now *in* today. Anglo-Saxon names are *out*. The poet LeRoi Jones assumed the African name Amiri Baraka. Nobel prize winner Simon Kusnetz, born Simon Smith, legally changed his name back to the original Russian patronymic that his father on coming to the United States had translated into Smith.

First names as well as family names may be undesirable for many reasons. Psychobiographers often speculate on the subconscious effect names have on individuals. Was Pearl Bergoff, a brutal strike breaker in the 1930s, moved to become a thug in order to prove his masculinity because he had a female name?

For many years it was fashionable to name girls typically masculine names like Frankie and Billy. Whitney and Kimberly are now popular names for girls. Few, if any, American boys are any longer given cross-gender names like Marion or Evelyn.

Most women, like most men, simply accept the name given

by their parents whether or not they like it. In infancy and child-hood most of us acquire nicknames, often suitable for a small child but inappropriate for an adult. How often have you smiled when a middle-aged man is called "Bobby" or a gray-haired woman is called "Muffie."

Since we age almost imperceptibly from day to day, we continue to live with names that become increasingly inappropriate and even embarrassing.

Most children live with their families—mother and father, or a mother or a father, or a grandparent—until the defining event of going away to school. This may be a boarding school, college, university, trade school, or professional school. At this point a girl or young woman is not only physically separated from her family and her childhood, she is psychologically separated. She becomes an individual, not simply someone's daughter.

This is the time when it is reasonable to think about more clearly defining your appearance, your future, your abilities. It is also a time to decide the name by which you want to be known in adulthood. "Sugar," "Cookie," and "Candy" are terms of endearment given by doting parents to pretty little girls. Is this the way you want to be perceived?

Many a forty-year-old woman today carries the name Scarlett or Amber because her mother read a popular novel during pregnancy. The name may suit you; but, it may not.

Often a female given name or nickname is extremely inappropriate. In many families girls are given the same name as their mothers. The daughter then becomes known as "little Louisa." When she is ten years old, the diminutive may be pleasant. When the daughter is sixteen and five inches taller than her mother, the sobriquet is sometimes ridiculous and embarrassing.

Some given names in time also not only become inappropriate but also become a handicap. If you are named Lily Belle or Lucy Mae and intend to become a doctor, a lawyer, an engineer, or a politician such a name can be disadvantageous. Ann Richards, governor of Texas, was given the name Dorothy Ann by her parents. When she was an adult she took the name Ann, clearly a more suitable name for someone in public life.

When you go away to school or begin your college or professional education you can change your name if you wish by simply assuming a new name. But when you receive your diploma or certificate or license to practice a trade or profession, it will be important to have your legal name on that piece of paper that will be your passport to your future career. *It is easier to make the legal change before you graduate or are licensed.*

Another defining moment with respect to your name is marriage. It is no longer unusual for young women to retain their own patronymic when they marry, rather than assuming the husband's surname. As in every choice, there are pros and cons.

When you marry, probably you hope and expect the marriage will last until death parts you from your husband. The sad fact is that one in every two marriages now ends in divorce. If you achieve success and prominence under your married name and later divorce, will you want to be known by your ex-husband's name? Will he object to your continuing to use his name?

If you have already established yourself in your career under your birth name, it may cause confusion and difficulties to change your name to your husband's name.

And if after a divorce you remarry, the acquisition of a third name will compound the problems. If you have established a career under the last name of your first husband, your second husband may find it an embarrassment. These difficulties can be particularly difficult when you and your first husband are in the same profession or when you live in the same town.

If you have children, the question of names becomes even more difficult. All of us have seen name cards on the roster of apartment buildings that read like this: "John Smith/Mary Jones/Billy and Jenny Brown." Billy and Jenny are Mary's children by her first husband. But to whom, if anyone is Mary married?

Some young now go the route of the hyphenated name. Jane Williamson marries Richard Witherspoon. They take the names Jane Williamson-Witherspoon and Richard Williamson-Witherspoon. In the present computerized world of identification cards and credit cards, a name of that length will not be easily accommodated.

Humorist Calvin Trillin speculates on the problems of marriage and nomenclature. He reports the real life wedding announcement of two Harvard graduates: Valerie Jane Silverman and Michael Thomas Flaherty. They adopted as a common family name "Flaherman." This is one solution.

Then Trillin discusses the names of the offspring of two fictional characters: Jennifer Morganwasser who married Jeremiah Christianson and Penelope Shaughnessy who married Nathaniel Underthaler. When the offspring of these two couples fall in love and marry will their names be Jebediah and Abigail Shaughnessy—Underthaler-Marganwasser Christianson?

And what happens in the event of a divorce?

A recent cartoon suggests an answer. It shows a lawyer explaining a divorce agreement to his client. The lawyer says, "As part of the settlement your wife is asking for any three of the six letters of your surname. You, of course, would retain the remaining three."

As in every decision a woman makes, there is no one answer that is right for every woman. You must decide what is right for *you*. That may depend on your occupation, your place of residence, your husband's occupation, the prominence of your respective families, and a solution that both you and your husband find comfortable in your particular milieu.

While it is now unexceptionable in New York or Boston for a professional woman to use her maiden name, Hillary Clinton found during her husband's tenure as Governor of Arkansas, that some constituents resented the fact that she practiced law under her maiden name. When the Clintons realized that this presented a problem in public life, she assumed his name.

The experiences of the women in this chapter will show you some of the pitfalls that the various choices can present.

Financial Problems

Lily was a successful business woman. She had a gold American Express card, charge accounts in many stores, a sizable bank account, and an automobile in her name. She also had an excellent credit rating. When Lily married she unthinkingly assumed her husband's name, as was the custom then. She changed all her credit cards and banks accounts to the name Mrs. William Russell (not her real name but a pseudonym used here to protect her privacy).

When Lily's first child was born she sold her business. A few years later she was divorced. When she went to the bank for a loan, she was refused. She had no bank account in her name, no credit cards, no indicia of her financial stability. She couldn't even rent a car. With considerable difficulty she transferred her assets back to her maiden name, threatened to sue the bank, and finally obtained a line of credit to start a new business that is now thriving.

Family Problems

Sophie is an ardent feminist. She determined to keep her own name. Her husband, Felix Remington, is a famous scientist. He believed that the choice of Sophie's name was her decision. When she had a baby, Felix was a proud and happy father until he arrived at the hospital and was dismayed to learn that there was no Mrs. Remington there. Sophie had insisted on being registered under her maiden name, Sophie Brown. The baby whom they had decided to name Felix, Jr., was listed on the birth certificate as Felix Brown-Remington, Jr.

Instead of joy over the birth of a healthy baby, a first child and first grandchild, dissension and unhappiness resulted for the parents and grandparents.

Sophie complained to me, "Why didn't I know the difficulties this would cause *before* . . . ?

Rachel Renfrou (a pseudonym) is a journalist. Her husband Jonathan Lerow is a banker in a conservative, staid investment bank. When they married Jonathan and Rachel agreed that they would keep their business lives separate and that she should keep her maiden name. Rachel is an investigative reporter, some might say a muckraker. Her articles would have embarrassed Jonathan and his firm if the name Lebow had appeared on the by-line.

They thought they had satisfactorily solved the problem of Rachel's nomenclature until their daughter, Theresa, entered first grade. The children were asked their parents' names. Theresa told the class, "My mother's name is Rachel Renfrou; my father's name is Jonathan Lebow." A few days later Theresa came home in tears. A classmate had called her a "bastard." The child had said that Theresa's parents weren't married because they had different names.

"Why don't you have Daddy's name, like all the other mothers?" Theresa cried.

Monica Zellinghast (a pseudonym) is the daughter of the leading citizen of her town. He is the political power in the county, the richest man in a close-knit community. Her mother is an ideal helpmeet for her husband. Monica is a different type of woman. When she received her MBA from the Wharton Business School and also control of the substantial trust her father had established for her as a means of avoiding taxes, she decided to go into business.

Monica went back to her home town and bought an abandoned factory and set up an electronics business. She named it *M Zellinghast, Inc.* Her business methods and philosophy were diametrically opposed to those of her father.

When she negotiated a contract with the union representing her employees, giving them health benefits and a company supported day care center, the workers in her father's factories struck and demanded the same kind of contract.

"We're all Zellinghast employees," they argued, "and we're all entitled to the same benefits."

Monica's father is angry and worried. His business is not as successful as hers. A similar contract would be disastrous for him.

"You didn't have to use my name," he accused Monica.

"But it's *my* name, too," she replied.

Monica no longer sees her mother and father. She misses the family Sunday dinners and holidays together. She is alone and lonely.

"If only I had known the problems a name could cause *before . . .*" she says.

Professional Problems

Lisa Aversa married Lawrence Richette when they were both young lawyers. She practiced law under the name Lisa Richette. She was politically active, a young attorney whose name was often in the press. Twenty years later, Lisa was appointed to the Court of Common Pleas of Philadelphia. The marriage, which had not been too happy, frayed under the stress of her new position and prominence and they separated. The ensuing divorce was unusually acrimonious.

Once the decree was final, Lawrence sued to get back his name. He argued that Lisa's activities prejudiced him and his legal practice.

Lisa resisted, claiming that she was known as Lisa Richette, that this was *her* name. A Pennsylvania court upheld Lisa, but the litigation caused further stress and embarrassment to Lisa, Lawrence, and their son. Other courts may favor a disgruntled husband.

Like most decisions in life, there are pros and cons in the choice of a name other than your birth name. Here is a list of issues you should consider when thinking of changing your name.

◆ Is my name a disadvantage or an embarrassment? A name identified in the public mind with a famous or infamous individual can be a handicap. After the rise of Hitler many men named Adolf changed their names either legally or unofficially. The names Capone and Dillinger are inextricably connected with notorious criminals. Such a name can cause problems.

Other names identified with famous persons also create difficulties. If you are named Elizabeth Taylor or Margaret Thatcher, whenever you are introduced, people will probably ask, "Not *the* Elizabeth Taylor?" or "Not *the* Margaret Thatcher?"

◆ Do you dislike your name? If you are named Ida after an aunt who has a nasty disposition, you will probably not be happy with that name. You may find Mary too plain a name for your taste or Esmerelda too exotic.

- Does your name cause unnecessary complications? Two classmates in law school were named Archibald Smith. Both intended to practice law in the same city. Anticipating the confusion that would result, they drew straws. The loser legally changed his name.
- Will your name adversely affect your career? If you have an unusual surname, you will be identified with your family even though you are engaged in a different occupation. If you plan to go into politics, practice a profession, or do something that brings you in contact with the public, it may make life easier for you and your family if you have a different name so that you are not identified with them.
- Will your activities adversely affect your husband or will his activities adversely affect your career? A different name will mitigate these problems.
- Will the abandonment of your family name or the refusal to take your husband's name cause emotional stress? This consideration may weigh heavily in your decision. The weight to be given is up to you.

The final piece of advice concerning names is that it is better to choose your name *before* you begin your career, marriage, or lifestyle than later.

You are legally entitled to take the name you want. It is *your* choice. Depending upon your foresight and sensitivity, that decision can eliminate problems, or it can cause difficulties that could have been avoided if you have considered your options *before* . . .

6

BEFORE YOU DECIDE TO MARRY

The ache of marriage . . .
looking for joy, some joy
not to be known outside marriage
two by two in the ark
the ache of it . . .

ELINOR WYLIE

Fairy tales end with marriage. In real life, that is when the story begins. Whether the couple will live happily ever after depends in large part on their expectations of each other. Are those expectations based on fact or fantasy? Do you really know what kind of life you want? Do you know what kind of life he wants? Are your respective desires compatible? Are they realistic?

Until the present time, it was expected that all women would marry. The unmarried woman's lot was to take care of her parents, her siblings and their families, to be an unpaid servant for her family, a grateful guest in the homes of those who gave her shelter.

Faced with that prospect, most young women tried to persuade themselves that they loved the men who offered them the status of wife, mistress of their own home, the prospect of children. Novels reinforced the notion that marriage was the only goal of a normal female by contrasting the differences in status of the wed and the unwed female. Rich or poor, a woman's goal in life was to get a husband.

Love outside marriage was a lifelong disaster. Consider the sad fate of Hester Prynne in *The Scarlet Letter*. Hester wore the red *A* for adultery blazoned on her breast throughout her life. Her lover, the Reverend Dimsdale, was the preacher of the town.

64

He was married and respected. This book was required reading in high school for generations of boys and girls. Think of the contrasting messages they received. The girls were graphically shown that love outside marriage was sin and brought degradation. The boys were told that they could get away with it.

Pamela or Virtue Rewarded by Henry Fielding brought home the message that the wise female would say "no" until the wedding ring was safely and permanently affixed to her finger. The more urbane, sophisticated novelist Henry James depicted a series of intelligent, cultivated, turn-of-the-century women deliberately devoting their energies to obtaining a husband as a necessary social adjunct. The husband usually was a fairly caddish creature.

And Charlotte Bronte's heroine Jane Eyre exclaims triumphantly at the end of the novel, "Reader, I married him!" What kind of a marriage would that be—life with a blind, ruined man who lied to and deceived a young girl?

Only a generation or two ago, female college graduates who received their A.B. degrees and their MRS. in the same week were considered successful. The money that their families had invested in their education had paid off.

Girls who could not afford college or did not have such aspirations were under similar pressure to marry on graduation from high school. A home of one's own seemed preferable to a menial, poorly paid job and living under the parental roof without sexual or personal freedom.

Today, Jane Austen would be a highly acclaimed author with ample funds to have her own home. She would not be expected to live with her parents or care for her relatives. She would probably be a professor of creative writing in a prestigious university, free to live her own life and follow her own inclinations whatever they might be.

Even though you may be less gifted, you are free to earn your own livelihood and live independently. Many contemporary feminist writers, however, present their readers with undesirable role models. Simone de Beauvoir, the icon of the early feminist movement, has written frankly about how she literally groveled before her lover Jean Paul Sartre. She even provided him with younger and prettier girl friends when he was no longer interested in her sexually.

Erica Jong, after writing several novels about strong, achieving women, in *Any Woman's Blues* presents the appalling picture of a highly successful female artist who submits to physical abuse, financial treachery, and sexual infidelity from a young, worthless lover and proclaims that she is happy.

These literary models of female life are no more realistic or helpful than the Cinderella myth. Let us look at facts. *Despite much media hype, there still is no shortage of male partners for females who wish to marry today.* Many women no longer feel the necessity to get married. They can be selective. The 1989 "New Diversity" poll by opinion experts Langer Associates and Significance Inc. reported that 90 percent of women believed they could have a "happy and complete" life without marriage.

In a national survey *Glamour* magazine found that 90 percent of women who had not yet married had made that decision because "they haven't wanted to yet." A 1985 survey of 60,000 women reported that only half of these married women would marry their husbands if they could relive their lives. *You need not be one of them;* this book will show you why.

There are many styles of marriage today. Some marriages still follow the traditional pattern in which the husband is the earner and the wife is the homemaker. And some husbands and wives live a continent apart. Others live in separate homes in the same city. Some couples consist of working wives and house husbands. In most marriages today, however, both spouses work. In many marriages the husband is the main breadwinner. And in some marriages, like that of Bill and Hillary Rodham Clinton, before they went to the White House, the wife is the big money earner.

Today you have many choices. You can follow any of these patterns or create one that suits you and your husband. You have many choices that your mother and grandmothers did not have. Examine those choices carefully before you make the decision to marry.

In a preceding chapter we set forth a series of questions you should ask yourself before you enter into a relationship with a man. You should ask yourself those same questions with respect to the man you contemplate marrying. You should also ask yourself many more questions with respect to the kind of marriage you want, what you expect of each other, your plans and dreams for the future.

◆ Do you want children? Does he? If you are not in agreement on this question, which of you is willing to compromise? He can become a father in his sixties. You cannot become a mother much later than your early forties.
◆ What kind of home life do you expect?
◆ Does he want a trophy wife? A housekeeper? A hostess? A breadwinner? Or does he want *you* as you really are, not some idealized or remade version of you to fit his pattern?
◆ What do you expect of a husband? Do you want a handsome escort? a good dancer? A party companion? A breadwinner? someone rich and famous or whom you think will become rich and famous, or do you want him as he really is, not as you hope to remake him? And if so, why?

Marriage is a far more significant step than a relationship. It has both emotional and legal consequences. It is complicated to terminate as we shall see in the next chapters.

Even though in the 1990s when one in two marriages in the United States ends in divorce, marriage implies a permanent commitment. Do not wait until the wedding ceremony to ask each other the traditional questions: "Do you take this man to be your lawful wedded husband, forsaking all others? Will you love, honor, and cherish him in sickness and in health, for richer or poorer, for better or for worse until death do you part?" These are awesome questions. Honest, ungrudging affirmative answers bind you to serious obligations.

If you have any doubts about your commitment to him and his commitment to you, it is better to find out *before . . . A good way to find out before is to rehearse this colloquy of the marriage ceremony long before the actual wedding.* Do it when you two are alone. Watch his responses to those questions. If he hesitates, you should hesitate, too. If you feel any reluctance in making those responses, think again.

I believe that most women's ideal life includes marriage. However, wise women realize that it is not the only life choice. The purpose of this chapter is to urge you look carefully *before* you marry so that you are not among the 50 percent of married women who would not marry their husbands if they could do it again. It is also to warn you of the limitations of your legal protections.

In no decision that you make is it more important to remember the New Commandments than in the decision to marry.

◆ **The First Commandment, "Protect thyself," is essential.** When you and your husband are alone in the privacy of your own home, how will he behave toward you? Today few, if any, women get married without having had intimate relations with their groom before marriage. But courtship is different from marriage. Do you know what he is really like when he is not seeking to please you? How does he treat other women? His mother? His female employees? Is it with respect or an attitude of command or condescension?

◆ **The Second Commandment, "Anticipate disaster," is also important.** No one knows how long he or she will live, whether it will be in sickness or in health. No one knows how secure employment is. Can you cope with such unexpected misfortunes as death, illness, or prolonged unemployment of your spouse? Can he?

◆ **The Third Commandment, "Act on your own best judgment" is perhaps the most important rule when deciding to marry.** Although parents no longer choose their daughters' husbands, we inevitably try to influence their choices. It is you, not your parents who will be living with him. They may find him charming; they may like his family; they may believe his financial prospects are good. But if you do not find him appealing, you are asking for unhappiness.

◆ **The Fourth Commandment, "Wear a velvet glove over an iron hand," in the context of marriage is a corollary.** Do not let anyone, no matter how well meaning, coax or coerce you into a marriage that you do not really want.

◆ **And the Fifth Commandment, dealing with the subject of money, cannot be ignored** even if both you and your fiancé are young and without any money or property. The poorer you are, the more necessary it is to live within your means. Is he a spendthrift who indulges himself? Or is he a miser with whom you will have conflicts over money?

The real life women you will meet in this chapter are not famous. They led ordinary lives. They were not stupid or mean or selfish. They came from all walks of life. Their decisions and how they handled the problems of marriage and its legal complications should help you in making your decision.

The Mistake of Acquiescing to an Importunate Suitor and Well-meaning Parents

Alison was a bright, attractive senior at Yale. She had dated Bruce on and off all through college. He was a medical student at Harvard. She was a science major and had received a fellowship to do graduate work in biology at Columbia University in New York City. Bruce had an internship in New Hampshire awaiting him.

Allison's father was a successful business man. Her mother wrote a column for the local paper. They had a pleasant suburban home and enjoyed their life and their family. Bruce's father was a successful doctor. His mother was president of her garden club. Both sets of parents felt that they had good lives. They hoped their children would replicate their lives.

Bruce came to New Haven for Alison's graduation. After dining with her parents the young people walked on the campus in the moonlight. Other happy young couples were strolling under the trees. Bruce took a small box from his pocket.

"Here is your graduation present."

It was a diamond ring. Alison looked at it in dismay.

"Oh, no!"

"Don't you love me?" Bruce asked in shocked disbelief.

"Of course, I love you. But—"

"But what?" he said angrily.

"But what about my fellowship? I want to be a biologist."

"You can be my wife and also be a biologist. We can get married next month and have a honeymoon in Europe before I have to begin my internship. You can go to graduate school in New Hampshire."

"But my fellowship? It's Columbia that I want, not some other university."

"Don't you want me?" Bruce said.

Alison had never seen him so angry. She was frightened. Was she throwing away happiness? Would she really make some important contribution to biology or was she just a foolish, selfish girl?

"Come, let's tell your parents we're going to be married so your mother can plan a wedding. We don't have that much time."

Alison's parents assured her they would pay for her tuition at Dartmouth. She needn't worry about the lost fellowship. And so they were married in a beautiful garden wedding.

The honeymoon was all that Alison could have wished, gondola rides in Venice in the moonlight, breakfast on a patio overlooking Florence, and a return to the United States on the *Queen Elizabeth*.

When they arrived in New Hampshire, Alison realized that the honeymoon was over. She started classes and he began his internship. Both were busy all day. But Bruce expected Alison to furnish a home completely and run it like clockwork as his mother did. Bruce's mother had a full-time maid and extra domestic help. Alison had an inefficient helper one day a week. Bruce's mother devoted her life to making his father comfortable. Alison had her own studies.

One evening he came home early from the hospital. Alison

was at school. Bruce was hungry. There was no dinner on the table for him. When Alison came home Bruce was furiously angry. He yelled at her.

"You can't speak to me like this," Alison declared. "Get out!"

Bruce left in a rage. About midnight he came back. Alison thought he wanted to apologize. Instead, he accused her of being selfish and uncaring. Alison called him a selfish brute. But she did not insist that he leave. In the middle of the night he demanded his "conjugal rights." When she refused, he raped her.

The next day she went to court and got a protective order barring Bruce from entering the apartment. Bruce ignored the order and came back whenever he pleased and forced himself on Alison.

She went back to court to get the order enforced.

"Call the police the next time he comes," she was told.

A few days later when Bruce appeared, Alison called the police. When they arrived they saw Bruce, nicely dressed, calmly sitting on the sofa and Alison screaming at him.

"Arrest this man," she cried.

"It's my apartment," Bruce told them and showed the lease.

"We haven't seen any crime," the police declared. They left.

Alison changed the locks on the apartment. But Bruce broke in. When she called the police she was told, "This is a domestic dispute. We don't interfere."

Finally when Alison realized that she had no protection, she left school and moved out of town. She lives in fear that Bruce will learn where she is and come back.

Alison ignored the Third Commandment. She took her parents' well-meant advice instead of acting on her own best judgment. She had misgivings about Bruce, his bad temper, his dominating manner. She also knew that she wanted to go to Columbia University graduate school, that this was of great importance to her.

Like most young women, she discussed Bruce's proposal of marriage with her parents. This was sensible, for often older people who have your interest at heart will see obstacles to a marriage—different lifestyles and backgrounds, different values, and character flaws that a young woman in love may overlook.

The Third Commandment teaches that you should act on your own best judgment. Alison did not do that. She allowed her will to be overborne by her parents. Their image of a good marriage differed from hers. She also knew character traits of Bruce that her parents did not. They had seen him only when he was on his good behavior. Only you can know what your suitor is really like, the person he is when he is not on public display.

After Bruce behaved brutally, Alison ignored the First Commandment. She did not protect herself. Like many wives, she hoped in vain for a change in her husband's behavior. She should not have permitted him to return to the apartment.

When she did seek legal protection she discovered, as all too many wives have, that the law affords only nominal security orders that are rarely enforced. She learned the hard way that she had to protect herself by leaving.

Acting on Your Own Best Judgment

Ruth knew what she wanted to do when she graduated from high school. She had seen her careworn mother burdened with six children and her hard-drinking father tied to the drudgery of a factory job, always worried about meeting mortgage payments, always afraid of losing his job.

Ruth wanted a different life, one that was more than getting up and going to work, coming home too tired to enjoy anything.

She was a bright, popular girl. When she graduated from high school she was offered a scholarship to the local college but turned it down. "I don't want to waste four years sitting in school," she said. "I've had enough of that. I want to be a business woman, have my own business and not be a wage slave."

Her friends were either going to college or getting married. Some who could not afford college were working in offices and stores, dead-end jobs, waiting for Mr. Right to come along. Ruth saw that all these women spent almost a fourth of their income on cosmetics, products that were terribly overpriced and not much better than what she bought in cut-rate drug stores. It was all a matter of packaging. This was a business she thought she could learn and master.

She got a job with a major cosmetics company and began to learn the business. After three years she was earning a big salary, more than her father had ever made.

She met Norman, a good-looking young man who worked in the same company. He was a college graduate who had a low-level executive job. He found Ruth different and exciting. They began to date. Both liked to dance. She loved jazz and he was content to go with her to the little, offbeat places she liked. Soon Norman was in love. He proposed marriage.

Ruth's parents were delighted with Norman. He was a step up on the social ladder, a nice-looking young man who cared for their daughter, and she seemed to like him very much.

"Now you can stop working, have your own home and a family," they said.

"I'm only twenty. I'm not ready," Ruth objected.

"Men like Norman don't grow on trees. You'll regret it when you see him with someone else," her friends warned.

But Ruth was not convinced. She knew Norman was a nice, good man. But he had no ambition. He would work for the cosmetics company until he retired or was fired. Although he had a moderate-paying, white collar job, he was too much like her father, tied to an unexciting job. And she would be like her mother, always worried about money, with no possibility of ever realizing her dreams.

She told Norman she didn't want to get married until she'd made her own life.

"Marriage to me will be a good life," he replied.

Ruth realized that this might be true for another woman, but he was not the right man for her.

Ruth and a friend in the cosmetics company opened their own business. They had to borrow money, scrimp, and save. But within four years she was making more money than she had earned in the big company. And the business belonged to her.

Norman married a year after Ruth refused him. He and his wife had a child. Shortly thereafter he lost his job when the company downsized. He is now working for Ruth.

She says, "In a few years, I'll be ready to think about marriage. The man I want isn't Norman, but someone more adventurous and brighter. And if I don't find him, I'm having a great life, doing what I want."

Ruth, like Alison, knew what she wanted in life. But, unlike Alison, she did not permit her parents' well-meant advice to override her own wishes. She realized that having a husband—even a nice, loving man—whose life values differed markedly from hers was not the most important consideration for her at that time in her goal-oriented young life. She obeyed the Third Commandment and is happy with her choice today.

There Is No Free Lunch

Grace was a bright, pretty girl. Her father's business had failed. He was having a hard time making ends meet. Grace's mother did dressmaking and alterations for her rich friends. They tried to keep up appearances. They borrowed the money for Grace's college tuition from a rich relative.

In her first year at college Grace met Max. He was the son of a successful business man. He was in his third year of college. He fell in love with Grace and courted her with flowers, candy, fraternity parties, and visits to his parents' country home.

Grace had also met Jim, a bright, handsome journalism major. He was an honor student but he was poor. He was attending college on a scholarship. He and Grace fell in love. He told her he wanted to marry her but that he could not marry for at least three years. After graduation he had to get a job, pay off his student loan, and help his parents. But he was sure that by the time Grace graduated he could afford to get married.

At the end of the school year, Grace was on the honor roll. Max was on probation. He proposed marriage. He suggested a fall wedding. Although Max was not very good looking and was certainly not very intelligent, Grace decided that she would like being his wife.

She was tired of the kind of penny-pinching life her parents led. She saw her mother, who had been pretty and vibrant, but was now worn and prematurely old looking and her father a tired, defeated man not yet fifty.

Grace's parents were delighted. Their daughter would have

a good, secure life, they thought. They would not have to borrow any more money for her education. They could help Grace's younger sister.

Max's parents were also delighted with the engagement. They liked Grace, her wit and charm. She was a prettier, cleverer girl than they had hoped Max would find. They envisioned smart, attractive grandchildren. They welcomed Grace into their warm, carefree family.

Max's parents gave a big dinner dance for Grace. She quit school and worked in a department store all summer to buy her trousseau. The wedding, given by Max's parents, was lovely. Grace was a beautiful bride and Max a happy but rather unattractive groom.

They had two daughters. One was smart and pretty like Grace. The other resembled Max in looks and temperament. Much as Grace tried to love both daughters and Max, the strain was too much. She missed Jim, his wit and fun, his intelligence. When Max made love to Grace she closed her eyes and thought of Jim.

Grace went to a psychiatrist. She tried to convince Grace to be more sexual, to enjoy Max. She also told Grace that she was foolish and selfish. She should appreciate her good fortune and make her marriage work. After two years of therapy, Grace was still unhappy.

Then disaster struck. Max's father's business was bought by a conglomerate. Within a few months Max was unemployed. Gone were the lovely home, the maid, and the psychiatrist. Grace went back to work in the department store.

Jim is now a successful journalist. He works for a major newspaper. He has a lovely wife and a fascinating life. Grace has the same penny-pinching, difficult life her mother had. She has little education and no job skills.

In desperation she consulted a lawyer about a divorce. She learned the bitter facts. Max earns little. Were it not for her salary combined with his, there would not be enough to support the children. She could not possibly divorce him. Alone, neither could afford child support.

"What about his father?" she asked her lawyer when she

consulted her. "When we got engaged he told me he would always see that we were well taken care of."

"That is not an enforceable promise," the lawyer told Grace. "Why didn't you have him set up a trust fund for you and the children?"

"I don't know anything about trust funds. I thought he would take care of us as he said he would."

Even though Max's parents are living as well as they always did, they have no legal obligation to support Grace or her children.

Grace is one of the 50 percent of wives who would not marry her husband if she had a second chance. She too says, "Why didn't I know *before* . . .?"

Grace, like most young women, wanted a carefree life with material comforts and pleasures. She thought marriage to the son of a rich man would give her what she wanted. But there is no guaranty that a thriving business will always flourish. There are recessions and depressions. Unless one is super-rich, the specter of bankruptcy and unemployment lurks in the unforseeable future.

◆ **Grace ignored the First Commandment. She did not protect herself** from the threat of poverty by acquiring learning and skill. She ignored the reality that the only true security for a woman is her own ability and skills.

◆ **Grace ignored the Second Commandment. She did not anticipate disaster.** She knew Max was not very bright, that he had a good paying job only because his father was the boss. When she married in 1980 she should have taken into account the possible vicissitudes of life—divorce, death, illness, and unemployment.

By an ironic trick of fortune, Grace has the very life she sought to avoid, because she ignored the First and Second Commandments.

Follow Your Bliss

Frances is one of the happiest women I know. She had a privileged childhood: private schools; summer camps; and vacations in Europe. She dutifully made her debut and then attended a Seven Sister college her parents had selected. There she suddenly discovered the excitement of the life of the mind. Despite her parents' protest she went on to graduate school.

Each time she came home for a holiday, her mother would ask whether she had met any "nice men." They could not understand why she wanted to go to Indonesia and study the life of some primitive tribes.

"How can you live in such a place? Where will you meet a husband?"

Nonetheless, Frances persevered. She spent several years in southeast Asia and then worked on an Indian reservation in Arizona.

When she was thirty-five she met Joe. He was twenty-six and was working in the desert studying hydrology. He was the first member of his family to attend college, a state university. He had worked his way through school as a handyman and gardener. He was tall, good looking, and brilliant. Although he had never been to an opera, never worn a tuxedo, had no social graces, he had the most exciting mind Frances had encountered. He was also a marvelous lover.

Frances brought him to Boston to meet her family. They were horrified. They disapproved of his age, his table manners, and his clothes.

"And what does your father do?" Frances's mother asked.

"He was just laid off from his job on an auto assembly line, ma'am," Joe replied.

"You can't marry this man," Frances's family exclaimed in horror. "We're not snobs, but you have nothing in common."

Her old school friends living their proper Bostonian lives expressed dismay.

"Sure, he's good looking. But that isn't everything," Gwen warned her. "My James was handsome when I married him, but look at him now."

Frances looked at James, a paunchy banker whose conversation was limited to stocks and bonds. She also looked and listened to her parents and her lifelong friends and knew she wouldn't trade places with any of them.

After ten uncomfortable days in Boston, Joe and Frances went back to Arizona, where they were married in the home of an Indian couple on the reservation. They live in an adobe house that Joe built.

Each morning when Frances awakens and looks out over the desert, she rejoices in the life that she has chosen.

If you follow the path prescribed by someone else, a parent, teacher, or friend, it will not lead to your bliss. Frances understood this message. She followed her bliss and achieved a rare happiness. By studying and working in her chosen field, she found a satisfying career. In the course of that work, she also found love and marriage.

Frances obeyed the Third and Fourth Commandments. She acted on her own good judgment in the choice of a husband. In discussing marriage with her family and friends she was polite but firm, a wise woman. As a result, she is also a happy woman.

Know Thyself

Martha is a physician. She had a long hard struggle working her way through college and medical school. While she was an intern she met a man who sold medical equipment to the hospital. He would wait for her when she got off duty and take her to dinner. He was pleasant and she was grateful to have someone who seemed to take care of her. She was tired and worn out from eight years of grinding work and schooling.

When she finished her residency and obtained a position with a physician on the hospital staff, Edgar proposed marriage. Martha did not find him physically alluring. In fact, although she had had many boyfriends all through school, she had never been sexually attracted to any of them.

She wanted to talk to someone about her strange lack of feelings, lack of desire. She talked to her married sister.

"Sex isn't everything. Is he kind and caring? Do you enjoy his company? Those are the qualities that count in the long run."

Martha also consulted a psychiatrist on the hospital staff. He was a kindly middle-aged man steeped in Freudian theory.

"You're just tired after all this hard work. You're in a man's profession. You probably have a subconscious penis envy. Don't you want a home and a family? Every woman does, even you career women. After you've been married a few months, you'll find you are more comfortable with sexual intercourse."

And so Martha and Edgar were married. They had two children whom Martha adored. But she found life with Edgar more and more distasteful. She became depressed. She felt her work would be affected if she didn't get away from Edgar.

When she told him she wanted a divorce, he was enraged. "You don't like men—you might even be a lesbian," he screamed.

And Martha realized that he was probably right. She had spent seven miserable years trying to force herself into a life that she hated.

She obtained a divorce without any difficulty. Edgar had never contributed to her support and she didn't ask for anything. Their marital assets were negligible.

It was the custody battle that was difficult. The lawyer she consulted told her that Edgar had already filed a petition to obtain custody of the children, to bar her from seeing them, and to demand child support from her. He alleged that she was an unfit mother because she was a lesbian.

"What if I am? That doesn't make me an unfit mother," Martha told the lawyer.

"The court won't see it that way," he replied.

Martha knew that Edgar was not a good father. The girls were bright. They should go to college. Edgar thought education for women was a waste of money. He would not know how to deal with the difficult adolescent years. She could not entrust her daughters to this man.

Martha paid the first lawyer his fee and got her papers. She told him she had not decided what to do and that she was not retaining him.

She consulted another lawyer who also told her that if Edgar's charges were proved, she probably would not get custody of her daughters.

"Make him prove it," she told the lawyer.

"You are sharing your apartment with another woman since Edgar left, aren't you?"

"Yes. Because I can't afford the rent and he doesn't pay any child support. Would it be better if I shared the apartment with a man?" she replied.

Martha fought her case through the courts and won. Her daughters are now in college. They have a warm, loving relationship with their mother. They see their father only occasionally. Martha is paying for their education.

Whether she is a practicing lesbian, I do not know. Apparently her daughters do not know either. They simply know that she is a good mother.

Martha said to me, "I'm a physician. I should have known what my real nature is and not spent all those miserable years trying to be the kind of person everyone expected me to be. But I thought when I was twenty-nine that if I didn't get married then, I would lose all chances of finding a husband. I never asked myself if I *wanted* one."

Martha did not know or acknowledge herself until an unhappy marriage opened her eyes. Martha acted wisely after she consulted her first lawyer. She learned from him how the law really operates and she used that knowledge *to make it work to her benefit*. Every woman who faces a legal battle should find out *before* she goes to court what the likely outcome of her claim or defense will be. Armed with that information, she is then in a position to protect herself. When she went to court Martha obeyed the First Commandment. *She protected herself.*

A Loan Often Loses Both Itself and Friend

Suzanne knew she wanted a husband. She wanted not just a husband but also a home and children, the happy life her mother had. When she graduated from college, she knew that she did not want a career. So she found a pleasant job where she would meet interesting people. She worked in an art gallery.

In due course she met Raoul, a debonair Frenchman with a very famous surname. He bought a good but modestly priced painting from Suzanne and then invited her for a drink to celebrate his purchase. His conversation was delightful and fascinating. He seemed to know all the important people in the art world that she read about in magazines. He knew what wines to order. He was a ballet aficionado. Suzanne was enchanted with Raoul.

When she brought him home for a weekend, he charmed her parents and even the crusty housekeeper. He was a good tennis player and a good dancer. He was an ideal companion.

When Suzanne began talking about marriage, her father asked, "What does he do?"

"Something about international finance. But he's really interested in art."

After a few months of steady dating Raoul presented Suzanne with an antique gold ring, a family heirloom, he told her. They set a date for the wedding.

"What about his family?" her parents asked.

"They're in France at their chateau; they'll come for the wedding, Raoul says."

"Still, I'd like to meet them before you get married," her parents said. "Doesn't he know anyone we know?"

"Oh, don't be old fashioned, Dad. Raoul is a love. I adore him and he adores me."

Two weeks before the wedding Suzanne called her parents and said she had to talk to them seriously, right away.

"I love Raoul, but—"

"But, what? If you have any doubts, now is the time to discuss them instead of later."

"Well, my friends say I'm crazy, suspicious, that I just have prenuptial jitters. Raoul is the answer to every woman's prayer. And I do love him. He's sweet and tender and caring—"

"But, what is wrong?"

"Somethings just don't jibe. He told me all about the family chateau near Blois. You remember when I spent my third year abroad. We were in Blois. I think I saw every chateau within fifty miles, but not his. I got out my old Michelin and my notes from school and asked him exactly where it was. He said I must have misunderstood him, it's not near Blois but Arles. I know I didn't misunderstand because we talked a lot about the Loire Valley and Arles isn't on the Loire. Also, he said he got a wire from his parents; they can't come to the wedding. And, Daddy, I lent him some money, $10,000. He hasn't paid me back. What should I do?"

"What's the name of this firm he works for?"

"I'm not sure—he says it fast in French, *Compagnie* something or other."

"I'm going to investigate him. I'll do it quietly so I won't embarrass you. I hope he's telling the truth. But if he isn't you want to know, don't you?"

Suzanne cried. "Yes, I want to know."

Raoul was indeed a relative of the famous family, but the black sheep. He had fled France after a financial scandal that the family had hushed. They had disowned him. He does work for a French company but is in debt and probably will lose his job.

Suzanne called off the wedding.

When she asked Raoul for her $10,000, he laughed. "That was a gift to me. I don't owe you any money."

Suzanne talked to a lawyer friend. "Do you have a note from him? Anything in writing? A promise to repay?"

"No. I trusted him," she cried.

"Well, I'm afraid the courts will think you were too trusting. But, we can try."

Raoul was an appealing witness, good looking, smooth, and charming. He told the jury all about the presents he had given Suzanne—the antique ring that she had returned, flowers, books, candy.

"I'm a poor man and she's a rich woman. If she wanted to give me a gift because she loved me, I would not hurt her feelings by refusing."

Suzanne lost her $10,000. The jury found that it was a gift.

Romance and money are uneasy partners. One outweighs the other. *Usually money predominates.* Whenever a man asks for money, remember the First Commandment: *Protect thyself.* If Suzanne had asked Raoul for a note acknowledging the debt when she agreed to lend Raoul money, she would have acted prudently to protect herself. If a female friend had asked for a loan, that is what she probably would have done. But because she confused money and romance, she failed to protect herself.

Suzanne also ignored the Fifth Commandment. She did not discuss money with Raoul. She should have had a frank talk with him about his job and his finances *before* . . . She would have avoided the embarrassment of a public engagement and a cancellation of the wedding. She would also have mitigated the pain of betrayal of love.

Marriage is no longer irrevocable. You can get out of an unhappy marriage—as we shall see in the next chapter. But it is seldom an easy or pleasant process.

American women usually marry for love. Indeed, we look with scorn upon a woman who marries for money alone. When you are in your twenties and still are unsure of your own identity, you are expected to make one of the most significant decisions of your life: the choice of a husband.

For centuries women did not have this right. They were given or sold into marriage by their fathers who selected their husbands. Sometimes the wishes of the bride were taken into consideration. Often she did not see her bridegroom until the day of the wedding. That is still the custom in many parts of the world. Love and marriage did not go together.

In *Fiddler on the Roof,* Teyve, the father, asks his wife of many years, "Do you love me?"

She is astonished. The thought has never occurred to her. She simply did her duty as a wife and mother without any expectation of love. No self-respecting American woman would want such a marriage. But, as many women discover, love, by which we usually mean sexual attraction, is not enough to create a strong, enduring marriage.

Margaret Mead suggested that every woman have five husbands in turn: one for love or sex; one for children; one for her career; one for companionship; and one to care for her in old age. Most women want one husband to fulfill all these roles.

You have the right to choose your husband. That right also

entails a responsibility—to discover whether your prospective husband is reliable, whether you two come from compatible backgrounds, whether you are intellectually and emotionally attuned to each other.

In Japan the custom of arranged marriage still prevails. The families of the prospective bride and groom carefully discuss these questions. If they are satisfied that the two would be compatible and that the families will be happy together then introductions are arranged. The man and woman get acquainted. If they are both satisfied, then the marriage takes place.

When he proposes marriage or, as is often the case, you mutually discuss the subject, you must do for yourself what Japanese families do for prospective brides and grooms.

Use This Checklist Before You Say "I Do"

Before you marry, ask yourself these questions:

◆ Do I love him? As Martha and Grace found out, marriage without sexual love is a tragic burden.

◆ Will he be a good father? If you want children and he does not, one or the other of you will be unhappy. An unwilling father is rarely loving or helpful. Children who feel unwanted bear lifelong scars. A woman who wants a child but does not have one spends a lifetime of regret. Often she resents the man who prevented her from becoming a mother.

◆ If you have a profession or want to have a career outside the home and he opposes you or is unwilling to assume any of the household responsibilities, you will encounter problems.

◆ Is he a good companion? What do you talk about? Is it always his business? Or is he also interested in what you do? Do you enjoy the same things? If he loves sports and you are bored by them, if he likes jazz and you like classical music, if one of you is a bookworm and the other wants to go out every night, you may have some problems with companionship in the years ahead.

◆ None of us expects to be sick or ailing. Unfortunately, most people do have periods of illness. If you should, will he be caring or will he find you a burden? See how he treats other people who are old or ill.

Then put yourself in his shoes and ask yourself how you would answer those five questions if he asked them of you. If either of you scores less than 80 percent stop and think *before* . . .

BEFORE YOU DECIDE TO MARRY

No marriage will succeed without love. If you love him and he loves you, that may not be enough to ensure your future. Here is a pre-marital checklist of areas where vital differences in attitude may indicate trouble ahead if you don't explore them now rather than later:

HOW DO YOU BOTH FEEL ABOUT . . .

◆ **Having a family?**
◆ **Handling money?**
◆ **Your lifestyle now and dreams for your future together?**
◆ **Your mutual career plans?**
◆ **Sharing responsibilities at home, socially, financially, in family life?**
◆ **Being open, not secretive, about yourself, your past, your everyday needs?**
◆ **How do you plan to settle the inevitable disagreements that crop up in every relationship from time to time?**
◆ **Your relations with one another's family(ies), close friends, your social life as a family unit?**
◆ **Religious observance?**

Obviously, these questions represent only the tip of the iceberg, but these are issues that I have seen arise as the basis of problems that bring couples to lawyers and court later in life, if not well understood before marrying. You need not agree on every point, but you both must understand and respect your differences and know ahead of time that you are committed to working them out for the good of the union.

7

BEFORE YOU DECIDE TO BECOME A MOTHER

I do not love him because he is good, but because he is my little child . . .

RABINDRINATH TAGORE

The decision as to whether or not to become a mother may be the most difficult and certainly the most irrevocable decision of your life. You are the mother of a child until death do you part, no matter how far apart you may grow. You can always quit a job you do not like. You can remake your body through surgery. You can have countless kinds of therapy to alter your mind and personality. You can divorce an unsatisfactory husband and marry again. But, as of the present time, you cannot divorce a child (although recently some children have started suing to divorce parents).

A few generations ago, when grandma married grandpa she had no choice as to motherhood. Nature made that decision. If she did not become pregnant, it was her fault. No one questioned his sperm count or his potency. She was a barren woman, a creature to be pitied. In many societies childlessness was a ground for a husband to divorce his wife, as it still is in many countries today.

If a woman had too many children that was her fault, too. The only way to avoid repeated, unwanted pregnancies was to refuse marriage. If married, the only option was to refuse sex. This was the birth control method of Sigmund Freud and his wife, George Bernard Shaw and his wife, and probably countless other couples who have not been the subjects of biographies.

Historically, childbirth has been painful and dangerous. In New England cemeteries one sees family plots with one grave for the father, two or three for his succession of wives and many tiny plots for the children who died in infancy.

Today in the United States childbirth is no longer a mortal danger for a healthy woman who has proper prenatal care and delivery. Nor is abortion dangerous or life threatening if it is performed legally and under proper auspices. Women no longer need be the victims of nature or society or deny themselves the natural pleasures of sex.

Motherhood, like sexual love, is one of the great experiences of life. Unlike sexual passion, which can vary, depending on life's vicissitudes, motherhood endures. When you are in your seventies and eighties you will still be a mother. If you are wise and fortunate you will have the companionship of children and grandchildren. Long after passion is spent this love will survive. Motherhood is not something to be rejected lightly. But it is not the right choice for every woman.

The purpose of this chapter is to inform women of the various options available today to those who wish to become mothers and the legal obligations and pitfalls these choices entail. Today, with little censure or stigma, a woman has many choices. She can marry and have a child by her husband. If she does not become pregnant she can try fertility treatments, artificial insemination, in vitro fertilization, or hire a surrogate mother. She can adopt a child. Or she can become a foster mother. Unwed women and lesbian women can also become mothers through such means.

Whatever your marital status, sexual preference, or method by which you become a mother, you will have legal responsibilities. In this chapter we point out many of the obligations the law imposes on mothers and the lack of legal protection for them.

If your marriage ends in divorce, you will have many problems with respect to custody, visitation, and child support. These are discussed in the chapters on divorce. In the chapter "Before You Marry Again" we discuss the problems of stepchildren. And in a later chapter we'll analyze the difficulties that mothers encounter with adult children as to control of money and choice of lifestyle as a mother ages.

Problems of child rearing, discipline, care of physically and emotionally handicapped children, and the role of the father are subjects beyond the purview of this book. It must be noted, however, that the major share of child care in most families still falls on the mother. If the child is a problem for any reason: emotional; physical; or behavioral; it usually is the mother who bears the blame for the situation and the burden of the extra care required. Such problem children and their special needs often become the precipitating factor in a divorce.

Happy families rarely have legal problems. The mother and father remain married and bring up the children together. They share the pains and pleasures of infancy, childhood, and adolescence. And they rejoice in the successes of their children and grandchildren. In old age they have the comfort of their families.

Not all women are so fortunate. Many women encounter problems with their husbands and their children. If the children are adopted or obtained through any of the newer conceptual methods there may be legal problems that should be anticipated. Although adoption is an old and well-established relationship, there are new legal regulations and rights to which all parties concerned must adhere. The natural mother and father have rights today to reconsider and to reclaim a child given up for adoption. Adopted children also are beginning to assert the right to know their birth parents. And adopting parents are also claiming rights against adoption agencies. These legal changes have created unprecedented problems, which are discussed in this chapter.

Motherhood is not simply a matter of emotional desire and fulfillment. It entails legal rights and obligations. If you become a mother by any means you have assumed legal obligations. Much as you may love this child, he or she is not your property. You can be deprived of the care, custody, companionship, and love of this child by the law. If you and your husband divorce, he may obtain custody, as we shall see in the following chapters.

If you and your lesbian companion agree that you shall bear

a child and you and this companion later separate, she may go to court to try to obtain custody of the child.

Children also have new legal rights and remedies against their parents, and parents have new obligations and new accountability to public authorities. If you are accused of child abuse or child neglect, you may lose your child. The court can place your child in a foster family, terminate your parental rights, and give your child up for legal adoption against your will and despite your protest.

The law with respect to parent and child is on the cusp of change. Its very uncertainties engender many problems. No one as of this writing can state with certainty how the courts will treat the competing claims of biological mothers and fathers, children, surrogate mothers, adopting mothers, and foster mothers. Despite legal contracts, representations, and the advice of lawyers, in many circumstances, the law may not protect the woman who becomes a mother.

By whatever means you contemplate becoming a mother, here are some of the issues every woman should consider *before* . . .

The First Commandment is *protect thyself*. Therefore, the first question you must ask yourself is, *Do I want to be a mother?*

As in every important decision you make, you must consider what *you* want, not the wishes of your husband, your parents, or your friends. Doctors, marriage counselors, and parents can give you good advice. But only *you* know what will make *you* happy.

If you are in your twenties, ask yourself, "Am I ready for the responsibilities of motherhood? Will I feel that I have been cheated of my youth and resent the baby?" Some women are mature at twenty and others are flighty and self-centered at fifty. Only you can determine for yourself whether you are ready to take on motherhood.

If you are a young married woman, your family and friends will expect you to have a baby. Your parents undoubtedly want to have a grandchild. Your friends who are parents want you to share their experiences. Probably your husband wants you to have a baby. And all the advertisements, the media, and society in general seem to be in a conspiracy to see that all young married women above the poverty level—and within certain social limitations—become mothers.

But, if you are poor or unwed or lesbian or if you have had any involvement with the criminal law, all the forces of society combine to discourage you from having a child.

Regardless of your age, marital status, sexual preference, or economic condition, it is *your* choice. The Constitution protects your right to bear a child and, through the use of contraceptives, your right not to bear a child.

The Second Commandment is *anticipate disaster.*

◆ Is your marriage firm and stable?
◆ Is your husband sufficiently mature and unselfish to assume the responsibilities of a family?
◆ Or will he become restive and resentful of the time you spend with a child and the child-care chores with which you expect him to help you?

No one has a crystal ball, and even the best marriage can fail. So ask yourself whether both of you are prepared to cope with any problems in your marriage that may exist or may arise, and a baby as well.

◆ If you are unmarried, can you afford to bring up this child?
◆ Will you be able to explain your decision to your child?
◆ If you have health problems, will you jeopardize your future by becoming pregnant? If you have concerns about this, consult the best physician you can find to give you honest answers. Then get a second opinion. Both you and your partner should have a checkup to find out if either of you has any genetic problems that should be taken into account.

The Third Commandment, *act on your own best judgment,* has in this instance been covered in the discussion of the First Commandment as it relates to motherhood.

The Fourth Commandment is *wear a velvet glove over an iron hand*. A baby can be a source of contention and disagreement between husband and wife. Many men believe they have the right to decide the family's fate. But motherhood is not fatherhood. If you really want a child and he suggests that you defer motherhood until it is more convenient for him, be firm. Motherhood is more difficult and more dangerous as a woman gets older. He can father a child late in life. It is extremely difficult to become a mother then.

Many men who initially want to defer having a family, like many women, change their minds. He may not want a baby now, but when it is too late for you, he can marry a younger woman and father a child. He will have a family; you will be alone.

If you are convinced that you do not want to have a child, be equally firm. You will be the one who is pregnant for nine months and who will give birth. Although many fathers now share in child care, most mothers still have the primary responsibility for care of the children.

The Fifth Commandment is *money is not a dirty word; use it*. A child is expensive. Medical costs unless you have adequate insurance are enormous. Child care is very expensive. You may have to make drastic changes in your lifestyle and stardard of living. You may not be able to continue to work full time. Discuss these facts *beforehand so that you are prepared to welcome and care for your baby*.

Most educated women in their twenties and thirties seriously contemplate motherhood. They rarely ask these questions. What most young women ask me is a question I consider irrelevant. They say:

"If I have a baby, will I jeopardize my career?"

My response to them is an unequivocal *"No!"*

And then I explain.

Look at the men at the top of your profession or occupation. Aren't most of them fathers? Why should you forgo what is a normal part of life, an experience that you want, when men do not make that sacrifice?

If the women's movement has succeeded, even in part, it should mean that women have the same rights to jobs and parenthood as men.

- ◆ You cannot be fired from your job if you become pregnant.
- ◆ You cannot be denied a job because you are a mother. However, you may have many problems. Day care is hard to find and expensive.
- ◆ As of this writing you are not entitled to parental leave in most states.
- ◆ And if you do take it, many employers will slide you over to the slow mommy track, where you will be unlikely to advance as rapidly as others after you return.

Also, you may not want to work full time after you have a baby. Many women want the pleasure of being with their children during their growing years. At age three, your child may well go to nursery school. A good part of his or her childhood will be spent in school. At age seventeen or eighteen, he or she will probably go away to college.

Your life expectancy is almost eighty years. What will you lose by taking off three or four years to be with that child? Only money.

You may find yourself a few rungs lower on the career ladder as a result, but if you are able and hard working, you can make up that time. Many employers will now let you work part time or flex time while you are rearing young children. Other women have been happy mothers and achieved brilliant careers. Supreme Court Justice Sandra Day O'Connor has four children. Congresswoman Patricia Schroeder is a mother. Cosmetics tycoon Estee Lauder is a mother. Opera star Beverly Sills is a mother. Nobel Prize-winning scientist Rosalyn Yalow is a mother. Five female Nobel Prize winners in science have been mothers.

New developments in family law are barely a generation old. They reflect the growing recognition of the claims of women and children to personhood and to juridical means to enforce these dawning rights.

For millenia fathers had almost absolute life and death control over their children to the exclusion of the mothers. In ancient Greece and Rome, fathers could and did order the deaths of unwanted or defective children. No legal liability or moral censure attached to those fathers.

In the Biblical tale, Abraham was prepared to sacrifice Isaac in obedience to God's orders. And in Greek mythology, Agamemnon sacrificed his daughter Iphigenia to appease the gods. Her mother Clytemnestra was powerless to save her. These fathers were considered exemplary, pious men.

In China well into the twentieth century, parents abandoned unwanted infants on mountaintops where sometimes they were rescued by compassionate missionaries. No legal responsibility was placed on those parents.

In the seventeenth and eighteenth centuries in Europe, it was a common practice for parents to place unwanted infants in foundling homes. In Florence, Italy, many churches had a kind of revolving door in which the infant could be placed and received without the persons in the church seeing who placed the child there. No legal blame or censure attached to parents who abandoned their children. Indeed, Jean Jacques Rousseau, the noted author and authority on child education, abandoned his own children as foundlings.

In England it was a common practice for poor parents to blind and/or maim their children so that they would be more effective beggars. In India this practice persisted into the twentieth century.

The widely accepted contemporary belief that parents have an obligation to rear their children and provide them with a loving, supportive home is a modern concept. For centuries wealthy parents hired wet nurses, nannies, and governesses to care for their children. English families who could afford to do so sent their children to boarding school at an early age. Winston Churchill acknowledged that he really did not know his parents until he was an adult. He then established a warm, loving relationship with his mother.

Royal and noble families and wealthy families married their

children off at very early ages, often long before puberty, to enhance family alliances and to strengthen commercial ties.

Parents who were not wealthy often boarded their children with other families or apprenticed them to strangers who brought them up. Many financially hard-pressed parents paid women who ran "baby farms" to care for their children. These women often sold the children's clothes and permitted them to die of starvation or neglect. It was not until the mid-nineteenth century that England enacted laws making such conduct criminal.

Today the law with respect to parent and child lurches between the concepts of status—parenthood and the family; and contract—the agreements between mother and father, government and foster parent, surrogate mother and contracting mother, biological mother, and adopting mother.

American law is just beginning to recognize that children are not the possessions of their parents but individuals with constitutional rights, albeit very limited, rights. The recent case of Gregory K., the boy who asked to terminate his mother's rights so that he could be adopted by his foster parents, is only a blip on the screen that portends drastic changes in the laws concerning parent-child relationships.

Today, when a poor woman who has no means to support herself and her child, abandons it in a bus terminal or a stranger's car in a parking lot, she is hunted by the police, prosecuted, convicted, and often imprisoned. *Rarely is the father prosecuted.*

Parents are no longer permitted to compel or allow their children to work until they are of a legal age to do so. (Children of migrant workers often are illegally employed.) Parents cannot physically abuse their children, although many parents do so under the benign terminology of "discipline."

If a *child* plays hookey from school, the child's *parents* may be punished for violating the compulsory school attendance laws.

If a child becomes ill and the parents do not provide medical treatment, the parents may lose custody of the child. They may also be criminally prosecuted for child abuse or neglect. If a child dies after being denied medical treatment by parents who believe in faith healing, or by parents who are opposed to blood transfusions, the parents can be prosecuted for homicide.

Under the law for most of this century, adopting parents, once the order of adoption was final, had the same rights and obligations as natural parents. The record of adoption was sealed. Neither the natural parents nor the adopted child had the right to examine the facts surrounding the adoption or to learn each other's identities. Today, with the increasing emphasis on the rights of the child and the desire of many adopted children to know who they are, these laws are under attack.

A mother who gives up her child for adoption under a promise of secrecy may later be confronted with that child who learns her identity and finds her residence. A woman who adopts a child under a similar pledge of secrecy may find that the child she considers her own will seek out his or her birth mother and reject the adopting mother. It is uncertain as to whether the law will enforce these promises of secrecy and anonymity.

Modern medicine, which seemed to offer the miracle of motherhood to many women who were infertile, had medical problems or genetic defects, creates problems. If you have a child through a surrogate mother, a woman hired to bear either your fertilized egg or hers, fertilized by your husband or by a sperm donor, despite the money you have paid and the agreement made with her drafted and approved by her lawyer and yours, you may not be declared the legal mother of that child with the right of custody.

A song entitled "Mommy Number Four," by Mae Richard, from a recent musical, *Cut the Ribbons,* describes the numerous modern paths to motherhood and the uncertainties that beset such a mother.

> . . . Your mom was a lady from Shenandoah
> whose husband had very weak spermatozoa
> so the doctor put her ovum in a petri dish
> with stock from some Yalie and they played go fish
> till his him hooked up with her her
> and there you were
> . . . the husband from Shenandoah
> consulted a specialist in spermatozoa

and he and his wife had a child of their own
... so adoption was their request
... now you're all mine, *I hope.*

The mother in the song plaintively sighs, "I hope," because there is no certainty that a woman will be permitted by law to keep her child whether she follows the old or the new methods of becoming a mother.

The notorious case of Baby M, in which the surrogate mother refused to relinquish the child to whom she gave birth was followed by a spate of legislation regulating the practice. Nonetheless, some family members have acted as surrogates for their sisters, and one woman for her daughter.

This relation of one woman bearing the child of another is so novel and has occurred so infrequently that it is difficult to draw any conclusions as to its desirability or the legal consequences that flow from such an arrangement.

The practice of the "handmaiden," however, the poor woman servant who becomes pregnant by her employer and bears a child for his infertile wife, has roots that go back to the Biblical story of Jacob and Rachel. Whether the practice is perceived as a benefit for the infertile wife, or a form of peonage for the poor woman who bears a child for a fee, has not been resolved by society or the law. Today the only certainty with respect to surrogate motherhood is that the law is uncertain. If you go this route you probably are buying a lawsuit as well as a baby.

The law with respect to foster parents is also changing radically. Until the present time, a foster mother had no legally cognizable rights. No matter how much she may have loved her foster child and no matter how close the bond between the child and the foster mother, she was treated as a contract employee of the state. She was paid a fee for services, albeit a minimal fee, to care for another woman's child. The contract could be terminated at will, either at her choice or that of the government.

The government, acting through its employees or a child care agency, had almost unlimited discretion with respect to the placement of a child. The government could remove a child from the foster parent, return the child to the allegedly unfit natural parent, or place the child with another foster parent, even over the protest of the foster mother who had cared for the child since birth. There is a current move to recognize to a limited extent the claims of foster parents. But there is no certainty that if you agree to be a foster parent you will have the right to care for that child for any given period of time, or that if the child becomes available for adoption that you will be given preference as an adopting parent.

The desire to love and nurture a child is deeply rooted in many women. Fortunately, for the survival of the human species, women who want to become mothers usually provide loving care for their own children and children entrusted to them under the law. Often they do so with great difficulty and little legal protection.

I hope that the experiences of the women whose problems follow—real women whom I knew as clients and in my years as a judge—will help you in making decisions about this crucial step in a woman's life.

You Can Be Happy Without a Child

Sara Beth is one of five children, born into a happy, loving family. Her husband Jim also had a happy childhood. When they married they confidently expected to have a large family.

Sara Beth was a physical education major and taught gym at the local high school. She and Jim lived on his salary and saved her salary for three years to buy a large house. They furnished one bedroom for themselves and one as a nursery. They left the other three bedrooms empty until they would be needed.

But Sara Beth did not become pregnant. Her gynecologist was of the old school. He told her not to worry. Just relax and nature will take its course. But nothing happened.

Then she went to a fertility expert. He examined her and Jim. Jim's sperm count was high. He suggested fertility drugs and assured Sara Beth and Jim that she would become pregnant. The side effects of the drugs were painful. But she persevered.

For five years they were on a roller coaster of high hope and then the slough of despond. The treatments were expensive. Jim began to work overtime. Sara Beth, who became too ill to work as a result of the drugs, used up her sick leave and went on leave without pay.

Finally, almost six years later she became pregnant. She was very ill. The doctor advised her to stay in bed. She did. Jim did the cooking and cleaned the house when he came home from work. In her fifth month Sara Beth miscarried. They discovered she had been pregnant with triplets and that they were seriously deformed.

Sara Beth's recovery was slow. She was depressed and weak. Jim was exhausted, worried about debts of more than $10,000.

When Sara Beth recovered, she wanted to try again. Jim insisted that she see another doctor. He advised her that she had serious medical problems, that if she became pregnant again she would probably miscarry.

Jim and Sara Beth consulted a lawyer. "If we had been told that Sara Beth would probably miscarry, we would never have spent all these years of illness and more than $30,000 in medical fees for Sara Beth to become pregnant," Jim told the lawyer. "I want to sue that doctor for malpractice."

Sara Beth and Jim learned that despite the oral assurances of the fertility expert, the likelihood of recovering damages from the doctor was minimal. The law assumes that doctors cannot guarantee satisfactory results. The treatments that Sara Beth was given were medically approved.

Sara Beth and Jim gave up their futile quest for a child, sold their big house and bought a smaller one. She returned to teaching.

When I saw Sara Beth a few years later she looked well and happy. She and Jim had just returned from a trip abroad, their first vacation since she began the fertility treatments.

"We're beginning to enjoy our marriage after all those years of anguish," Sara Beth said. "Why didn't some one tell me we could be happy without a child *before* . . .

Many couples like Sara Beth and Jim spend years and thousands of dollars trying to have a child. Some women who take fertility drugs encounter problems. Others try in vitro fertilization with the husband's sperm or with the sperm obtained from a friend or from a sperm bank.

Recently it has been learned that some doctors surreptitiously use their own sperm to impregnate patients who believe that the sperm is from their own husbands. These doctors are prosecuted criminally. But monetary redress for the gulled mother does not compensate her for giving birth to a child she falsely believed was that of her husband. Nor is there any guaranty that an anonymous sperm donor does not carry a genetic defect.

At present all these methods of becoming pregnant are risky, unpredictable, and expensive. As of 1992, 19,079 in vitro fertilizations had been performed in the United States but only 3,110 babies had been born.

Before you spend years of frustration and thousands upon thousands of dollars, consult several specialists. Learn the risks and probabilities of success. Then make an informed, intelligent decision.

Mother May Not Always Be Right

Mollie and Hank had a charmed life together for almost twenty years. They were college sweethearts. When Hank was graduated from Yale and Mollie from Smith they married. In due course they had a son, Hank, Jr., and a daughter, Lauren. Both children were good looking and intelligent like their parents.

Hank was president of his own company, a small but thriving high-tech operation. Mollie ran an art gallery that Hank financed. The children went to private school. An au pair from France lived with them and taught the children French.

When Hank Jr., was in his last year in prep school, Hank was killed in an airplane accident. He was piloting the company plane on his way to a meeting. Mollie and the children were devastated. Life without Hank, big, cheerful Hank who took care of everyone and everything, was unthinkable.

A few weeks after the accident, Hank's lawyer called Mollie. For the first time she learned that the business was not successful. In fact, it was losing money. Hank had pledged his shares to a bank for a loan which was coming due. The bank intended to take over the company. Hank had no pension. She then learned that the house was heavily mortgaged. Both cars belonged to the company. Hank had let his life insurance lapse. The only assets Mollie had were Hank's Social Security, the household goods, her engagement ring, and a claim against the airplane manufacturer for an alleged defect in the plane. Their life savings in securities were also pledged to meet the company debts. Mollie was shown the documents she had signed. She had only a few hundred dollars in her own checking account.

Mollie sold her art gallery and realized a few thousand dollars. She sold the house. After paying off the mortgages she received less than $50,000. She and the children moved to a tiny apartment. Mollie got a job at the local community college that paid barely enough to cover the rent and food. But she managed to pay the tuition for the children until the end of the year.

Hank, Jr., had been accepted at Yale and confidently expected to go there and live the carefree life his father had so often described. Mollie and the lawyer explained to him that this was no longer possible. If he worked all summer, got a grant, and a scholarship, he might just barely be able to attend the state university.

The boy was furiously angry. How could his dead father and his living mother do this to him?

"You have $50,000 from the house," he said. "Why can't you use that to pay for my tuition at Yale? Besides you'll collect at least a million dollars on the suit against the plane manufacturer."

"The manufacturer says the plane ran out of gas. That's why it crashed. The suit won't come to trial for at least three years," Mollie told him. "This money is our only asset. What if I become ill and can't work? What about your sister? She has only one more year at Harrington prep. She's entitled to finish there."

"I'm entitled to go to Yale. Dad promised me," Hank Jr., rejoined. "Lauren isn't much of a student. She'll never get into Smith. The tuition is wasted on her."

"She needs help more than you do," Mollie explained. "You're smart. If you work hard your first year at State perhaps you can get a scholarship to Yale your second year."

"It's not the same being a transfer student. I want to go to Yale in the fall. You can afford it. You just would rather spend Dad's money on Lauren than me."

Hank Jr., went to a child advocate law office and persuaded them to sue Mollie to compel her to pay his tuition to Yale.

Mollie thought the lawsuit was so preposterous that she did not retain a lawyer. She went to court to defend herself.

Meanwhile Hank Jr., had been in touch with Yale and obtained a partial scholarship for sons of Yale alumni. But the balance of the tuition and fees for one year was still more than $10,000.

The judge, a Yale alumnus, agreed with Hank, Jr. He concluded that a son who had the ability to be accepted at Yale and whose parents were graduates of Ivy League and Seven Sisters colleges was entitled to a comparable education. The mother, he decided, owed that to her son.

Other judges have held that wealthy parents are not required to pay for their childrens' college education. The law is unsettled and varies from state to state. But, it is clear that a child has the right to sue a parent not only for necessaries but for private schooling and other amenities in keeping with the family's standard of living. Beware—a mother's judgment as to what is best for her children can be overruled by a court today.

Elmira is a willful teenager. Although she is only fourteen she looks much older. Despite her mother's rules, she wears heavy makeup and sexy clothes. She stays out late. She does not do her homework. Her mother Marilyn cries and scolds. She worries about drugs, AIDS, pregnancy. Elmira's father Jeb has washed his hands of her.

"If she wants to ruin her life, let her," he tells Marilyn. "She's not going to ruin my life."

When Elmira did not come home until after four A.M., Marilyn locked her in her bedroom and said that Elmira could not come out until she promised to behave.

At eight-thirty in the morning, when Marilyn and Jeb were getting ready for work, Marilyn asked Elmira if she would promise to behave. Elmira refused to answer.

"Well, you can just stay in your room until we come home from work," Marilyn said. "It won't hurt you to be hungry for a few hours. Think about what I've told you."

About noon Elmira decided she was hungry. She also wanted to meet her boyfriend, a school dropout. The door was securely locked. After banging and screaming, Elmira realized she was home alone. She opened the window and slid down the water pipe and walked to the police station.

When Marilyn came home after work, there was a summons for her. Marilyn rushed to the police station thinking Elmira had been arrested. She discovered that she was under arrest, charged with child abuse. Elmira had been placed in a foster home.

Marilyn had to post bail to obtain her daughter's release. She and Jeb had to retain a lawyer, get witnesses, and go to court three times before they could prove that they had not abused their daughter, and to reclaim her. But Elmira holds the threat of further child abuse charges over her frightened parents.

Mollie and Marilyn were good parents. They did everything they reasonably could for their children. What they did not do was follow the Five Commandments. They did not protect themselves from self-indulgent children. They permitted their children to hold them hostage. Mollie also violated the Fifth Commandment. She did not discuss money with her son. She should have explained the family's financial situation to him earlier, carefully and completely, and perhaps have had her lawyer and accountant talk to the boy.

Mothers must heed the Five Commandments in their dealings with teenage and adult children as well as with their husbands.

Why Do You Want a Child?

Norbert and Alma are a busy couple. Their names are in the society page regularly. They contribute to countless worthy causes and attend innumerable fancy functions. He is a successful architect. She is an acclaimed hostess.

After Norbert had designed and built them a dream house and Alma had decorated it with rare and lovely antiques, they decided they should have a family. It was an expected part of their life style.

But Alma did not become pregnant. They consulted several fertility experts and were told their prospects were poor. Alma would have to spend a year or more undergoing treatments. She did not want to interrupt her rapidly moving life. So they turned to adoption.

The licensed agencies told them that the likelihood of getting a healthy white baby within the next five years was remote. At that time Alma was already thirty-five. At forty her chances would be even less. The agencies told them that there were many nonwhite infants and older children available for adoption. But Alma and Norbert could not envision a nonwhite child. How could they take such a child to their clubs? The child could not go to the exclusive dancing classes the children of their friends attended. The older adoptive children they saw did not meet their expectations of a tall, blond son who would go to Princeton and join Norbert's eating club.

A friend put them in touch with a lawyer who promised them a healthy white child, the offspring of a pregnant unwed student at a Seven Sisters college and a married man who was a graduate of an Ivy League university. They paid the lawyer an enormous fee.

Several months later Alma and Norbert met the plane, accompanied by a nurse and expensive receiving garments. The lawyer handed them a blond, blue-eyed baby boy. The adoption papers were duly filed and the decree entered.

When the baby was a year old, their pediatrician told Alma and Norbert that Norbert, Jr., had serious problems. Although his physical development was only slightly below average, the boy was not normally responsive. Hadn't they noticed that?

They hadn't because he was under the care of a nurse, who rarely spoke to the child.

"I think he's a fine baby," Alma declared. And she changed pediatricians.

By the time Norbert, Jr., was two both Alma and Norbert knew that something was wrong. They then learned that the boy had been obtained from a mother in Eastern Europe. The child had evidently suffered a birth injury. He would never go to Princeton.

Norbert brought suit against the lawyer for fraud and deception. The case was thrown out of court. Norbert tried to annul the adoption. The court refused to set aside a valid and binding adoption.

As the child became older, he was disruptive and was dismissed from the schools in which they placed him. Norbert and Alma argued and argued about what to do with the child. Finally, distraught over the experience, Norbert divorced Alma.

She was awarded custody of the child by the court, although she would have preferred that Norbert have the responsibility of caring for the boy. Alma placed him in a school for learning disabled children. Year in and year out she is in court attempting to collect the enormous support payments necessary to pay for the child's upkeep.

Many couples who have adopted children through agencies about which they know nothing have had similar experiences. They have not been told of the problems the child has or have been given no information about the child's parents. When these disappointed couples have sued the agencies for fraud and deception, they have rarely succeeded in getting the adoption set aside. Occasionally a court has awarded the couple damages for the extra medical expenses of caring for the child. But an unhappy couple is left with the burden of caring for an unwanted child for the child's life. And the unfortunate child is left with adopting parents who do not want him or her.

Jane and Elmer Jenkins, a couple I represented many years ago, wanted to adopt a child whom they had obtained from an unlicensed agency. They thought the infant was adorable. I urged them to have her examined by a physician and a physical anthropologist. The child had normal intelligence and no serious physical problems. But the anthropologist told them that the child was a mulatto. This couple did not want a nonwhite child and refused to go through with the adoption. They could not recover the fee they had paid the agency even though they had specified that they wanted a white child.

Other couples have experienced problems when the adopted child reached adolescence. Philadelphia psychiatrist Marshall Schechter, author of *Being Adopted: A Lifelong Search for Self,* reports that although adopted children make up fewer than 2 percent of the population, they constitute 25 percent of the children in inpatient mental health programs he studied.

Before you undergo the long and often frustrating process of adoption, ask yourself why you want a child.

◆ Is it to satisfy your concept of yourself or your ideal family? Or is it because you really want to love and cherish a child?

◆ Are you and your husband emotionally and financially able to cope with a child who has special problems and may need an unusual amount of care?

◆ Are you prepared to love and care for a child who may have some disabilities?

Of course, a biological child can also have many problems that the parents do not anticipate. Often such a child is the cause of divorce. And it is almost always the mother who is left with the care of the child. Many parents, however, are able to give such children, whether adopted or their biological offspring, the love and care they need and find their own lives enriched by the experience. Are you wise and unselfish enough to be one of them?

If you truly want a child and are prepared to love him or her, no matter what the child's problems may be, by all means adopt. If you are not sure, then do as the Jenkinses did; have the child carefully examined by competent experts *before* you adopt.

In the 1990s there are very few healthy American infants available for adoption. Before 1973, 19 percent of the babies born to unmarried white women were given up for adoption. From 1973 to 1981 only 8 percent of unmarried white women gave up their children for adoption. Among unmarried black women fewer than 2 percent gave up their babies for adoption.

Few unwed Hispanic women give up their infants. Whether the number of American babies available for adoption will increase with the recent barriers to legal abortion, no one knows.

It is more likely, however, that unmarried women like the fictional Murphy Brown will choose to keep their babies and rear them as single mothers. As more young women are given sex education and learn about birth control, it is likely that there will be fewer unplanned pregnancies and fewer children available for adoption. Foreign countries are also becoming concerned about the traffic in babies and are placing controls on adoption procedures by American women and their agents and lawyers.

The Single Mother

Marci is a thirty-five-year-old divorcée. She has a responsible position in a large corporation. When she married her childhood sweetheart at age twenty-three she wanted to have a child, but he did not. After seven years of marriage she realized that her husband was a Peter Pan, a young man who did not want to grow up. He was irresponsible in his job. She was intelligent and hardworking. If she stayed with him, he would be her child, someone she had to support, care for, and cater to. This was not the life she wanted. And so they divorced.

Years passed and she did not find a man she wanted to marry. But she did want a child. After discussing the problem with her doctor and a psychiatrist, Marci decided to have a child by artificial insemination. After she became pregnant, she told her family and friends.

Although her parents at first were horrified, she assured them she was able financially and emotionally to care for a child and that she was not going to deny herself this important experience. She told them that single motherhood has long been the practice in Scandinavia, where bearing a child out of wedlock carries no social or legal stigma.

In the 1990s birth of a child out of wedlock is no longer a secret, shameful situation. In the year 1990 more than 23.3 percent of the babies born in the United States were born to unwed mothers. Two-thirds of teenage mothers were not married.

Marci had her baby in a hospital. When I visited her, she was surrounded by friends and family. Her colleagues had given her a baby shower. Her employer gave her three months' maternity leave. Marci is a happy, fulfilled mother. Her daughter is a delightful toddler who has many friends in her nursery school. They are a charming family.

Jodi is one of the teenage mothers whose pregnancy was unplanned. When she discovered she was pregnant, she was already in her second trimester. The obstetrician she consulted advised against an abortion at that late date. Jodi is a good student. She wants to go to college and eventually become a scientist. She decided to give the baby up for adoption.

With the help of a social worker, she found a nice, intelligent young couple who agreed to adopt her baby. The baby's father, a handsome, ne'er-do-well classmate of Jodi's, had never suggested marriage. He had not offered to help with her medical expenses. He was a high school student who had no money. By the time the baby was born, Jodi was no longer interested in him. The baby was the result of a careless night, not an abiding relationship.

However, the boy went to court to oppose the adoption. He claimed that as the father he had the right to custody of his child. He said that his parents would bring up the baby in their home while he finished high school and then he would get a job and support his child. Jodi was appalled. The boy's parents were lazy, uneducated people. She did not want her baby reared by them.

The court, however, decided that the father's parental rights could not be terminated in the absence of proof that he was an unfit father and scheduled a hearing on that issue.

Jodi is now fighting to regain possession of her own child. Her plans for college have been deferred because she cannot afford both counsel fees and tuition and the lawsuit takes all her time and energy. Meanwhile the baby is in foster care. The woman who had agreed to adopt the baby attends the hearings anxiously waiting to learn whether she will have the child she so desperately wants.

The Foster Mother

Bertha lives with her husband, Joe, and two teenage sons in a modest section of a wealthy suburb. They moved there at some sacrifice so that the boys could attend a good public high school. Bertha is a registered nurse. She realized that she should be home in the afternoons when her sons and their friends began to "hang out" at her house. And so she looked for some means of earning money at home. A friend suggested that she become a foster mother.

When Bertha called the government agency, she was welcomed with open arms. A registered nurse was a godsend for failure-to-thrive babies who required skilled care and were difficult to place.

Bertha was given Dawn, the daughter of a fourteen-year-old drug addict, who is the daughter of a thirty-year-old drug addict. The baby had been in the hospital for almost three months and had finally reached a weight of six pounds. A scrawny, crying little bundle was given to Bertha.

At first Joe and the boys resented all the time Bertha had to spend caring for Dawn. But, after five or six months Dawn weighed seventeen pounds and was an adorable, dimpled, smiling little brown-skinned girl. The entire family was enchanted with her. By the end of the year Dawn was an integral part of the family and a delight. She called Bertha and Joe Mom and Pop. The boys discovered she liked to sing and could recognize their favorite jazz songs. Soon they were teaching her to dance.

During the more than eighteen months Bertha had cared for Dawn the child's mother had never called or come to see her. The social worker who paid a visit every three or four months was delighted with Dawn's progress.

Shortly after her last visit she called Bertha to inform her that Dawn was placed for adoption and that the agency had found an adopting couple. Dawn would be taken from Bertha the following week.

Bertha, Joe, and the boys were dismayed. "We'll adopt her," they decided.

Bertha promptly called the social worker who informed her

that it was against their policy to place a black child with a white family, particularly a family that lived in a white suburban neighborhood. The policy was inflexible.

The social worker told Bertha that if she wanted to adopt Dawn, she should have taken action *before* the agency had arranged an adoption with what it considered a suitable family. If there were no other family in the picture to contest Bertha's claim, she would be more likely to succeed.

Bertha and Joe retained a lawyer to claim their right to adopt Dawn. The court appointed a child advocate to represent Dawn's interest. Civil liberties groups entered the fray on both sides of the issue which was phrased as "What is in the best interests of Dawn, a black baby? Is it to be brought up with a white family or a black family?"

The fact that Bertha and Joe are the only parents Dawn has ever known was deemed irrelevant. Dawn was taken screaming and crying from Bertha's arms and placed with a different foster mother. Bertha has not been permitted to see Dawn while the court is hearing learned arguments and painfully attempting to reach a Solomonic decision. Whatever way the court decides, there will be an appeal. Dawn will probably be three or four before her fate is finally decided.

Meanwhile Bertha, Joe, and the boys suffer the loss of a little girl who had won their hearts. Bertha is working in a hospital to pay the not inconsiderable counsel fees required to attempt to establish the rights of a foster mother. And Dawn is an unhappy, lonely, confused child.

Most of the women whose quests for motherhood I have described had unhappy experiences. Successful relationships between children and parents are not the subjects of litigation. As in medical malpractice cases, lawyers and judges are called in *only when something goes wrong*. We do not see the countless operations that restore sight, the use of limbs, and provide new hearts for defective ones. Nor do we see happy adoptions, successful fertility treatments, and natural parents who rear their children well. Fortunately, the successful relationships *far* outnumber the unsuccessful ones.

The women whose problems I have recounted began their quests for motherhood in good faith and with high hopes. But the law did not protect them.

Good marriages are not made in heaven but by intelligent human beings. Not all happy families are produced by nature. Your life as a mother or potential mother can be happy or unhappy whether you are a married woman and have a biological child or are childless; or are an unwed mother, you can be happy or unhappy with an adopted child, and you can find fulfillment— or not—as a foster mother. In many instances the outcome will depend upon the intelligent questions you ask—and the choices you make as a consequence of the answers to these questions— *before* . . .

8

BEFORE YOU DECIDE TO DIVORCE

Whosoever shall marry her that is divorced committeth adultery . . .

MATTHEW 5:32

For decades the marital knot was supposed to be a binding tie no matter how sorely it chafed. Divorce was a tragic aberration, an evil to be avoided at all costs.

Sometimes the costs to women were physical abuse, degradation, insults, loss of one's children, and almost always poverty. Sometimes the cost was loss of freedom. As recently as the mid-twentieth century, husbands unhappy with their marriages found an easy solution by incarcerating the hapless and helpless wife in a mental institution.

As late as the 1920s two famous writers took this path to rid themselves of their wives, as did the husbands of several of my clients. I was able to obtain the release of these clients only after difficult, protracted, costly hearings.

Until modern times it was very hard for a woman to obtain a divorce, but remarkably easy for a man. Anglo-American law gave a husband control of his wife's property and custody of their children. Even if he was a drunkard, a wastrel, or a roué infected with venereal disease, the law protected him but not her. Consequently, few women were willing to divorce and risk losing their children and enduring a life of poverty and a loss of social status. Having no real choice, they submitted to cruelties and indignities.

In many parts of the world today females are still sold into a marriage that they cannot terminate except by death. By contrast, the husbands can terminate the marriage at will. Under Islamic law a man can divorce any or all of his wives by simply saying three times, "I divorce you."

Today American women have real choices although the various options may not be the happiest. Since the early twentieth century American wives have been able to obtain divorces on many grounds. It was not necessary to prove adultery or physical abuse in most states. Nonetheless, as the result of a campaign spearheaded by a small group of women, no-fault divorce laws became popular in the 1970s. Today almost every state has some form of no-fault divorce.

The theory is that no couple should be chained together in a loveless marriage. In fact, almost any man or woman who wants a divorce in these states can obtain one, and many couples do. Depending on the laws of the state in which she is domiciled, an unhappy wife can allege that her husband has subjected her to cruelty, or indignities. These charges are easily proved. A shove or push can be interpreted as physical cruelty. Indignities can be proved by recounting an insulting remark made in the presence of a friend, relative, or a worker in the household. Some states permit divorce on the grounds of incompatibility. Only a few jurisdictions require proof of adultery. With a cooperative spouse and a slight disregard for truth, even that is easily proved.

In most instances, it is the husband who wants his freedom. And the laws permit, indeed encourage, the wife to demand a satisfactory monetary settlement before the divorce is obtained. Wives of wealthy men demand and get substantial sums of money before they consent to a divorce.

However, in the past the law as to custody clearly favored the wife. If the children were young, the law presumed that a child of "tender years" should live with its mother. Unless the mother was an alcoholic, mentally deranged, or lived an openly lewd and promiscuous life, she would be awarded custody of the children at least until they were in their teens.

Today all that is changed. Under the guise of "general" laws, there is no presumption that a mother shall have custody of her children. The new law is that the courts are to be guided by "the best interests of the child," a vague standard at best. Often it is interpreted as favoring the parent who can give the child the best housing and physical care. This depends upon the relative finances of the parents. Since most husbands have a greater earning capacity and more money than their wives, husbands who seek custody are favored.

The wife whose husband wants a divorce has lost her bargaining position. He can get a divorce whether she agrees or not. Child custody, child support, and alimony for the wife are treated separately from the divorce. *This is not a level playing field for most women.*

Many very poor women both before no-fault, and now, simply ignore the entire legal process. They do not marry; they do not divorce. Many have long, stable, loving relationships with persons other than their spouse. Others are transient. Since neither man nor woman has any property, there is nothing for a court to distribute.

The problem for most women prior to no-fault divorce was not getting a divorce, but obtaining adequate support for herself and her children. This is still the problem today, but it has been exacerbated by the law. *More than half of divorced men do not pay child support.* Children are among the largest and fastest growing segment of the poor. And the new law of "equitable distribution of marital property" has left many women much poorer than they would have been under prior law.

The media have made most Americans aware of the Bel Air divorcées who live in their automobiles. These once wealthy women are members of the new poor, while their former husbands maintain their lavish life styles. Countless middle-class women are also members of the new poor. Some live in shelters with their children. Others are bag ladies. The majority work long hours for little pay and lead unhappy, exhausted lives.

Whether an unhappy or rejected wife should get a divorce is a serious issue, raising not only questions of love, sexual satisfaction and compatibility but also economic, social, and family questions.

Formerly in many communities a divorced woman was shunned by family and friends. Her lot was not a happy one. Today there is little stigma attached to divorce for a woman. She can lead whatever kind of life she wishes, without censure or ostracism. However, many divorcées find that there is a kind of purdah for the woman without a husband. She probably won't be invited to the dinner parties given by her married friends— although her ex-husband will be. An extra man is a social plus; an extra woman is an extra. These are relatively minor issues to be considered when contemplating divorce. Many divorced women remarry. Some are happy and some are not.

Prior to no-fault divorce laws money and custody were usually settled by both parties through a process of bargaining before going to court for a decree in divorce.

Under no-fault the divorce is granted and then both parties fight over support and custody and division of the property. Obviously, when a man knows he can get a divorce without the consent or cooperation of his wife, he is unlikely to be generous about money or cooperative about custody.

Although some men genuinely want custody of their children, the question of custody is often used as a ploy to reduce the wife's claims for alimony, child support, and equitable distribution of the marital property. Rather than face a prolonged custody fight in which the children will be examined and forced to testify, and which the wife may lose anyway, many women forgo their rights to adequate alimony and support. Even if the husband concedes custody, the question of visitation with the children raises acrimonious problems.

Most importantly, under no-fault divorce, the wife no longer can refuse to give her husband a divorce. Today, under no-fault laws it is almost as easy for an American man to rid himself of an unwanted wife as for an Arab. Nonetheless, wives still have some choices. Here are some questions a wife thinking about divorce might ask herself:

- ◆ If she is unhappy with her marriage and he is not eager for a divorce, should she obtain one?
- ◆ If he says he wants a divorce, should she attempt to salvage the marriage?
- ◆ If she does not contest the divorce, a fruitless action in most jurisdictions, should she put up a legal fight for money and custody?
- ◆ Or should she try counseling, mediation, arbitration, or other quasi-legal remedies?
- ◆ How vigorously should she pursue her property and alimony claims?

There is no one correct answer for everyone. You must decide what is in your own best interests after realistically examining the facts and the law and most importantly your own wishes.

Here are a few useful rules to follow when contemplating a divorce. Study the following questions, and on a sheet of paper, answer them as truthfully as you can. Do not show the paper to anyone. It is solely for your guidance.

◆ **"Do I want this man as my husband?"** Obvious though this question is very few women seriously ask themselves that question. Even fewer answer it honestly.

◆ Many women dread divorce. They view it as evidence of their failure instead of an opportunity to rectify a mistake. They blame themselves. If he no longer wants her, she believes that she must have done something wrong, lost her allure, failed to be a good wife or a good mother.

This conditioning to assume the blame instead of blaming her husband is deeply ingrained in many women and reinforced by the flood of literature and TV shows urging women to be attractive and charming. If your husband says he wants a divorce, don't blame yourself. Maybe you were not a perfect wife. No one is. Probably he was not a perfect husband. No one is. It takes two to tango and two to make a marriage work.

The second question you must ask yourself is,

◆ **If I do want him, what should I do to keep the marriage intact?**

◆ If I don't want him, what property rights and support do I need? In order to answer this question, you will have to find out how much money and property he has, and how much money and property you have jointly. To get honest answers to these questions you will have to consult a lawyer and do some sleuthing on your own.

Then ask yourself:

◆ **"What kind of life will I have as a divorcée?** Can I support myself and the children? How much money do I need? How much money can I reasonably expect from him? What are my job options? What about child care? Health insurance? Do I need further education? If I move, will I have a network of friends?

The next question pertains to the children.

◆ **Do I want custody of my children? Will they and I be happier if they live with him or with me??**

Many women think that it is demeaning or grasping to demand adequate support. They are more concerned with emotions like lost love and pride than the practicalities of daily living.

Most women believe it is unnatural not to insist on having custody of one's children and that there is a stigma attached to a mother who does not insist on being the principal caretaker of the children. In many instances, particularly when a child is a teenage boy, the father may be a more appropriate caretaker. Remember, the principal caretaker has the quotidian problems of discipline and homework, finding caretakers, and more. The other parent has the fun of vacations, dating, weekend treats. There is no one right answer for every woman.

Whenever a tearful female client has come to me to represent her in a divorce because her husband walked out on her, my advice has been:

"Don't be sad; be mad. Turn your hurt feelings against him—*not* against yourself. Think positively. It's not the end of the world. It can be the beginning of a new and possibly better life if you think about these issues *before* . . .

In the next chapter we shall discuss the nitty gritty of the actual divorce proceedings and the choices you have. For now, this chapter is designed to help you decide whether or not you want a divorce and what to do if your husband says *he* wants a divorce.

A Divorce Can Be the Beginning—Not the End

Sylvia was a pretty, petite fifty-year-old woman, one of many weeping clients. She was immaculately dressed, but her clothing was inexpensive. Her husband Herman was a well-known, successful business man. They had been married for twenty-seven years and had three grown children. She had been a schoolteacher but had not worked since the first child was born.

Herman had presented her with a fait accompli. He was going to get a divorce and marry his secretary. His lawyer told him that Sylvia had to have her own lawyer, a legal technicality he did not approve.

Her friends and sisters urged her to fight for her home and family.

"Don't give him a divorce," they advised.

Her three adult sons worked for their father. They urged her not to fight him, but to take the settlement he offered.

"When Dad is crossed, he can get mean," they warned. "You may end with even less than what he offered."

When she came to see me she was confused by this contradictory advice.

"You tell me the right thing to do," she begged.

"You tell me what you want," I said.

"I want to save my marriage. It's all I have," she wailed.

"Tell me about your marriage and Herman. Describe him to me."

She paused for a while. "It's a long time since I even thought about my marriage or Herman. I just accepted them. That's the way life is. What is my marriage like? Since the boys are grown and married, my life is lonely. Herman never talks to me. He isn't interested in the things I care about—books and the theater. He's only interested in business and his country club."

"Don't you go to the country club?" I asked her.

"Yes. I go but I don't enjoy it. I'm not a good golfer and so we don't play in a foursome. He plays with the men. Occasionally we have dinner there with his friends."

"What about your friends?"

"I see a few women for lunch and we go to the theater, matinees. Herman is stingy and I have to scrimp on my allowance to buy theater tickets and to go to lunch with the girls. I'd like to go back to teaching but Herman won't let me."

"What is he like?"

She paused as if she were trying to remember. "He—he's fat, bald. He smokes a big cigar. His clothes are always dirty, spots on his tie. His grammar is poor—"

She stopped suddenly. "That's Herman. What do I want him for?"

"You are an attractive, educated woman. Look at this as an opportunity for a better life, for independence."

She wiped her eyes and looked more cheerful.

"Now we have to talk about money," I told her. "If you are going to begin a new and better life at age fifty you will need some financial security. What is Herman's income? What assets does he have?"

Sylvia, like many middle-aged women, did not know what her husband's income was. She signed a blank tax return. She had only the vaguest notion of his business affairs and property holdings. She said her sons thought his offer of $500 a month support without security was fair.

"I've never had $500 in my whole life to do with as I want," she told me. "Before I was married I lived with my parents and gave my paycheck to my father. After I was married I gave my paycheck to Herman. Since our first child was born and I quit work, I've been dependent on Herman for everything."

"Do you like that lifestyle?" I asked her.

"No, I hate it. I want to feel like a person, to do what I want sometimes, not always what he wants."

Sylvia was no longer tearful. She was beginning to think about herself, her future.

"When we meet with Herman and his lawyer I want you to look your very best. Buy a new dress and charge it to him. He's responsible for your bills until the divorce is final. Get your hair done. We'll come together. I don't want a weeping client but a self-sufficient woman who will stand up for her rights."

For the first time Sylvia smiled.

Herman was exactly as she had described him. When he saw Sylvia striding self-confidently into his lawyer's office, Herman was amazed.

"What happened to you? Why are you looking so happy?"

"Because I am happy," she replied.

"Happy that I'm leaving you?" he exclaimed!

"Yes," she replied.

This occurred before no-fault divorce laws were enacted. He had expected a weeping wife who would tearfully agree to his terms. His lawyer soon advised him that Sylvia would not be a pushover.

Herman not only had a girlfriend, he also had a great deal of money, which Sylvia learned about through legal discovery. *Regardless of the divorce laws of your state, you through your lawyer are entitled to see the books and records of your husband, the businesses in which he has an interest, all his assets.*

Our first victory was an agreement for temporary alimony pending the divorce proceedings. This is very important because a wife, especially one who is not employed and has no personal funds, must have money to live on while negotiating for the final settlement or property distribution under no-fault laws. It also gives a strong clue as to how amenable or how stingy her husband will be. Under the laws of most states today, a wife is entitled to temporary alimony until the divorce decree is entered.

The temporary alimony Sylvia obtained was substantial. At my urging Sylvia bought a new wardrobe and went on a cruise with a girlfriend, the first vacation of her choice in twenty-seven years.

The final settlement was adequate. Sylvia resumed teaching part time. She moved from her gloomy house to a cheerful apartment downtown near theaters and shops. Three years later she brought her fiancé to meet me. They came with her three sons. Now that Sylvia was no longer dependent on Herman they had become closer to her. They realized that she was an interesting, attractive person. They enjoyed her company. The boys were her friends for the first time since they had become adults. They were happy in her happiness. The fiancé is a school teacher, a widower. He is not rich but he shares her interests.

"My divorce gave me a new life," Sylvia said.

Although Sylvia had been married for twenty-seven years, she was wise enough and sufficiently resilient to see her divorce *not as the end of her life, but the possibility of a new beginning,* a life of *her* choosing.

Sylvia also *obeyed the First Commandment. She protected herself financially. She obeyed the Third Commandment. She did not take the advice of her sons* to accept the inadequate settlement that her husband offered. She acted on her own judgment.

Once she separated from her husband, Sylvia did not sit home. She set out to live the kind of life she had always wanted. In middle age she found the happiness she had been denied in marriage.

Freedom is Worth Buying

Peg is a thirty-five-year-old lawyer. I was the judge to whom her case was assigned. My state, like most other states, has a no-fault divorce law. Under the old law, the one who wanted the divorce, usually the husband, had to pay for his freedom as Herman did. As I mentioned, under no-fault the parties bargain over the division of marital property. Under both systems, the judge usually has only a ceremonial function. The lawyers work out the settlement and the custody arrangements and simply present the judge with a decree to sign.

Peg and Warren have two children and a house that she had

bought. She is a successful, hardworking lawyer who has a six-figure income. Warren is lazy. He had just quit or lost the latest in a series of jobs. He had no income and no assets other than the marital property that she paid for. But, he wanted his freedom *and* support. Although Peg would not have put Warren out of the family home, when he said she "stifled" him, she agreed not to place obstacles in the path of his divorce. Peg agreed to give him half the value of the house in cash and an income of $5,000 a month for five years. She was to have custody of the children and he would have visitation twice a week.

Warren pretended to be very unhappy about giving up *his* home and custody of the children. I asked Peg whether she wanted child support.

"My parents think I should fight him, make him pay support for the children. But I don't want to. I know he'll never pay and I don't want to be bothered with him. I'm glad to buy my freedom. Do you think I'm right?"

"It's your decision, not your parents'. You're a sophisticated lawyer. You know that most divorced men have to be sued again and again to collect child support. Of course, he should pay. The question is not what is the right thing for Warren to do but what is the right thing for you."

"I'm going to forget about child support. The less I have to do with him the better I'll like it."

Peg didn't ask for child support and he didn't contest custody. The divorce was granted without any unpleasantness. Peg didn't miss any time from work. The children didn't have to testify. She was satisfied despite the substantial alimony she agreed to pay for five years.

Warren's tennis game improved greatly after the divorce, when he stopped pretending to look for a job. He saw his children sporadically. But when the five years expired and his support from Peg ceased he brought a suit to obtain custody of the children, a ploy to get more money from Peg. His petition was withdrawn without a hearing; I suspect that she paid him again. When last I saw Peg she was addressing the bar association.

Peg is another wise woman. She knew that freedom was more important than vindication of her rights. *She obeyed the Second*

Commandment. She anticipated that her husband would not pay child support and so she avoided an unpleasant hearing that would have been required if she had asked for support.

She also obeyed the Third Commandment. She followed her own judgment instead of taking the advice of those who told her to ask for the child support to which she was legally entitled.

Freedom and peace of mind are worth buying if you can afford the cost. Peg could and she does not regret her decision.

Some Marriages Are Not Worth Saving

Louisa was the debutante of her year, the year after she graduated from prep school. She is tall, blonde, and fragile looking. When she was in her twenties she was extraordinarily beautiful. When I saw her in court she looked worn, ill, and terrified. One could only dimly discern traces of her lost charm.

Two years after her coming out party, Louisa married Brock, a tall, handsome Princeton athlete, the scion of a prominent family. His parents and Louisa's belonged to the same clubs; they had summer homes in the same exclusive colony in Maine. It appeared to be a marriage made in heaven or in the board room. In due course, Louisa had three children. She and Brock bought a large estate with a swimming pool, tennis court, and stables. The children went to their parents' respective prep schools. But after a few years cracks began to appear in the lovely picture.

Louisa's best friend Muffie testified before me in criminal court. The charges against Brock were aggravated assault and assault with intent to kill. Louisa came to court in a wheelchair, attended by a nurse.

"We noticed that Louisa looked ill," Muffie told the court. "She seemed to have one accident after another—a broken arm, a broken nose, black eyes. She looked awful. When I asked her what happened she would say, 'I'm accident prone.' I never suspected that Brock was beating her. That sort of thing only happens in the slums, I thought."

Louisa's mother also testified, but unwillingly. The prosecutor had to subpoena her. It was she who had called the ambulance to take Louisa to the hospital. Her mother had arrived at Louisa's home and found her bleeding on the floor, Brock standing over her beating her with his fists.

"Was this the first you knew that they were having problems?" she was asked.

"No. Louisa had told me she was unhappy, that she wanted to leave Brock."

"And what did you do?"

"I told her to try harder to make her marriage work. Marriage is not always smooth and easy. We had never had a divorce in our family. But I had no idea he was beating her."

The mother wept.

Louisa testified that Brock had been abusing her for several years, that on her mother's advice she had gone to a marriage counselor but had not told him that Brock beat her. She was ashamed. Brock had been gambling and had dipped into company funds. He wanted money from her trust funds. When she refused to give him money he beat her until she agreed to get money for him.

Several times when Brock beat her she called the police. Once she even obtained a protective order from family court prohibiting Brock from hitting her. At the hearing he abjectly promised the judge that he would behave, that he truly loved Louisa. They went home together.

Brock promptly tore up the court order that was given to Louisa. The next time she called the police she told them she wanted the protective order enforced. They asked to see the order which, of course, Louisa could not produce. They left and advised her to go back to court.

The last episode occurred when she told Brock she couldn't get any more money for six months. The bank that held her funds refused to make any more money available.

Louisa did not bring criminal charges against Brock. The physician at the emergency ward of the hospital filed the complaint. She and her family were still trying to keep up a front. They did not want the family name marred by divorce.

Brock is serving time in the penitentiary. Louisa is undergoing painful reconstructive surgery on her face which will probably be permanently scarred. Their children are in therapy. I do not know whether Louisa ever sued Brock for divorce.

Brock did not testify. But many abusive husbands who appeared before me did take the witness stand. One man, a police officer, who had twisted his wife's arm until it broke, angrily took the witness stand.

"I'm not a criminal," he declared. "I arrest criminals."

"If you saw a man breaking someone's arm, wouldn't you arrest him?" I asked him. "Assault is a crime, you know."

"This was no crime," he replied. "It was only my wife."

Abuse is a crime. Even though most husbands, like Brock, ignore protective orders issued by the courts, you do not have to remain in your home and be beaten. There are shelters for abused women in most communities. You can prosecute. And you can sue for support and damages. The most effective protection against an abusive husband is not a protective order but a criminal prosecution.

At least for the period that Brock is in prison, he will not molest Louisa. When he is released he may come back and beat her again. Many husbands do. And many wives find that their only protection is not the law but escape. They move to another community, assume another name, and hope that their abusers will not find them.

Most marriages are begun with love and high hopes. Some women invest so much of themselves in the marriage that they will try almost anything to save it. Probably many marriages could be saved with a little more effort on the part of both parties. But some marriages are not worth saving. When a husband physically assaults his wife or molests his children, the wife should leave him.

Louisa violated the First Commandment. She did not protect herself.

She violated the Second Commandment. She did not anticipate disaster, that after the first assault he would beat her again. Unfortunately, most wife beaters are addicted to this type of behavior. I have seen scores of husbands who violated protective orders, were jailed for contempt of court, and on the day they were released went home and beat their wives again, even more brutally. Although all of us hope that wrongdoers will be reformed and we want to give them a second chance, it is not wise or safe to give a wife beater another opportunity to assault his wife.

Louisa violated the Third Commandment. She knew Brock was violent and dangerous but instead of acting on her own good judgment, *she followed her mother's advice.* I fear for her safety when Brock leaves prison.

Some Marriages Should Be Saved

Mary Alice had been married for about ten years, and had two children. She and Bob lived in a pleasant suburban house. She loved gardening. She was president of the PTA. She was a happy, contented woman until Bob announced that he wanted a divorce. He said he was bored with marriage and suburbia. He wanted adventure.

Mary Alice was heartbroken. She loved Bob. His departure came as a shock. She did not know that he was having an affair with a neighbor. She had no money. She has never had a job.

Mary Alice and Bob were childhood sweethearts. They married the day after she graduated from college. Her mother and her friends were outraged when they heard that Bob had walked out.

"He's a shit. Take him for all the money he has," they urged.

Mary Alice went to a lawyer who told her the sad facts of life. Although Bob was a physician earning more than $150,000 a year, he had no assets other than their heavily mortgaged house in the suburbs. At most he could be ordered to pay Mary Alice alimony for a few years until she obtained some job skills. He is legally obligated to support the children through high school, but perhaps not to pay for college and graduate school and probably could not be required to pay for tuition at their expensive private schools, she was told.

The lawyer, a college classmate of Mary Alice, was sympathetic. "Go to a marriage counselor," he suggested. "Perhaps your marriage can be saved."

Mary Alice talked it over with her parents. Her father, a

successful business man, offered her money. "You don't have to go back to that man after the way he treated you," he said.

Her mother said, "You're pretty. You were always the most popular girl at school. You'll find a better man than Bob."

No one asked Mary Alice what she wanted. Bob continued to pay the mortgage on the house. He sent her $300 every week. Bob's girlfriend went back to her husband and Bob was alone. After a few months of bachelor life, Bob got tired of eating in restaurants and hanging out with his friends in bars. He missed his home and his children. He missed Mary Alice.

When he came to take the children out he suggested that perhaps the marriage could be resumed.

Mary Alice expected him to apologize, to promise that he would be faithful forever. He didn't do so. He just said, "I think I'd like to come back home."

"It isn't your home any more," she replied.

A year after Bob left he called with startling news.

"I'm filing for divorce tomorrow. Melissa (his new girl friend) is pregnant and I'm going to marry her."

Mary Alice's lawyer worked out the best deal he could. Ten thousand a year for Mary Alice for five years, title to the house and one car, and $150 a week support for each child until graduation from college. Bob adamantly refused to obligate himself for graduate school. "I have a new family to support," he declared.

Mary Alice soon discovered that she could not afford to live in her house and maintain a garden and a swimming pool. Her membership in the country club ceased. The new wife now belongs. Also, she has no medical coverage, although Bob keeps the children on his medical insurance.

Mary Alice was fortunate to obtain a job at her alma mater in the admissions office. She meets a few men but she is usually too tired to go dancing and have fun.

She and the children live in a small apartment. They resent their new life style and prefer their weekends with Bob in his big house and playing tennis at his country club. While they are out Mary Alice cleans the apartment and does the laundry.

Her father has retired. Her parents now live in Arizona. They send the children lavish presents and occasionally buy Mary Alice expensive clothes. But her life is hard and lonely.

Mary Alice asks plaintively, "Why didn't I know what my life as a divorcée would be like *before* . . .?

Mary Alice violated four of the Five Commandments.

◆ **First, she did not protect herself.** When her lawyer told her the sad state of the law, that she could not get adequate support for the children or an adequate property settlement and alimony, she should immediately have taken action to effect a reconciliation with Bob or to institute divorce proceedings.

At that time Bob did not have another girlfriend. He wanted to come back to Mary Alice. He would have been more willing to make a fair arrangement than when he was adamantly seeking a no-fault divorce.

◆ **Mary Alice violated the Second Commandment. She did not anticipate disaster.** She might have expected that Bob would find another woman after she rebuffed him.

◆ **Mary Alice violated the Third Commandment. She did not consult her own wishes** as to effecting a reconciliation with Bob but simply followed her family's advice.

◆ **She also violated the Fifth Commandment. She never discussed money** with Bob. He did love his children and he cared for her in his selfish way. She might have persuaded him to be more generous than the meager requirements of the law.

Most disastrously, she never really asked herself what she wanted. Obviously she was hurt and heartbroken by Bob's infidelity. It is hard to trust a man who has betrayed you. Love cannot be the same again. But in a less than ideal world, a flawed marriage may be preferable for a mother of young children than no marriage. These are poor options but if those are your only choices, at least you should make the decision and not let events foreclose your choice.

Being Right Is Not Enough

Jennifer, like Mary Alice, was a happy housewife and mother until her best friend, Sue, told her that she had seen Roger at a Club Med in the Caribbean with his secretary. He had told Jennifer that he was going away on a business trip.

She confronted Roger with the facts.

"I love you. This was just a one-time fling," he protested. "It won't happen again. I don't want to lose you and the children."

"Give me time to think about this," Jennifer said.

She talked to a lawyer who gave her much the same advice as Mary Alice's lawyer had. She talked to her married friends who were outraged by Roger's treatment of Jennifer.

"Throw him out, the two-timing bastard," was their advice.

Jennifer also talked to several divorced friends who told her of their problems—the support checks that were always late, the men they dated who thought every divorcée was fair game. No one mentioned love.

Before the children were born Jennifer had been a social worker in a family service organization. She knew from her clients the loneliness and hardships of single women with children and little money.

Her parents said they would help, whatever she decided, but that they could never feel close to Roger again.

"You're an attractive young woman; you're intelligent; you don't have to put up with such treatment. This is the 1990s. You're entitled to your own life," they said.

It is my life, Jennifer decided. She carefully reviewed her life before Roger. She had had many boyfriends but none as charming, as loving, as much fun as Roger. She reviewed their marriage of ten years. There had been rough spots when Roger quit his job as accountant for a successful firm when they wanted him to "adjust" the books. The two years when he opened his own firm had not been easy. She had kept her job and postponed having a baby that they both wanted very much.

Two years later when she had a miscarriage, Roger had been loving and caring. The past few years had been wonderful. Roger was a good father, a good lover. He was still the most interesting man she knew. His betrayal hurt her deeply. But one weekend out of the eleven years she had known him was not so terrible that she should give up all those joys. She could get over her disappointment with Roger and her wounded pride. She knew she still loved Roger and if he still loved her, as he said, that was all that mattered.

When Sue saw Jennifer and Roger at the theater together laughing and obviously having a good time, she was aghast.

"How could you take him back?" Sue asked. "Don't you know he wronged you?"

"Being in the right is not the most important thing," Jennifer calmly replied. "Doing what I *want* is more important."

In a traditional marriage ceremony, the bride and groom promise to forsake all others, in other words to be faithful to each other. Not many women want to have an open marriage in which neither party is faithful. When a husband has an affair, it is very hurtful to his wife. Depending on the circumstances, infidelity may be forgivable.

Again, this is a decision only you can make.

Jennifer and Roger talked about his infidelity openly, after Jennifer initiated the discussion in a nonjudgmental way. He assured her that it was a one-time fling, not a serious affair. Jennifer knew that he had been faithful for more than eleven years.

She examined her own mind and heart and admitted to herself that she had been attracted to other men, that her faithfulness may have been lack of opportunity to have an affair rather than lack of desire. But all the time it was Roger she loved. And when he said that she was the only woman he really loved, she believed him.

Jennifer told me that she never regretted her decision. They now have a good marriage again.

Half a Loaf Is Better Than None

Gertrude and Lewis met in college. They were both bright and attractive. Her family was comfortable; his was poor. When Gertrude told her parents she wanted to marry Lewis they welcomed him. Her father gave him a job in the family business. In due course they had two children. Under Lewis's able direction the business expanded enormously. Suddenly Lewis was wealthy and Gertrude's family were out of the business.

Lewis was then ready to rid himself of Gertrude and move into the fast lane with a new, trophy wife. Gertrude's lawyer worked out a fair property settlement and an agreement that she would have custody of the children.

A few years later when Lewis discovered that his second wife could not have children, he decided he wanted his children by Gertrude. He filed a petition for change of custody.

Lewis retained a famous and expensive psychiatrist who examined the children. Lewis then applied for an order requiring Gertrude to submit to a psychiatric examination. She protested. "There's nothing wrong with my head."

The judge to whom the custody case was assigned examined the children privately in chambers, with counsel present but not the parents. Lewis Jr., who was only seven, told the judge that "Mommy cries a lot."

The boy did not know that Gertrude had breast cancer. He only knew that Mommy was unhappy. Gertrude had not told her lawyer about her medical problems so he could offer no explanation for her weeping spells. The judge ordered a psychiatric evaluation.

Gertrude's lawyer told her that she should retain her own psychiatrist to examine the children.

"I don't want them put through this ordeal. Why should they be subjected to prying questions? It upsets them."

"If you don't counter Lewis's expert's unfavorable opinion with an opinion supporting you, he will get custody," the lawyer advised.

And so reluctantly Gertrude took her children to a board certified psychiatrist who spent forty-five minutes with each of the children and charged Gertrude $500. His fee for testifying in court was $750.

The judge held one hearing. Lewis asked for leave to bring in other experts. This was granted. Gertrude then discovered that Lewis had paid a maid she had discharged $1,000 to come and testify that Gertrude had a temper, that she yelled at the children, and that she was often away from home. Of course, she was away from home for her radiation treatments.

Lewis also brought in the children's teachers. Since he was paying the tuition for the children to attend private school, they testified that he was a caring and concerned father, that he showed more interest in the children than most fathers.

Meanwhile Gertrude had uncovered some of Lewis's dishonesty in the business. He was under investigation by the Internal Revenue Service for tax evasion and by the SEC for stock fraud. The court ruled that this evidence was immaterial. Lewis' business morals had nothing to do with his ability to be a good parent.

Gertrude called her psychiatrist again. He reexamined both children, another $500. He told her that the court proceedings were upsetting the children. Gertrude knew that the boy was having nightmares and her four-year-old daughter was unhappy because her brother was unhappy. He testified again, another $750. The judge still did not reach a decision. He ordered a third hearing.

Gertrude was running out of money. She could not afford more counsel fees and more fees for the psychiatrist. Although every person accused of crime is entitled to free legal counsel for his or her defense, a woman who wants custody of her children is not entitled to free counsel. The Supreme Court has held that the custody and companionship of her children is not a fundamental right protected by the Constitution.

Although there are women's law centers, legal aid associations, and public defenders, in most jurisdictions it is almost impossible for a woman to obtain free counsel to represent her in a custody case.

Gertrude was not only out of money. She was exhausted from her cancer treatments and the custody battle. She told her lawyer she could not go through another hearing; he should try to work out an arrangement with Lewis.

Lewis agreed to shared custody—one month the children lived with Gertrude and one month with Lewis and his new wife. It was an arrangement that satisfied no one. The little girl cried to Gertrude, "Which is my own home?"

Shared custody is popular with many family court judges. They think it is fair. Both parents should be involved with their children and should share in all the decisions: school, summer vacations, religious instruction, health care. Of course, every one of these decisions causes more dissension and unhappiness for both parents and for the children, who believe that they are the cause of all the problems.

In despair, Gertrude gave up the fight. The children now live with Lewis. She sees them once or twice a month. They now call Lewis's wife "Mom."

Gertrude could not fault her lawyer. He fought for her as valiantly as he could. But she told me that if she had known what the custody hearings would do to the children, she would never have put them through that ordeal. She would have come to some accommodation with Lewis.

King Solomon suggested to the two women who each claimed that a baby was hers that he divide the infant. A judge in a custody case cannot divide a child. He or she can only divide the time spent with each parent. Within a year of three hundred sixty-five days there is always the opportunity for compromise.

Most parents are secretly glad to have some respite from the care of their children. Wealthy parents send their offspring to summer camp or boarding school to have some time for themselves.

The fashionable phrase today is "quality time." You can be close to your children without being with them all the time. Often it is better to have less actual time but more pleasurable and meaningful time. And surely it is better to avoid dissension if at all possible.

If Gertrude had agreed to generous vacation time and weekly visitation, she could probably have avoided the psychiatric examinations of the children and the distressing court appearances. She knew that Lewis was physically stronger than she and much richer. In this struggle, it was not a level playing field.

◆ **She violated the First Commandment. She did not protect herself.**

◆ **She violated the Second Commandment. She did not anticipate disaster.** She should have known that Lewis could outspend her and outlast her in a court contest.

In the end, both she and the children suffered to no avail.
She, too, said, "If only I had known *before* . . .

In matters of divorce and custody, every women should remember the Five Commandments and do what is in her own best interest. She must also know *before* how the legal system operates in her case and what a legal battle entails in emotional wear and tear and in money.

Divorce is still easier for men than for women. This is a fact that is hard for many women to accept in the 1990s, when they have been led to believe that women have equal rights.

Most men are able to maintain their former lifestyles after divorce. They belong to their clubs; they have housekeepers. Their ex-wives are not members of the club. They do their own housework and take care of the children, and hold down a job.

You must decide what is right for you *before* you act or by inaction permit the situation to get out of your control. The advice of family and friends is well meant. But it is you who will have to live with your decision. Heed what you have read here, and think carefully *before* . . .

BEFORE YOU DECIDE TO DIVORCE

5 Things He May Say or Do That Could Be a Warning Signal	5 Ways to Protect Yourself Against These Warning Signals
1 When he says, "You won't like what I have to tell you—I'm in love with someone else," this may be a trap to get you so angry that *you* file for divorce, a disadvantageous situation.	If you don't want a divorce, suggest you wait six months to see how you can rearrange your lives. He may change his mind. You may also change yours. If he wants out and you don't, make him fight for his advantage every inch of the way.

5 Things He May Say or Do That Could Be a Warning Signal	5 Ways to Protect Yourself Against These Warning Signals
2 When he says, "Let's have a trial separation. I'll pay you $—— a week, while we decide what to do," back up! He is setting you up to accept the amount of the eventual support order—at just what he wishes to pay you. It may not be anywhere near what you will need.	Refuse to agree to a fixed amount. Tell him you do not know how much you will need for support, and proceed to investigate that carefully with *your* advisors.
3 If he says, "You can have custody of the children if you don't fight the divorce (which he wants and you don't)," this may be a trap to get you to accept a ridiculous settlement.	Get your lawyer to draw up a binding custody agreement—and *then* negotiate a financial settlement.
4 When he says, "We don't need expensive divorce lawyers," beware! He probably means that he doesn't want attorneys examining his finances.	Suggest he write down exactly how he proposes to take care of you so that there won't be any misunderstandings. Then take this to *your* attorney to have it reviewed.
5 When he says, "I feel miserable that I hit you, I'll never do it again," this probably is a promise that will be broken.	Suggest that he go with you to a marriage counselor or therapist. If he refuses, you know he has no intention of changing his ways.

9

BEFORE YOU SETTLE THE DIVORCE

Litigious terms, fat contentions, and flowing fees . . .

JOHN MILTON

Most women fear courts. They have heard about long delays, enormous counsel fees, and unjust results. Most have seen countless TV programs about fictional trials and have observed portions of actual trials aired on the media. They have seen the brutal cross examination of Anita Hill and other women who dared to challenge men and male versions of the facts. It is not an encouraging picture.

Recently, a widespread popular movement has evolved encouraging people to use private individuals and organizations instead of courts to resolve their differences. This is called alternative dispute resolution. It includes arbitration, mediation, and conciliation.

Although these procedures differ from each other, all are informal, out-of-court means of settling disputes. They are essentially based on the principle of getting the parties to agree rather than to have a decision imposed on them by a court. As we know from mediation in international disputes, it is successful only when both parties want to reach a fair solution.

Arbitration is the closest to a court proceeding, for the arbitrator bases the decision on legal principles. As in all alternative dispute resolution proceedings, the procedures are informal. Neither rules of evidence nor rules of procedure are observed. No record is made.

Mediation is more informal. The result is based on the mediator's notions of fairness, which the parties are encouraged to accept.

Conciliation is an attempt through a neutral individual to get both parties to agree. In divorce actions the aim of the conciliator is often to preserve the marriage.

There are both advantages and serious disadvantages to these alternatives. Remember that a decree in divorcee must be entered by a court and an order of custody will also be a court order. These orders have binding effect and far-reaching consequences.

Despite manuals and books on "do-it-yourself" divorce, *it is always advisable to have a lawyer.* If you believe you cannot afford a lawyer, you are in a very difficult position. Although every person accused of crime has a right to counsel provided and paid for by the state, there is no right to counsel in divorce or custody proceedings.

If you do not have a lawyer and your husband does, in a court proceeding the judge will probably try to protect you and see that inadmissible evidence is excluded. The judge may also try to protect your financial interests by helping you cross-examine your husband. A judge has to be concerned with the legality and fairness of the trial because a record is made and the decision can be appealed. An appellate court will reverse a decision that is based on inadmissable evidence or that violates the law. In alternative dispute proceedings *there is no record* for a court to review.

Often arbitrators, mediators, and conciliators believe that lawyers are an unnecessary impediment and they will encourage you to proceed without an attorney. This is a very risky undertaking since you will have no means of protecting yourself and will not know if your rights are violated.

If you cannot find a legal aid or legal services organization that will help you, check out the women's support groups in your area, many of which offer legal counseling and support. If they will not provide you with a lawyer, they may provide a lay advocate who will at least be a witness to the proceedings.

Look in your local phone book under *Woman* or *Women*. In many communities there is a women's legal defense group. If you are the victim of spousal violence and are seeking a divorce, organizations to protect battered women may help you. Call your local bar association and talk to someone on the committee on family law. If you live in a very small town or rural area, get in touch with the county or state bar association. You can always write to NOW (National Organization of Women)'s Legal Defense Fund in Washington. They do not represent individual women but they can offer useful advice.

To what organizations do you belong? Your church, your political party, your PTA? All these groups have knowledgeable people who may be able to help you.

Although lawyers take cases on a contingent fee basis (they are paid only if you win), this is not permitted in divorce and custody proceedings. If all else fails, beg or borrow the money for an attorney.

Often women believe that a simplified, private procedure without legal technicalities will be less painful, cheaper, and more desirable. A divorce trial is heard in open court. Alternative dispute resolution proceedings are heard in a private office. The public is not admitted. However, unless you are a movie star, a multimillionaire, or public figure, it is extremely unlikely that anyone will be in the courtroom during your divorce hearing.

In most jurisdictions, custody proceedings are not heard in open court.

Under both court litigation and alternative dispute resolution procedures in custody matters, your children may be required to testify. They may be required to submit to psychiatric examinations. There is little you can do to avoid the stress and trauma of this experience for your child unless you and your husband can agree on issues of custody and visitation.

When you have firmly decided that you want a divorce or have concluded that your husband is going to get a divorce regardless of your wishes, you will have to decide how you wish to proceed.

In some states mediation is a required precondition in custody cases. In other jurisdictions it is offered as an adjunct to the court system. In most jurisdictions arbitration, mediation, and conciliation are available on a purely voluntary basis. You cannot be compelled to forgo your rights to a court hearing, nor can you compel your husband to do so.

In essence, you must ask yourself whether you want a negotiated settlement or a decision based on legal rights.

In considering this choice these are some of the things you should know *before*—

Private or Public Adjudicator?

A mediator, arbitrator, or conciliator is in a business and is paid a fee for each case. You or your husband or both of you will be paying his or her fee. Like all business persons these individuals and their organizations advertise. Their literature presents glowing pictures of the advantages of using their services. They have a vested interest in reaching a result because an aborted arbitration, mediation, or conciliation—that is one in which the parties refuse to proceed—is considered a failure. Therefore, there is a subtle, perhaps unconscious, effort to coerce an agreement.

If the mediator is appointed by the court, as is the practice in some jurisdictions, the mediator's likelihood of receiving further appointments may depend upon his or her success in getting an agreement.

Judges are public servants, paid by the taxpayers. Judges have more than enough cases and are under no pressure to get more business. Consequently, judges are more detached. They are not concerned with which party will be paying the fee nor do they usually attempt to force an agreement on the parties. You must decide whether it is to your advantage to have an agreement negotiated for you or whether you will fare better by receiving what the law allows.

Divorce in Haste and Repent at Leisure?

One of the advantages of alternative dispute resolution is speed. The cases can be heard sooner and more quickly. If you are in a hurry to remarry, then this is an important consideration.

However, if you are not in a hurry, you should take ample time to find out what the law and practice in your jurisdiction are.

- ◆ What is the usual division of property under equitable distribution? Is it fifty-fifty or forty-sixty, or does it depend upon which spouse earned the money?
- ◆ If you have children, what is the practice with respect to award of custody? Is the mother preferred or does the court follow the "best interests of the child" rule?
- ◆ Does this approach mean which parent can offer the better physical and monetary care?
- ◆ What is the practice with respect to child support? Will the court consider the needs of the parent as being more important than those of the child?

Hearings in alternative forms of dispute resolution are often very quick, sometimes taking less than a day. Consider carefully the evidence you will want to present with respect to your financial needs, and if you have children, their emotional as well as financial needs. You should also review your situation, investigate your husband's finances, and investigate the job market for yourself if you will need to support yourself after the divorce.

If you have children, consider carefully their needs. You may want to talk with their school teachers, counselors, and other people who can advise you. *Haste is rarely advantageous to you.*

PERSONAL PARTICIPATION OR RELIANCE ON COUNSEL

Alternative dispute resolution is conducted informally. You will be encouraged to speak directly with your husband. This is sometimes considered empowering the litigant. However, most wives have arrived at the position where a divorce is inevitable because they have not been able to communicate effectively their husbands. Often a wife finds that the most empowering phrase she can use when dealing with her husband is, "See my lawyer." You know better than anyone whether you are more likely to win in a direct confrontation with your husband or through a tough lawyer who speaks for you.

Legal fees in alternative dispute resolution are often less because less time is involved and witnesses are often not used. But, unless the financial results are as good as those likely to be obtained through litigation, this is being penny wise and pound foolish.

While lawyers are necessary, they are not an unmixed blessing. Lawyers are trained to win. Sometimes a wife and husband have reached an amicable agreement that is upset by nitpicking, intransigent attorneys who want to obtain the last dollar possible and the greatest number of hours and minutes of visitation rights with the children. Remember that the lawyer is your agent not your master. If you are aware of all the facts and the applicable law and are satisfied with the agreement you have reached with your husband, do not let your attorney prolong the agony of the proceedings and create more dissension by insisting on provisions that you consider unnecessary. In fact, many women need protection from their divorce lawyers, a situation emphasized in 1993 when Chief Judge Judith S. Kaye of the state court of appeals announced a series of new regulations governing divorce proceedings and the conduct of divorce lawyers. Among the rules, sex between divorce lawyers and their clients was banned, with the thought that at the time of divorce women tend to be extremely vulnerable. It was expected that other states would follow with divorce reforms preventing the exploitation of female clients.

THE GENDER BIAS PROBLEM

Many judges are gender biased, whether they are men or women. So are many mediators, arbitrators, and conciliators. In most cities and large counties, you cannot be sure which judge will hear your case. It is the luck of the draw. In some small communities, there is only one judge who hears divorce and custody matters. If that judge has a reputation for being hard on women, then you may be wise to consider alternatives.

A judge will decide your case based on the admissible evidence and the law. A record is made of the proceedings. If the judge betrays obvious prejudice or deviates from the established law, you have a right of appeal.

If you choose arbitration, you through your lawyer can influence the selection of the person who will hear your case. You can veto an individual you do not want. In mediation and conciliation you may not have that choice. In some jurisdictions you will have to accept the individual designated by the court to hear your case.

Because there is no record of the conversations in alternative dispute proceedings, you will have great difficulty in proving that the person who heard your case was biased or prejudiced against you. And if he or she does not follow the law, you probably will have no effective recourse.

In domestic relations matters, including divorce and custody, most mediators, arbitrators and conciliators are not lawyers. They may be psychologists, therapists, educators, or house-wives—people who have taken a course of probably not more than six months in arbitration, mediation, or conciliation. They can and often do allow hearsay and unreliable evidence at the hearing. You cannot challenge the admissibility of such testimony no matter how prejudicial it is.

DO YOU KNOW THE EXTENT OF YOUR HUSBAND'S ASSETS?

Under these alternative dispute resolution programs usually there is no provision for discovery. You have few rights and fewer means to discover any hidden assets your husband may have. As I have noted, if you are not familiar with your husband's business affairs and investments, you should make *a thorough investigation of his assets.*

This is not easy to do. It takes time and clever sleuthing. The place to begin is the income tax return. Almost every married couple files a joint tax return because it saves money. You are entitled to see that return. Go to the local office of the Internal Revenue Service and ask for it. Look at the sources of income. If there is real estate, a realtor can give you a ball park estimate of the value of the property. Check the stock exchange for the value of the securities.

Make a list of how much your family spends each year collectively and individually on housing, food, automobiles, entertainment and *all* other expenses. If the outgo is more than the reported income, he probably has hidden assets.

A court can order him to produce records. When he testifies he is under oath and a record is made so that if he lies about any material fact, he can be prosecuted for perjury. This is a powerful incentive to truthtelling. In alternative dispute resolution proceedings, there is not the same coercive threat to induce truthful testimony.

THE ISSUES TO BE DECIDED

When a dispute is over money (does *A* owe *B* a certain number of dollars, and the parties have relatively equal bargaining power) arbitration and mediation do save time and money. These alternatives relieve the overburdened courts of litigation and reduce the backlog. They save the taxpayers money because the litigants pay the fee of the mediator, arbitrator, or conciliator. For these reasons many courts urge the use of alternative dispute resolution procedures.

A divorce presents complex problems. Here are some of the issues that must be decided in most divorces.

DISTRIBUTION OF ASSETS

What assets do you and your husband have? In no-fault jurisdictions the marital property will be "equitably distributed." Which of your properties will be considered "marital property" varies from state to state. Find out the practice in your jurisdiction. And what is considered equitable? If the assets include an ongoing business or professional career, how will that be valued?

CUSTODY AND VISITATION

If you have children, custody and visitation can be the most difficult questions to be decided. Shall there be joint legal custody? Joint physical custody? Or custody in one parent?

If one parent is awarded physical custody, what rights of visitation shall the other parent have? If the parents live in different cities, who shall pay for the children's transportation for visits? What rights shall each parent have over the choice of schools, religious education, summer vacations? Which parent shall have the children on holidays?

Support

Support presents many questions:

◆ The amount to be paid weekly for each child.
◆ If they attend private school, the tuition.
◆ What higher education, if any? If father, for example, is a doctor, must he pay tuition for his children to attend graduate or professional school?
◆ What support will you receive for yourself and for how long? Many courts award support only for a limited time in order to permit a non-working ex-wife to become employable. What education and training will you need? How much will it cost? How long will it take?

Health Care

Health care is a serious and expensive problem.

◆ Which parent shall pay for health insurance and for how long? Once you are divorced you cannot be included on your former husband's insurance policy. The children can be included if you insist.
◆ Will he pay for your health insurance?
◆ How much will it cost and what will it cover?
◆ Who will pay for dentistry?
◆ Who will pay for eye care?
◆ Who will pay for prescription drugs?
◆ Who will pay for physical and/or psychiatric therapy?

Bargaining

Under alternative dispute resolution, the outcome may be determined by bargaining between you and your husband, either directly or through your attorneys. Spouses are rarely in equal bargaining positions. Usually the husband has more money than the wife. Usually the husband is more sophisticated in dealing with financial and legal matters. Only you can decide whether you have an equal bargaining position.

APPELLATE RIGHTS

Under alternative dispute programs, you probably give up your right to appeal an unjust decision. Although you have limited rights to appeal mediation and conciliation, it is more difficult to overcome an unfavorable decision or recommendation than to make a fresh record. Arbitration may be binding and unappealable, except for fraud and illegality, which are difficult and expensive to prove.

The experiences of the following divorcées may help you to decide how you wish to proceed.

WHEN MEDIATION IS PREFERABLE

Janet and Leonard had been married more than thirty years when Leonard suddenly decided that he wanted a divorce. He had fallen in love with an associate, Verna. Janet was shocked. She thought they had a happy marriage. They had two grown daughters who were happily married to successful men. They had three grandchildren whom they adored. Janet and Leonard had lovingly built a beautiful home; they were avid tennis players; they collected primitive art. They had no financial problems.

Leonard said he wanted an amicable, quick divorce. He would agree to whatever reasonable requests Janet made. She was furiously angry. For the first time in their married life she screamed at Leonard. She accused him of disloyalty and stupidity. He walked out of the house.

"I'll see you in court," he yelled and banged the door.

When Janet tried to speak to Leonard over the phone, he hung up on her. The chance for an amicable agreement was irrevocably lost.

Janet had been a very pretty, popular, wealthy girl. When they were first married Janet worked because Leonard could not support them. She used $50,000 of her inheritance to buy their first house.

Leonard was a poor boy who worked his way through college by going to school at night. His academic record was mediocre. But he had over the years risen to a good position in a successful corporation.

Verna was only a high school graduate, not very attractive. But she adored Leonard and thought he was the most brilliant man she knew.

Janet and Leonard lived in a state that had a no-fault divorce law. Janet knew she could not stop Leonard from getting a divorce and marrying Verna. But she determined to make it as difficult and expensive as she could. She retained a bright young lawyer who suggested mediation, to which Leonard reluctantly agreed.

Janet had inherited an estate of about $250,000. Leonard had, through his employer's stock option plan acquired stock worth $1,000,000. The house which was jointly owned was then worth $750,000. They also had other securities owned jointly, worth about $100,000. They also had their furniture and art collection.

The mediator proposed that Janet receive the house and the furniture because Leonard and Verna were planning to move to the West coast and buy a new house and new furnishings. Janet would retain her own estate. The art collection would be appraised and divided in kind. The jointly owned securities would be equally divided. Leonard would get three-fourths of his company stock and Janet one fourth. Janet would thus have assets worth $1,300,000 plus half the art collection. Leonard would have $800,000 plus his pension, which was worth about $400,000. Thus the parties would come out approximately equal and Leonard would have a quick and easy divorce.

After some grumbling, Leonard agreed. Janet rejected the proposal and fired her lawyer. She wanted half of all the property.

A year later Leonard obtained his no-fault divorce and promptly married Verna. Janet's new lawyer attempted to negotiate an agreement, but Leonard was no longer interested. "We'll go to court," he told Janet's lawyer.

Janet fired this lawyer and after much unpleasantness paid a fee of $5,000. She then retained another lawyer. Janet was still living in the house. But the real estate boom had busted and the house was worth only $500,000.

After a lengthy, contentious hearing that lasted almost a week, the court entered the following order: Janet's estate was part of the marital assets, as were the house and the furniture. Since Leonard had contributed the major part of the assets, the judge awarded 60 percent of the assets to Leonard and 40 percent to Janet. The house, furniture, and art collection were to be appraised and their value included as part of the marital assets. Leonard's pension, he ruled, was not part of the marital property. Thus Janet received $640,000 plus 40 percent of the value of the art and the furniture.

Leonard received $1,160,000 plus 60 percent of the value of the art and furniture.

Janet fired that lawyer, who demanded a $30,000 fee. No other lawyer would take the case, of course, until the previous lawyer had been paid. Janet resentfully paid his fee and retained a lawyer who appealed the order of the court. After a hearing and fees of $10,000 the appellate court dismissed her appeal.

Whenever her daughters visit Leonard, Janet is angry with them. Her relationship with them has deteriorated. She is a lonely, unhappy woman. Although she is not poor, she has much less money than Leonard. She bitterly complains, "Why didn't someone explain the law to me *before* . . ."

When a husband is eager to remarry, he will usually agree to a more favorable settlement in order to obtain his freedom as soon as possible. Obviously Janet could have made a better arrangement with Leonard then than after he had his divorce and remarried.

Janet violated the Second Commandment. She did not anticipate disaster. She should have asked her lawyers what the worst possible result could be. There is no guaranty of the outcome of any law suit. That is why most cases are settled. Both parties assess the best and the worst likely results and try to arrive at a medium figure.

Once Leonard had his divorce, he was willing to gamble on

the outcome of a trial. Had Janet realistically weighed the chances, she would have settled. *Her lawyers did not have the same incentive to settle. They were paid regardless of the result.*

PROTECT YOURSELF BY MAKING A DEAL

Helen and Bill had been married fifteen years when he decided he wanted a divorce. Their children were eight and ten years old. Like many husbands, Bill had left the rearing of the children to Helen. Maggie, the eight-year-old, was a sunny child seemingly without problems. Billy Jr. was a bright child but he had mild dyslexia. It made the boy unhappy because he could not keep up with the other children. His sister read much better than he. Bill was impatient with the boy. He simply couldn't understand why a bright kid had so much trouble with school work.

Aside from disagreements over Billy, Helen and Bill's marriage had been placid and pleasant. But the excitement for both had vanished. After a few days of weeping and blaming herself for not keeping Bill interested and happy, Helen realized the marriage was over.

Although Helen was shocked and hurt, she told herself that a divorce might be the best for all. She would go back to work at the advertising agency that occasionally called her when they had a rush job. She was happier when she had some work of her own instead of sitting alone evenings, waiting for Bill to come home, which he did less and less frequently. And when he was home they had little to talk about.

Helen decided the best thing would be to get through the legalities as quickly and painlessly as possible.

"Let's be civilized. I don't want any more unpleasantness," she told Bill.

"I agree," he said happily.

Helen's best friend had just been through a long, hostile divorce. She urged Helen to do anything to avoid a trial. Helen's father had been a lawyer who had always talked about the fairness of the law. Helen consulted other divorced friends who also recounted horrible tales of trials in which they were subjected to brutal cross-examination.

When Bill suggested mediation, she agreed with some misgivings. Bill did not want anyone prying into his finances. And so they went to a mediator.

Helen assumed that she would have custody of the children and that the only issues to be mediated were the division of their assets and the amount of support for the children.

The mediator appointed by the court was a pleasant middle-aged woman who had been a psychology major in college. In midlife she had taken a course in mediation. She was not a lawyer and knew nothing about law or finances.

At the first session, Helen said brightly, "This should be a simple matter. All we have to decide are monetary questions: how much I need for myself and the children."

The mediator, who firmly believed in shared custody, was shocked.

"The important question is the welfare of the children, who shall have custody, not money," she exclaimed indignantly.

"But custody is agreed upon," Helen said.

"Oh, no. It isn't," Bill declared. He immediately recognized that this was a huge bargaining chip he had not counted on.

For the first time Bill demanded not simply shared legal custody but primary physical custody. Helen tried to explain to the mediator that Bill and Billy did not get along well, that Bill did not understand his son's learning problems.

The mediator recalled a long-ago course in Freudian psychology and concluded that Helen and Billy had an Oedipal problem.

"The boy needs his father. You are overprotective," she told Helen.

At this point Bill became alarmed. He did not want the daily care of his children. He wanted his freedom. He graciously suggested that shared custody would be fine.

The mediator was impressed with Bill's generosity. Helen did not know how to bring up the subject of money. She feared that the mediator would think she did not care about the children.

Bill presented their joint tax returns for the previous year. It showed that he had earned $110,000 and Helen had earned

$17,000. Their house was heavily mortgaged. The return showed savings and securities of $50,000. There was no indication of Bill's ownership of a share in a real estate trust because the trust had not paid any income. He was not questioned about any assets other than their automobiles.

The mediator decided that Bill should keep his car, a new Mercedes, and Helen should keep her car, a six-year-old Toyota. She proposed that they sell the house and divide the proceeds.

"Sell the house?" Helen exclaimed in horror. "This is our home, our children's home."

"You don't need a big house. You can't afford to maintain it. A small apartment will be better for you. After all you won't be entertaining clients. And the children will be with their father half the year."

"What about support? Health insurance?"

Bill promptly interjected that he would keep the children on his health policy. It was paid for by his employer and cost him nothing.

"You will be going back to work and will get insurance on your job," the mediator told Helen.

"But I don't have a job yet. And I'm not sure I can work full time and take care of the children. What about support for them?"

The mediator concluded that $200 a week for the weeks the children were with Helen would be sufficient.

"I will have to pay rent twelve months a year, even though the children are with Bill," she protested.

The mediator was not impressed. She divided the securities equally.

Helen was afraid to protest lest she lose custody of the children. The mediation was concluded in less than two hours.

Helen went home and tried to make out a budget. There was no way she could pay for rent, food, and clothes for herself and the children on $10,400 a year. She had no job and no medical insurance. Then she consulted a lawyer.

He immediately filed exceptions to the mediator's report. The judge dismissed the exceptions.

"The mediator heard the evidence. I trust her," he told Helen's lawyer.

Shortly thereafter the decree in divorce was entered.

Six months later Helen read an announcement of Bill's marriage to a young real estate broker. Then she learned that Bill and his bride had gone on a honeymoon to the Orient and bought an apartment for $500,000. But it was too late to open the decree.

With much difficulty she went back to court and got the support raised to $300 a week.

The children think Bill is wonderful because he lavishes gifts on them, while they live in a tiny apartment with Helen, who can barely afford to pay for their necessities.

Helen sadly told her lawyer, "If only I had known the facts *before . . .*"

Helen violated the First Commandment. She did not protect herself. Even though she wanted to avoid unpleasantness, she should have consulted a lawyer before making any decisions. A lawyer would have at a minimum obtained Bill's agreement as to custody of the children. A lawyer would have had Helen make out a realistic budget before any hearing. And a lawyer would have inquired into Bill's assets. If Bill had been evasive, the lawyer would undoubtedly have advised a court trial where Helen would have had the right to discover the extent of Bill's assets.

Helen was able to afford an attorney. It is penny wise and pound foolish to proceed into the unknown thickets of the law without legal counsel. When a husband says, "We don't need attorneys," *that is a red flag, warning that he fears what a good attorney may do.*

The time to see your lawyer is *before . . .*

CONTROL YOUR OWN CASE

Marie and Mark have two children. They have been married ten years. Marie was a high school teacher. She earned $45,000 a year. She had good health benefits that covered Mark and the children. If she wanted to teach summer school she could earn an additional $8,000. Mark had a small electronics business. He earned about $30,000. He had no benefits and no vacation pay. Their house was heavily mortgaged.

Marie is an energetic, active person. She was taking night courses to get her master's degree. She loved to go camping with the children. She was active in community affairs.

Mark is a quiet, reclusive man. He spent his evenings watching television or reading science fiction. He resented the time and money Marie spent entertaining friends. He objected to going out evenings. For the previous two summers he had refused to go with Marie and the children on their summer vacation trips.

When Marie was invited to give a paper at an education conference, with all expenses for her and the family paid, he flatly refused to go with her. She and the children went and had a marvelous time.

On their return, Marie asked Mark, "Didn't you miss us?"

He replied, "No. I didn't. It was nice and peaceful here."

Marie realized that she hadn't missed Mark either. In fact, she had a better time when he was not with her and she didn't have to try to placate him and make excuses to her friends for his surliness. There was no point in trying to keep the marriage alive.

When she suggested a divorce, Mark was shocked. After a few weeks he told her that if she really wanted to leave him, she should go ahead and get a divorce. He would not contest it. He agreed that she have custody of the children. He would be content with visitation once a week and two weeks in the summer.

Marie consulted a lawyer who informed her that a court would probably order Mark to pay a small sum like $30.00 a week for support of each of the children. Since she earned more money than Mark and since they had few assets it would be wise simply to make an agreement with Mark and present it to the court. There was no point in having arbitration or mediation. He advised her to tell Mark to get a lawyer and he and Mark's lawyer would draw up an agreement.

A conference was held with Mark and Marie and their lawyers. Mark's lawyer demanded half the equity in the house and half the furniture as well as the car that was in his name. Marie's lawyer countered with a demand for a hundred dollars a week support for the children. The discussion soon became heated.

Marie suggested that they adjourn and meet again. She asked Mark to go out and have coffee with her.

"Mark," she said, "Why don't you go through the house and make a list of everything you want. Let's have the house appraised and see what our equity is worth. We may not be talking about more than a few dollars. I don't want to fight with you."

"I don't want to fight either," he agreed.

"How much support do you think you should pay?" Marie asked him.

Mark thought about that and suggested $20.00 a week for each child.

The realtor who sold them their house told them their equity was worth at most $20,000.

Mark and Marie instructed their attorneys to draw up an agreement providing for custody of both children for Marie and visitation once a week and two weeks in the summer for Mark. He would pay $40.00 a week support for both children and the furniture would be divided according to their wishes. Marie agreed to pay Mark $10,000 for his share in the house over a three-year-period. When Mark's lawyer demanded interest on the $10,000, Mark said he didn't want it. Mark's lawyer prepared a note that Marie signed. The divorce was concluded without a hearing and without acrimony. Counsel fees were minimal.

Mark rented a small apartment in the neighborhood. He took enough furniture and household goods to provide him with what he needed. When Marie's parents came to visit they were dismayed at the bare-looking house.

"Why didn't you demand your rights? What kind of a lawyer did you have?" they expostulated.

"A few chairs and tables aren't worth fighting about," Marie told them. "I can always replace them when I have the money. An amicable divorce is worth much more to me."

Mark visits Marie and the children once or twice a week. They have dinner together. Sometimes Marie cooks the dinner. Sometimes Mark takes them to a restaurant. Occasionally he brings a present. The children know they have their mother *and* their father.

Marie obeyed the Third Commandment. She acted on her

own best judgment. She was not influenced by her parents or her lawyer to insist on unimportant matters that would have made the divorce more difficult.

Divorce is rarely a happy or easy proceeding for a woman. She is plunged into an alien world of law and finances without a map to guide her or an understanding of her destination. Often she feels that she has lost control of events.

If you are involved in a divorce, remember that you do have choices. You can negotiate. You do not have to accept whatever your departing husband offers or demands.

This is a time to be mindful of the commandments.

Protect thyself: Be sure that you and your children have the necessities of life—income, health care, and security.

Anticipate disaster: Be sure that arrangements are made to cover the situation in the event your ex-husband defaults on the payments.

Act on your own judgment: Do not be influenced by family, friends, or your lawyer to make unreasonable demands or to have an unnecessarily hostile situation.

Wear a velvet glove over an iron hand: Probably your husband once loved you. Do not destroy whatever kindly feelings remain by acting shrewishly. But be firm about important matters.

Discuss money: If you have a thorough discussion of your financial situation and his, you may be able to reach a better accommodation.

A fair and relatively unacrimonious divorce is possible many times if you obey the commandments. And after such a divorce you should be ready to begin another and better chapter in your life.

BEFORE YOU SETTLE THE DIVORCE

5 Things He May Say or Do That Could Be a Warning Signal	5 Ways to Protect Yourself Against These Warning Signals
1 Beware when he says, "We can work out a financial settlement ourselves." Be sure it won't work in *your* favor as well as one determined by good lawyers and accountants on your side.	Tell him a divorce is a legal act, not just a private agreement; that both of you will be better served by having knowledgeable lawyers and accountants who know the consequences of such important decisions.
2 When he says, "Why get involved with courts, let's go to a conciliator," this can be a mixed signal. *Does he want to reconcile with you or does he want to side-step a legal proceeding that will protect you?*	*If you don't really want a divorce* tell him a conciliator can reconcile people only when they want a reconciliation. If he wants to be reconciled with you, he should just say so and forget the divorce. *If you want a divorce,* or he says he doesn't want a reconciliation, then tell him that you will proceed according to law and that his lawyer should talk to your lawyer.
3 When he says, "Let's be civilized. Instead of a court battle, let's go to a mediator or an arbitrator," this is a warning that he's trying to hide information from you and the court.	Tell him you want to be civilized, too. Since he is not Woody Allen, it's unlikely there will be any publicity. You are willing to avoid litigation if he will present your lawyer with a fair written offer of settlement. If he is not willing to do this, then litigation is inevitable. If he does make an offer, here is a checklist to present to your attorney covering the most important items in any offer of settlement: Temporary alimony and counsel fees

5 Things He May Say or Do That Could Be a Warning Signal	5 Ways to Protect Yourself Against These Warning Signals
	Permanent alimony and security in case of his premature death Medical insurance for you Custody of the children Child support, including medical insurance, school fees, summer vacations, higher education Division of your property— homes, cars, securities, household goods, and other valuables.
4 If he says, "I'll tie you up in court proceedings for years if you don't accept this offer," don't be intimidated, fight.	If you and your lawyer think his offer is unfair, tell him your lawyer is prepared to fight as long as necessary and demand counsel fees from *him* for as long as the litigation takes.
5 When he says "Let's leave it all up to the judge," this is a red flag. A negotiated agreement is always preferable to taking a chance on what a neutral judge might decide. You can assume that he has some assurance that the decision will be favorable to him.	Tell him you prefer to have your lawyers negotiate an agreement but if he insists on going to court your lawyer is prepared to demand extensive discovery of his assets and produce an array of witnesses that he may find embarrassing.

10

BEFORE YOU DECIDE TO MARRY AGAIN

Yet the light of a whole life dies when love is done . . .

SONG FROM THE MUSICAL *FANNY*
FRANCIS WILLIAM BOURDILLON

One of the most charming weddings I officiated at not long ago included eleven youngsters—the six children of the bride and the five children of the groom. After the ceremony in my judicial chambers, the bride and groom and all the children went to the zoo, where they had a wedding lunch of hot dogs and Cokes.

Both bride and groom were divorcées. They had met at the corporation where both were employed. When I saw them recently they were planning the wedding of one of the eleven children. They were happy and contented with their large combined family.

On the other hand, at some remarriages I can predict a divorce within a year or two. Either the bride or groom is attended by a sulky, unhappy child or a hostile young adult who obviously hates the thought of a stepparent.

Another charming and gala wedding at which I officiated took place in a retirement home. The bride and groom, both in their eighties, had met there. The residents gave them a magnificent wedding feast complete with champagne and music. Almost all the residents joined in the dancing and fun.

Second or third marriages can be successful and happy provided the couple avoids the pitfalls *before* . . .

If you and your prospective second husband are both young and if neither of you has children then you are in approximately the same legal posture as a couple marrying for the first time. You can skip this chapter. If, on the other hand, either or both of you has children, then you should seriously consider an antenuptial agreement.

Anglo-American law, even as modified by statute in most states, is predicated on a one-marriage situation. When a spouse dies the survivor is entitled to a share of the deceased's estate, despite any provisions of a will excluding the spouse. This is known as "taking against the will." In most jurisdictions if the couple has no children, the survivor gets half the estate. If there are children, the survivor gets one third. Each state has slightly different provisions so it is essential to get legal advice *before* . . .

When two people who have children remarry, it is natural that they should want to provide for those children. You do not want your property to go to his children rather than yours. Probably he wants his property to go to his children. For this reason the antenuptial agreement has been devised. It can be your greatest protection or your undoing. *It depends upon the agreement you make.*

First marriages I think of as a duet sung by the wife and husband. Second or third marriages are more often a trio or quartet or small ensemble composed of the couple and their offspring. The success of these marriages depends upon the harmonious blending of all these voices in one chorus.

When one or both of the bridal pair has children there are many complications, both emotional and financial. Unless the pair is old, he probably has financial obligations to the children of his first marriage. He, and sometimes she, will also have financial obligations to the first spouse. She probably has custody of her children by the first marriage. One or both usually has money and property.

No book can tell you how to be a loving friend to his children or how to make him a kind and supportive friend to your children. Note that I do not use the terms *mother* and *father*. If you are a divorcée, your children have a father. Your second husband is not their father. If he is a divorcé, his children have a mother, no matter how poor a parent he may think she is. You are not their mother. But you are inevitably a part of those children's lives. Try to make your participation happy and helpful.

This chapter can show you how to avoid the emotional and legal stumbling blocks in the path of a second marriage. They deal not with love and nurturing but with money and property. It shows you how to avoid these contentious issues *before* . . .

Some second marriages have a better prospect of success than first marriages. A recent study by a New York–Cornell Medical Center psychiatrist reports that almost 80 percent of remarried couples have an appreciably better sexual relationship in their second marriages than in their first. This is encouraging news for women who contemplate remarrying.

Some second marriages are happier because both parties have learned from their unhappy experiences. In other cases, they replicate their mistakes again and often again in a third marriage.

Most women and men who marry a second time do so because they are lonely. They like the companionship and comfort of a spouse and a home. If both parties have approximately the same social status and share the same friends, the marriage is likely to be stable and satisfying, even though it may lack the elements of passion and romance of a first marriage. In many instances, second marriages are more loving and caring than first marriages because the husband and wife are not so pressured by the needs of their careers, the care of infants, and the lack of money. They have more time to be caring of each other.

Much as a woman who has been married for a number of years may have been annoyed by extraordinary demands and acrimonious discussions, silence is oppressive. Cooking a meal for one person seems to be a waste of time and effort. How often can one make a hamburger or a TV dinner a satisfying meal? Evenings with female friends seem to lack the sparkle of mixed company.

When an eligible new man appears on the scene she often fails to appraise him critically. She cooks delicious meals for him; she laughs at his stale jokes. She fears that if she doesn't accept this offer, there may not be another.

Divorcées are more likely to marry than other women (even though the rate has been dipping a bit). The census figures for 1987 disclose that the rate of marriage per thousand women in the United States is 58.9 for single women and 80.7 for divorcées. The median age for a first marriage is 23.6; for a divorcée who remarries, 33.3; and for a widow, 53.9. It is never too late for love or companionship.

Many women marry a second time for financial security. They see the real value of Social Security, their pension, and other funds diminishing. At age fifty or over it is difficult to enter or reenter the job market, despite laws prohibiting age discrimination. A second husband who is well-to-do is very desirable.

Whether you are romantically in love, or desire companionship, or seek security, when you contemplate remarrying, you must remember the Five Commandments.

All the advice in the chapters "Before You Get Involved in a Relationship" and "Before You Marry" are equally applicable to a second or third marriage.

This is a time when you need a good lawyer, since much more complicated legal and financial issues are involved than those clarified *before* . . .

If you are not well off, it is even more important to have a good lawyer who will see that you are protected. When a woman remarries not only for companionship but also for financial security, she often is disappointed. She may find that she has paid dearly for a very small sum of money.

Whether your first marriage was ended by divorce or death of your spouse, your friends will urge you to date, to look for another man. When they introduce you to someone who is available, they think you should be grateful and accept him. This is a time to obey the Third Commandment and act on your own best judgment. *They* may find this man a good golfing partner, a good business friend or colleague, but they cannot know whether he will appeal to *you*, whether you will find his conversation interesting and his company pleasant.

On the other hand, your family may compare this man unfavorably with your first husband. Your children will undoubtedly believe that no man could equal their father. However, *you* may know that your ex-husband was not always a Prince Charming. This new man may be the right person for you.

The real life women you meet in this chapter faced the problems that you may encounter when you contemplate a second marriage. The way they handled the problems of a prenuptial agreement should be of help to you.

The Advantages of a Prenuptial Agreement

Leon and Sybil had both lost their spouses of many years. Both were in their sixties and wealthy. Their children were grown and married. After Leon and Sybil had been dining together and going to the theater together for some months, he said, "I think your lawyer should talk to my lawyer."

That was his way of proposing marriage.

The lawyers did meet and satisfactorily worked out all the details of the financial arrangements of these two lonely people. The agreement provided that Leon's property would go to his children and Sybil's property would go to her children. Neither would have a claim on the other's estate. Because Leon was going to move into Sybil's home, he agreed to pay her half the value of the home. Before they married they showed the agreement to their children, relieving them of any anxiety they might have about their futures.

Leon and Sybil lived happily together until Leon's death at age seventy-nine. By leaving the questions of money to their lawyers, Sybil and Leon avoided the distasteful mingling of affection with discussions of money. Sybil's lawyer knew her financial situation, her desire to protect her children and grandchildren, and he was able to see that she was adequately protected.

The Disadvantages of Not Having a Prenuptial Agreement

Marietta was in her late fifties when she and Sam decided to marry. Sam was in his late sixties. Sam's wife, Marietta's best friend, had recently died. Sam and his wife had lived lavishly. Marietta's husband was in moderate circumstances. Their marriage had not been happy. She longed for a more glamorous lifestyle, trips abroad, jewels, and elegance. When Sam suggested that Marietta leave her husband and marry him, she was delighted and promptly obtained a divorce. Marietta and her first husband agreed to sell their house and divide the proceeds. He also agree to give her one-third of their savings. Marietta also kept the small trust fund her father had established for her.

Sam and Marietta each had two married children. Sam wanted his estate to go to his children. When Sam suggested an antenuptial agreement, Marietta refused.

"I am younger than you. Women live longer than men. When you die, I won't be able to maintain our lifestyle on my income," she said.

And so they married, much to the displeasure of both sets of children. Marietta promptly refurnished Sam's home. They had a busy, luxurious life for a year or two. Then Marietta was diagnosed as having cancer. She died a painful death a year later without the comfort or companionship of her children. During that year, Sam's business failed. He went into bankruptcy.

Marietta's will left all her property to her children. But Sam, as was his legal right, took against the will. He received one-third of her property. Sam died shortly thereafter and his children inherited Sam's property, a third of which consisted of Marietta's estate.

Marietta thought she was protecting herself, but actually she was being unfair and selfish. *She also ignored the Second Commandment. She did not anticipate disaster.* No one knows how long she will live or how long her husband will live. Statistics apply to huge numbers of people. Even if 90 percent of all women live to a certain age, you may be one of the 10 percent who don't.

A marriage based on selfishness is not likely to be happy. When it is based on the denial of natural expectations of the children of either husband or wife, there will be dissension. This can be avoided by a fair and sensible prenuptial agreement.

The Role of a Stepmother

Stepmothers have not had a good press. In fairy tales the step-daughter is always the victim and the stepmother the villain. In real life it is often the reverse. Children inevitably resent the woman who takes first place in the affections of their father. Many daughters resent their own mothers and prefer their fathers. It is to be expected that there will be friction between children and a new stepmother.

Sometimes this can be alleviated by affection and goodwill. Often stronger measures are needed. If your husband's children are going to live with you, the roles of each member of the family should be clearly understood *before* . . .

Pamela did not do this and her marriage foundered. She had been divorced for almost ten years when she met Jerome. She had two grown children, a good job, a lovely home, and a host of friends. She was not looking for another husband. They met at a party given by mutual friends.

The next day she was astonished to receive a call from Jerome, to whom she had spoken only a few words. He told her she was the most fascinating woman he had met in years. He wanted to see her every day and every night. She went out with him a few times and found his company pleasant. He had a dry wit; he liked music and the theater. He was an avid gardener and so was she.

The following month Pamela went to Europe, a long-planned visit with an old friend who lived in Paris. Two days after her arrival, Jerome appeared in Paris. He stayed a week, during which he took her out every night and often for lunch. Before he left, he asked her to marry him.

Pamela was amazed, flattered, and perturbed. She really knew nothing about Jerome except that he was divorced and had two teenage daughters. She told him they would have to get better acquainted before she could think of marriage.

Jerome met her at the airport on her return. He continued his pursuit. Pamela went to his beautiful country estate, where she met the girls Jill and Jacqueline. They were pretty but sullen.

Pamela realized that they were indulged and pampered by their doting father.

The housekeeper also indulged their every whim, as did the parlor maid and the gardener. Each girl had her own horse. They attended school when they felt like it and stayed home when there was a race or a gymkhana. Homework was not in their vocabulary.

"Don't you want to go to college?" Pamela asked them.

"Oh, that's a bore. We want to have fun," they replied.

When Pamela tried to discuss the girls with Jerome, he told her not to worry about them. The housekeeper, who had been with him since the girls were infants, took care of them. Pamela need not concern herself about them or the house and grounds. Everything was taken care of. She had only to enjoy herself with Jerome.

"Don't you think they should go to a more demanding school? Perhaps a boarding school where they would have to do their homework?" she suggested. "After all, girls are now expected to have careers. I do. My daughter does."

"They'll never have to work," Jerome explained. "I have set up trust funds for them."

"But work is personal satisfaction, not just a means of earning a livelihood," Pamela told Jerome. "What does their mother think about their futures?"

"The girls don't get along with Marianna. They prefer living with me," Jerome explained. "Don't worry about them. They'll go off and get married. Just think about you and me and all the good times we'll have together."

The girls were fourteen and fifteen. Pamela knew they would probably not get married for at least five or six years, perhaps more. She did not approve of their indolence and ignorance. But, as Jerome told her, they were not her problem.

And so Pamela and Jerome were married in a lovely wedding at his estate and went off to the Greek isles on a honeymoon. They were having such a delightful time that they stayed an extra week. On their return Pamela was met by two hostile young females.

"Daddy, you promised us a holiday in Spain during our

school break. You didn't come home. And we were stuck here with nothing to do while you and Pamela were off enjoying yourselves. Don't you love us anymore?"

Jerome promptly promised to take them to Spain.

"Just the three of us," the girls said pointedly.

A few weeks later Jerome took his daughters to Spain while Pamela remained at home. The girls knew they had won the first round of what was to be a three-year war. Nothing Pamela did was right. Every suggestion she made was deemed an interference. She could not even move the furniture in her room without their objections.

Pamela realized she was not the mistress of the household, that Jerome, much as he professed to love her, put the girls and their wishes first. She obtained a divorce.

Pamela's problems were not legal. She and Jerome had a prenuptial agreement. There is nothing the law can do to help a woman when her stepchildren are determined to oust her from her proper role as wife and head of the household.

Pamela ignored the First Commandment. She did not protect herself. The warning signals were clear. *When a man tells a woman not to worry about a subject she wants to discuss, whether it is money or property or family members, that is a clear sign of a problem.* It will not disappear simply because you are told not to worry about it. Instead it will fester.

When you marry again if your husband's children are going to live with you, the family rules *must* be laid down in advance. You are not their mother, but when children live in your home they must know that they are subject to your rules. And you must assert your authority *before* . . .

The Role of the Stepfather

Frequently, a second wife's children live with her and her second husband. This poses difficulties that should be discussed in advance. Do you know whether this man's ideas of child rearing and discipline are compatible with yours? Is he a martinet? Does he believe in corporal punishment? Will he begrudge the money spent on your children?

The monetary problems can be avoided by a prenuptial agreement that specifies who will pay the household expenses, babysitters, child care, and other expenses concerning the children. As we have seen in the chapters on divorce, the fact that you have a support order or a divorce settlement that specifies that the father of your children will pay for certain expenses is no guaranty that he will, in fact, do so or that he will make the payments promptly. When an emergency arises your second husband may have to help with the care of your children and their expenses.

Angela had two boys, Billy, who was eight, and Rod, who was twelve, when she married Ferdinand. He had a son and a daughter who lived with his first wife. During their courtship Ferdinand was warm and loving to the little boys, but Rod missed his own father, and resented Ferdinand, who ignored him. Angela told Ferdinand that the boy would get over his coldness and they would be a loving family.

She didn't know Ferdinand's children. They lived in a distant city and he saw them for only a few weeks during the summer. She did not know what kind of father he was. She knew that Ferdinand was an intelligent, ambitious man. He had been a poor boy who had worked his way through college and through much hard work had built a successful business. He was an exacting employer. But he was gentle and loving to Angela.

Ferdinand bought a new house for his family in an upscale suburb where the schools were excellent. Angela was delighted. She thought her boys would have a good education and a good life. She did not anticipate the problems the older boy would have moving to a new neighborhood where he had no friends, and to a new school where the academic standards were much higher than at his old school.

When Rod came home with his first report card, three Ds and one C, Ferdinand was furious.

"There will be no TV for you, young man, not until you improve your school work."

Rod went to his room and silently wept. He phoned his father who lived in another state and told him how unhappy he was.

But Angela had custody of the children and there was nothing that could be done.

When Rod received his second report card that was no better, Ferdinand spanked the boy, hard and with a cold fury. Angela was horrified.

"Don't you lay a hand on my son," she said.

"As long as he lives here, he'll do as I say," Ferdinand replied.

Two days later Rod ran away from home. He was picked up by the police on a transcontinental bus, going to his father.

Ferdinand went to the police station to get Rod and beat him again before he brought the boy home.

The school guidance counselor asked for a conference with Ferdinand and Angela.

"Rod is having difficulties adjusting. You must be patient with him," she said. "Harshness will not help him."

"He's spoiled, indulged kid. At his age I was working after school and on Saturdays and I was first in my class," Ferdinand replied. "What he needs is discipline. And I'm going to see that he gets it."

Friction between Rod and Ferdinand continued. When Rod broke his leg playing ball, Ferdinand blamed the boy.

"Why weren't you home studying?" he asked.

Angela realized that she had to choose between Rod and Ferdinand. The boy was being destroyed by a stepfather who was convinced that his methods of child rearing were right and that Rod was just being willful and lazy.

"What do you want?" Angela asked Rod.

"I want to live with my father," the boy sobbed. "I love you, Mom, but I can't go on living here."

Reluctantly Angela let him go. It was a choice she never anticipated having to make.

"What could I have done?" she asked the school counselor.

"Didn't you discuss the children with him before you married?" the counsellor replied.

Angela then talked to Ferdinand about his own children. She learned that his wife had left him because he whipped the children. He expected them to work as hard as he had worked as a boy. And she would not let him impose his will on her and the children.

"If only I had known what kind of a father he was *before* . . ." she wept.

When to Say "Yes"

Rona was widowed when her children were in their teens. Her husband's insurance was sufficient to provide the basic necessities for them. But Rona went back to work to pay for her children's college education. She met Robert, whom she liked very much and who was attracted to her. When he proposed marriage a year and a half after her husband's death, Rona told her children.

"Have you forgotten Dad so soon?" they exclaimed in shocked dismay.

"I loved your father very much," Rona explained. "But I'm lonely."

"You have us," her children said.

And so Rona did not marry Robert. Three years later both children were away at college. Rona was even more lonely. But Robert had married another woman.

Rona ignored the commandments. *She did not protect herself. She did not anticipate disaster,* that Robert would find another wife. She allowed her children to influence her *instead of acting on her own judgment.* She is a woman who says unhappily, "If only I had known *before* . . .

Consult Your Lawyer Before . . .

Minerva is an intelligent woman who was divorced by her husband of twenty years. Although she is educated and had a good job, she was worried about money. Minerva's children were being supported by their father. But she had an elderly, sick mother. It was difficult to work all day and care for an incontinent old lady at night. Nurses were expensive and Minerva was tired.

When Walter proposed marriage, Minerva was delighted. He was an intelligent little man who thought Minerva was beautiful and intellectual. Her former husband did not have as high an opinion of Minerva. And Walter was well-to-do and generous. He readily agreed to pay for a nursing home for Minerva's mother.

Walter did not suggest an antenuptial agreement. Since Minerva had very little money, she did not think of consulting a lawyer. The marriage was happy for more than five years.

Then Walter became very sick. His doctor said he did not have to stay in the hospital. In fact, he would progress better at home. Walter had to be catheterized. He needed enemas. He sometimes had to be fed. Minerva hired nurses around the clock. After a few weeks, one of her checks was returned marked "insufficient funds." Minerva called Walter's lawyer. She then learned that his business had been sold. Walter was paid in part in stock. The new management was not nearly as competent as Walter. They had not paid dividends for two years.

Minerva is now giving Walter the nursing care she did not want to give to her mother. She does not know how long they can afford to pay for her mother's nursing home.

When Minerva finally consulted her lawyer, she told him, "Walter promised to pay for Mother's nursing home until she died. How can I enforce that promise?"

"If he doesn't have any money, there's nothing you can do. You should have asked Walter to set up a trust fund for your mother. He had plenty of money when he married you and he could have done it."

Minerva is now faced with the care of two very sick invalids. Although Walter has substantial assets, he has very little income. She is another woman who says, "If only I had known *before* . . .

A Marriage of Convenience Is Not Always Convenient

Elsie was sixty-four, a widow with a married daughter and son. She was a librarian who, since her husband died, had been employed in a private research laboratory for ten years. Although the salary was not large, it was sufficient for her needs. She had a small, pleasant apartment and a circle of close friends.

Then she met Martin, a wealthy, successful, seventy-six-year-old doctor whose wife Matilda had recently died. He was a vigorous, dominant man who led a very busy professional and social life. He lived in an elegant town house, staffed with a cook/housekeeper and a butler/chauffeur. Although his creature comforts were well supplied, Martin needed a wife, someone to grace his dinner table, arrange his parties, and accompany him on his many speaking engagements. He was accustomed to being cared for.

An old school friend of Elsie's invited them both to a dinner party. Elsie looked pretty and elegant in a quiet, understated way. Martin led the conversation. Occasionally Elsie in her soft voice made a perceptive comment. Martin looked at her critically and decided his quest was over. He was tired of the pursuit.

To Martin finding a wife was like hiring a secretary or a housekeeper, a wearisome but necessary process, one that required vigilance and caution to avoid mistakes.

Elsie had not been drawn to him. He seemed to be self-assured to the point of arrogance even though he was undeniably intelligent. Her hostess had told her how wonderful Martin was: rich; successful; a devoted husband. When Martin called to invite Elsie to dinner and a concert she was pleased and flattered. She bought an expensive new dress that strained her budget.

Soon she was attending banquets, balls, and charitable functions with Martin several times a week. Martin invited her to dine in his home. She was impressed with his antique furniture and his art collection. She liked being served by a butler. But the food was not to her taste—too many sauces and everything cooked too long.

Elsie invited Martin to dinner at her small apartment. She made a perfect soufflé and served a French wine, a luxury she could ill afford.

A few days later Martin proposed marriage. He did not say he loved her but that he thought they were compatible and he could give her a good life, a home with servants, an exciting social life, trips to Europe and the Orient. He made it sound glamorous. Martin did not mention what he expected of Elsie.

She told him that she had never considered remarrying, that she would have to think about it.

Martin was not pleased with her reply but said he would wait a few weeks for her answer.

Elsie was perturbed. Her well-ordered life was disrupted by Martin. She was exhausted from working all day and accompanying him on his round of functions every evening. She was also worried about finances. In the few months she had known Martin she had spent more than her budget for an entire year. Either she had to marry Martin or stop seeing him.

Elsie stifled her doubts and yielded to the advice of her friends and children.

Martin took Elsie to his lawyer's office where she was presented with an antenuptial agreement. The lawyer told her to show it to her own attorney before she signed it.

Elsie showed the antenuptial agreement to a young lawyer who said it was a standard contract. It provided that Martin would support her for the duration of the marriage. If he predeceased her, she would have an income of $10,000 a year for life, secured by a trust fund. At her death the principal of the fund would revert to his children. All the household goods and Martin's other possessions including the house and his securities would go to his children. Elsie would have no claim on his estate.

Martin gave up all claims against Elsie's estate if she predeceased him.

"I suppose this is fair," Elsie said. "We both renounce claims against each other."

"How much money does he have?" the lawyer asked Elsie.

"I don't know," she replied.

"Shouldn't you find out? From what I hear, the doctor is very rich. You have nothing but a small pension."

"I don't want to discuss money with him," Elsie said.

"I'll talk to his lawyer," Elsie's lawyer replied.

A few days later he reported to Elsie that Martin had agreed to raise the sum to $25,000 a year and to include Elsie on his health insurance policy for the duration of the marriage and for her life if he predeceased her.

"It was not a pleasant conversation," the lawyer told Elsie. Nonetheless, she signed the agreement. She gave up her home and divided her possessions among her children. At Martin's insistence, she quit her job.

"I want you to be free to travel with me," he said.

When Elsie tried to suggest simpler menus to the cook, Martin admonished her not to interfere with *his* staff. He also made it clear that when he came home he did not want to see her friends.

Elsie complied with his demands. Since there was nothing for her to do in Martin's home she volunteered to tutor underprivileged high school students.

One afternoon Martin came home and found Elsie in tears. The butler had refused to admit a shabby young boy whom Elsie had been tutoring. When Elsie went into the kitchen to make herself a cup of tea, the cook insulted her.

"If you are unhappy, my dear, you don't have to stay," Martin said calmly.

Elsie went into Matilda's dressing room, the only place she had been able to take for herself, and sat down with a pencil and paper and the antenuptial agreement. For the first time she realized that there was no provision in the event she divorced Martin. She knew he would not be generous if she left him.

Elsie realized that she could not leave. She had no home, no furniture, and only $8,000. At her age it would be difficult, if not impossible, to get a job.

She was too weary to undertake the emotional strain of a divorce suit and too physically tired to move. No matter how unhappy she was, Elsie knew that she would have to conceal her misery and lead the life Martin wanted.

Elsie wept silently, "If only I had known *before* . . ."

Elsie, like many older women, believed that it was unladylike to discuss money with a suitor. She violated the Fifth Commandment. If she had been willing to talk to Martin frankly about her financial situation, she might or might not have been able to protect herself. But she would also have been able to find out what kind of man Martin was, whether he cared for her or whether he was only interested in an unpaid hostess. She would have been in a much better position to make an intelligent decision.

She also violated the Second and Third Commandments. *She*

did not anticipate disaster, that the marriage would be unhappy. *She did not rely on her own judgment* but took the advice of her friends and her children.

The Unenforceable Promise

Philippa was Wilfred's secretary for many years, his faithful girl Friday. When Wilfred's wife died after a long, painful illness he asked Philippa to marry him. Wilfred's three children were grown, married, and wealthy. They were delighted that Philippa would take care of their father, who was a difficult man.

Philippa had never married. When she was young, she had had to care for her elderly parents and send her younger brothers to school. The years passed and life seemed to have passed her by. With all her family obligations, Philippa had no savings. She was fifty years old. And she was fond of Wilfred.

Wilfred told Philippa he wanted to retire. When she was his wife she would not have to work. He would support her.

"Do you think we should have an antenuptial agreement?" she asked him.

"It's not necessary. I'm going to leave everything to you in my will," he said. "The children don't need anything and I want you to be protected.

Philippa was happy for five years until Wilfred became ill. She nursed him devotedly for another five years until his death. Then Philippa discovered that he had not made a new will. Everything was left to his children. After she consulted a lawyer, Philippa learned that a promise to make a will is not enforceable. She had to sue to obtain her widow's third of Wilfred's estate, which had been greatly depleted by the expenses of his illness. Philippa's Social Security payment is small because she stopped working at age fifty. At age sixty she is now looking for a job.

She, too, says, "If only I had known *before* . . ."

A second or subsequent marriage, like a first marriage, has the promise of love, companionship, a home, and financial security. Because a woman has been disappointed in her first marriage is no reason to believe that her second marriage cannot be better.

You can learn from your mistakes. If you had a good first marriage and were widowed, you can find happiness again. Countless women do.

Often the difficulties in second marriages arise from problems with money and the children from prior marriages. Many of these unpleasantnesses can be avoided by having an adequate and fair prenuptial agreement.

In entering into such an agreement, remember the commandments.

◆ **Protect thyself.** You are not a naive child. It is your responsibility to see that your needs are taken care of.

◆ **Anticipate disaster.** A second marriage can also fail. Illness, business reverses, and other vicissitudes can occur. Be sure these possibilities are covered in your prenuptial agreement.

◆ **Act on your own judgment.** Just because your friends and family think you should marry again does not mean that this is a wise decision for you.

◆ **Wear a velvet glove over an iron hand.** Be pleasant but firm in the prenuptial negotiations. You are showing a different side of yourself to him; be sure that it is a pleasant one. And you are also having an opportunity to see what kind of man he really is.

◆ **Discuss money.** A frank discussion of your financial situation and his and the needs of your respective children will not mar romance or friendship but establish a firm foundation for your life with a new husband.

Lawyers cannot create a happy marriage. They can, however, avoid many problems that cause dissension. If you and your prospective second husband are fair and honest and are compatible, you can have a happy second marriage at any age if you act wisely *before* . . .

BEFORE YOU DECIDE TO MARRY AGAIN

5 Things He May Say or Do That Are Warning Signals	5 Ways to Protect Yourself Against . . .
1 When he presents you with a prenuptial agreement without disclosing his financial situation, that is deceitful. What may be a fair and even generous agreement for a man with assets of $100,000 is grossly unfair if he has assets of $1,000,000	Tell him you have instructed your lawyer to show his lawyer a statement of all your assets and liabilities and that you would like his lawyer to give the same information to your lawyer so that they can prepare a mutually satisfactory agreement.
2 When he says, "We don't need a prenuptial agreement, I'll leave everything to you in my will," that is an unenforceable promise. If he doesn't do so, you will have to sue to take against the will and may receive only a modest percentage of his estate.	Tell him you don't want *all* his estate, you want him to be fair to his family, as you expect to be fair to your family, and that everyone will be happier with a properly drawn agreement.
3 When he says, "You don't have to work after we're married. I'll take care of your old mother or sick child," he probably *means* to do so. But *what* will happen if he dies prematurely or has business problems, or if you predecease him?	Tell him you appreciate his generosity but that you will not have peace of mind about these obligations unless you have some permanent arrangement— a contract, a trust fund, an insurance policy, or whatever he can suggest that will take care of your dependents in the event of unforeseen conditions.
4 When he says, "I'll be a father to your children," this may mean that he will love and cherish them or it may mean that he wishes to control and discipline	Tell him your philosophy of child rearing and your plans for your children and see if he agrees with you.

5 Things He May Say or Do That Are Warning Signals	5 Ways to Protect Yourself Against . . .
them. There are many kinds of fathers—martinets, child abusers, fathers who expect young children to work, as well as loving and nurturing fathers.	
5 When he says, "We'll be one big, happy family all living together—your kids and mine," remember that resentful or hostile children can sabotage even the best marriage.	Suggest a prenuptial vacation with all the children and see how they behave together, how his children treat *you* and how he treats your children.

11

BEFORE YOU GO TO COURT

Law is a bottomless pit . . .
DR. JOHN ARBUTHNOT

Here are some truths about our justice system that every woman should know *before* she decides to go to court—or is summoned there.

Anglo-American law was created long ago. It is a system of men, by men, and for men. The legislators who enacted the laws were men. The lawyers who developed the law were men. And the judges who administered the law were men. Inevitably the legal system reflects the male point of view and the dominant male attitudes toward females.

As previously mentioned, American common law is based is built on a fiction: the "reasonable man." In order to determine whether a plaintiff or a defendant in a civil suit should recover, the court must decide whether that person acted as a reasonable man would have under the circumstances. The same rules prevail in a criminal case. Did the accused act as a reasonable man would have done? The test of reasonableness makes sense. We do not hold individuals to a standard of the most intelligent or bravest person but of what an average, reasonable individual would or would not do.

Recently the wording of the standard has been changed from

177

178 ◆ WHAT EVERY WOMAN NEEDS TO KNOW BEFORE . . .

that of a reasonable *man* to that of a reasonable *person*. But, such a gender-neutral standard, like many gender-neutral laws, does not always yield equal justice to women. This is particularly true in cases based on common law precedents—what other courts have decided—rather than on statutory law. Until the present time, those cases were based on the reasonable man doctrine.

The words, *reasonable person,* may be gender neutral, but the facts of life are not. The average American male is 5 feet, 9 inches tall and weighs 172 pounds. The average American female is 5 feet, 3 inches tall and weighs 144 pounds. When two men are face to face in a contentious situation the reasonable man will defend himself. When a man and woman are in a similar situation, the reasonable woman will retreat if possible. When a man is arrested for an alleged crime, he calls for a lawyer. When a woman is arrested, she asks for her children. The differences between the conduct of the average woman and the average man have not yet been defined by statute or judicial decisions. Consequently when you go to court, it is likely that your cases will be decided under the age-old doctrine of the reasonable man.

Recently a few courts in sexual harassment cases have adopted a *reasonable woman* test. But the myth of the reasonable man still dominates American courts.

Even today the members of the Congress and the state legislatures are overwhelmingly male. Although 50 percent of law students are female, legal practice is still dominated by men and reflects masculine values. And the judiciary is still predominantly a masculine preserve. In 1990 women constituted only 14 percent of all lawyers and judges. Despite many local ordinances and state and federal laws designed to give women the same rights as men, judges, both male and female, and juries, often retain age old mind-sets that are prejudicial to women.

Many women in the legal profession have been co-opted or brainwashed by their male professors, mentors, and colleagues. Law schools claim they teach their students how to think "like lawyers." Too often they succeed in teaching women law students to think like male lawyers. An able woman judge told me she sees no reason why female offenders should not be sentenced exactly the same as male offenders. Many women offenders are pregnant. Most women prisoners are the sole caretakers of their young children. Women coconspirators although equally guilty under the law are often the dupes of their male lovers and husbands. *The law does not recognize these significant differences between most male and most female offenders.* It treats them all as *reasonable men.* Similar unfairnesses are also endemic in civil law.

Although the Constitution declares that "no *person* shall be denied equal protection of the laws," there is many times an enormous chasm between this noble principle and the law as it is actually administered in the courts. The entire panoply of legislatures, lawyers, and courts is designed and maintained for the purpose of affording *all* the people equal justice. But in the day-to-day operation of the courts *they frequently do not provide equal justice or even a "rough average justice" for women.*

When you go to court this is a most significant occasion in your life. It can have drastic consequences. You may lose custody of your children; your marriage may be terminated; you may lose your liberty. You may lose your home and/or your property. The consequences may drive you into poverty for the rest of your life. Of course, you may win. You must remember that important as the case is to you, you are only one player in a large cast. Your interests are not the same as any of the other parties. You want justice for *yourself.*

While lawyers and judges are also concerned with justice and the rule of law, their roles and their interests are very different from yours. When you are a plaintiff in a civil action, naturally the defendants and their lawyers want to defeat you regardless of the justice and merits of your claim. They will use the rule of law, if they can, to defeat you and win. The same is true in the reverse situation when you are the defendant rather than the plaintiff.

The judge's duty is to follow the law and, if possible within its parameters, to do justice. The judge is also concerned with problems of court administration, the crowded calendar, and disposing of as many cases as possible. If your case takes a month to try, scores of others with equally valid claims are being denied a right to a "speedy trial." Consequently, there is always a desire, conscious or subliminal, to dispose of your case as quickly as possible. That usually dictates a settlement rather than a trial.

Your lawyer's sworn duty is to represent you to the best of her ability and to obtain the best possible result for you. Your lawyer also has to earn a living. Her fee must cover not only her time and overhead but also a profit. If your case takes too long or is too complicated for the fee that you can afford to pay, your lawyer will want to settle when you may want to litigate.

In every civil action, whether it is for alimony, breach of contract, sexual harassment, or a zoning violation, the bottom line is money. If you are injured either in an accident or through the negligence of your doctor, the only remedy you can obtain in court is money. The court cannot give you perfect and natural new limbs for damaged ones; it cannot give you a pain-free body. If you are cheated by a competitor, you cannot be given lost business opportunities. All you can be awarded by a court is money to compensate you as nearly as possible for those losses and sufferings. Even in libel cases, while a court may occasionally require a defendant to publish a retraction of a false and libelous statement, your most important recovery will be money damages. In wrongful discharge cases, whether for gender or age discrimination or sexual harassment, you may be awarded your old job, if you still want it, but money damages are probably more significant and useful to you.

Many plaintiffs say, and probably honestly believe, that they are suing for vindication, to clear their names, or to establish a legal right. The fact is that most people want what the law best provides: money damages. An Iowa study of libel cases asked the plaintiffs why they were suing.

Most replied, "To clear my name."

But when these plaintiffs were given the choice of a quicker and simpler action for a declaratory judgment that the allegedly libelous statement was false instead of a suit for money damages, no one was willing to forgo the possibility of an award of money.

So, ask yourself what you really want from your lawsuit. Is it vindication or justice? Or is it vindication *and* money or justice *and* money? If you answer this question honestly, you will make more intelligent decisions with respect to the conduct of the case and the acceptance of an offer of settlement.

If you decide to sue, you will have to pay counsel fees and court costs. You may have to pay in advance. Even if your lawyer takes the case on a contingency—that is, her fee will be a percentage of your recovery if you win and nothing if you lose—your case must have the likelihood of generating a large enough recovery to pay expenses and a fee. If you are offered a settlement, you may wish to take it and avoid a trial, but your lawyer may not want to do so if her fee is insufficient.

If you are sued, you have very limited options. You'll probably have to retain a lawyer to file an answer to the complaint. Then you must decide whether you wish to fight the claim or attempt to settle. Again, the bottom line is not justice or vindication but money. Can you afford to litigate? Or will it be cheaper and easier to pay to settle the case? If you are insured, your insurance carrier will make this decision. No matter how unjust the claims against you may be, if the insurance company wants to settle to avoid the costs of trial, you will have to agree or risk losing your coverage.

Litigation is a means of livelihood for lawyers and the entire court system, including the judges. For the litigant it is not a profession, a business, or a game. For most women it is a painful ordeal, something to be avoided if possible. If the person who has allegedly wronged you is a man he probably is counting on the fact that you will be reluctant to sue. If you do, he and his lawyers will make it as painful and difficult as possible for you.

Each lawsuit, like each litigant, is unique. The facts in your case may be overwhelmingly in your favor. The law may clearly be on your side. And you may be a strong person who will not find cross-examination too unpleasant an ordeal.

However, few cases are open and shut. Facts are often slippery and hard to prove. Witnesses have unreliable memories. The most truthful individuals often make poor witnesses. They stammer, hesitate, blush. They look guilty and the jury does not believe them. The law may appear to be clear. But every statute is subject to interpretations. If your case is extremely clear, your opponent will probably want to settle. Then you will have to decide whether the money offered is sufficient, whether vindication is more important than compensation, and whether you want to undergo the rigors of a trial.

Some types of cases are more impersonal and less likely to cause you emotional stress. They can be proved by objective evidence rather than relying heavily on your testimony. In such cases, if the money involved is sufficient to justify the costs of a lawsuit, you probably should sue, not merely to recover the money you are entitled to but also to establish or reinforce a legal principle. Such cases include the following types of lawsuit:

- ◆ Denial of a loan or mortgage because you are a woman
- ◆ Denial of a job or promotion because you are a woman or a member of an ethnic minority or both
- ◆ Denial of equal pay because you are a woman or a member of an ethnic minority or both
- ◆ Denial of a residence, either to purchase or lease, because you are a woman or a member of an ethnic minority or both
- ◆ Denial of insurance or overcharge of premiums because you are a woman or a member of an ethnic minority or both
- ◆ Breach of contract for goods or services
- ◆ Breach of warranty of a product or warranty of habitability of a rental premises

Most such cases can be proved by documents, your own documents, and the records of the company. There are, however, risks even in these lawsuits.

When the Law Is on Your Side

Laurel was a supervisor employed by a large insurance company. After working there for four years and having excellent ratings she discovered that the female employees were paid at least 20 percent less than the male employees doing the same work. Laurel was outraged. She consulted a lawyer who advised bringing a class action with Laurel as named plaintiff on behalf of all the female employees.

This was a wise move because the damages for lost wages for several thousand female workers were substantial. The lawyer could afford to take the case on a contingent fee based on a percentage of the total recovery. Because the case involved many people it was legally significant and would receive publicity and, therefore, help all women.

Laurel won the lawsuit but lost her job. Since she was obviously the ringleader the company was determined to get rid of her. Laurel's ratings plummeted from excellent to fair and then to unsatisfactory. A year after the suit was settled Laurel was given the choice of quitting with a satisfactory recommendation or being fired.

Laurel's attorney recognized that this was a mean and vengeful act on the part of the company. For Laurel to sue would require a great deal of time and money. Laurel would be cross-examined with respect to every single action over the past few years, every phone call, every day of leave, every letter, every dispute with her superiors. And what would her recovery be if she won? Reinstatement and lost wages for the time she was unemployed, less any money she had earned during the period. Laurel really didn't want her job back because she knew her supervisor would make life very unpleasant. If Laurel got a good job and earned as much as she would have earned at the company she could not recover any damages. If she could not get another job, or only a job at a lesser salary, the court might conclude that she wasn't such a competent employee. It was a typical catch 22 situation.

Laurel resigned her job. She is now working at another company earning slightly less than her fellow employees at the original company, all of whom benefited from the class action. But she does not regret bringing the law suit because the other women benefited even though she did not.

This is the kind of case every woman should bring. The lawyer took the case on a contingent fee basis, so that Laurel had no out-of-pocket losses even if she lost the case. The issue was of real importance. The trial would not involve any personal trauma to Laurel, no delving into her private life, no smearing of her reputation. And, because she was a competent person, Laurel knew that she could get another job. The possible gains far outweighed the possible losses.

When Your Reputation Is at Stake

More difficult and painful cases are those for sexual harassment and medical malpractice. Every woman who watched Senator Arlen Spector cross-examine Anita Hill received a lesson in the gender biases of the law. Anita Hill is an extremely intelligent and self-possessed woman. Ask yourself if you could retain your poise under such a withering cross-examination, because that is what will happen to you if you bring a suit for sexual harassment. Remember that Anita Hill did not reveal her charges until *after* she had tenure at the law school where she was teaching. Certainly it would have been foolhardy and stupid to make a complaint against her own boss while she was still working for him. If you can be fired from your job, you must ask yourself whether you can afford both the emotional costs and the loss of employment.

Even when you win, you may lose. Lynn is an experienced attorney. When she was offered a position at twice her salary by a large law firm, she promptly accepted. Four years later when she was not made a partner, she sued for job discrimination. She won.

But the trial was long and painful for everyone involved.

The law firm already had several women partners. At the time Lynn was denied a partnership another woman was made a partner and a man was also denied a partnership. Therefore, it was necessary for Lynn to prove that she was qualified to be a partner, that she met the exacting standards of professional competence that the firm demanded. Some partners testified that she did. Others testified that she did not. These opinions of her ability and skills were widely reported in the daily press and in legal journals and newspapers. Every other employer she might have applied to if things did not work out now knew that some people in the law firm did not think she met the partnership standards.

Four years after her victory, the appeal had not been decided. Lynn told a friend that the case had been very costly to her career. It did not cost her any out-of-pocket money because her lawyer took the case on a contingent fee basis.

She is a heroine to many feminist leaders. But what has she done to her own career?

- ◆ If the law firm is required to make her a partner, will she find it a pleasant place to work?
- ◆ If she loses the appeal, what other law firm will hire her?
- ◆ If she recovers monetary damages, will they be sufficient to compensate her for the loss of income during all the years she waited for a decision?

If you contemplate a law suit for job discrimination these are questions you should ask yourself *before* . . .

Muriel Siebert, the first woman permitted to buy a seat on the New York Stock Exchange, in 1967, told the *New York Times* that equality on Wall Street will come only when women who gain power begin to use it on behalf of other women.

"Law suits won't do it," she said. "It will take the decided effort on the part of major firms to make sure that women are advanced according to their abilities. And it will be up to the women who rise to the top to see that they make that effort."

If you are strong and determined, you can be one of those women who make the effort for others. But calculate the costs in time, money, emotional stress, and your own career *before* . . .

Can You Withstand Questions About Your Past?

Even in ordinary negligence and malpractice cases, women plaintiffs are at a disadvantage when the defendant is a man. Alicia's malpractice suit is not unusual. It reveals the kind of perfectly legal but grossly unfair questions that are usually asked of female plaintiffs.

Alicia has been in several accidents. Once she was a passenger in an automobile that was involved in a head-on collision. Alicia was injured. She sued both drivers and recovered damages for the cost of her medical treatment, loss of earnings, and pain and suffering, as was her legal right. Some years later she fell on a greasy floor in a restaurant and again suffered substantial injuries. The insurance carrier for the restaurant recognized that the restaurant was liable and settled her claim to avoid unfavorable publicity.

When Alicia tripped over a loose wire in her own home, she broke her leg. The orthopedic surgeon who treated her put her leg in a cast for three months. Although Alicia complained repeatedly that the cast was painful, the surgeon refused to remove the cast to see if anything was the matter. At the end of three months when he did remove the cast, the leg was twisted and an inch and a half shorter than her other leg. It is painful and she must walk with a cane. Alicia sued the surgeon for malpractice.

She thought it was an open-and-shut case. The jury would be able to see her deformed leg and the difficulty she had walking. The doctor knew that if he lost this case, he would lose his insurance and the ability to practice surgery. He prevailed upon his insurance carrier to offer Alicia a settlement of $100,000. Alicia had never been in a courtroom. She had no idea what the trial would be like. She detested the surgeon who had maimed her for life. Despite the advice of her attorney, Alicia turned down the offer.

The surgeon retained the best lawyer in town, in addition to the insurance company lawyer.

Alicia was the first witness. She was a middle-aged woman in a neat but inexpensive dress. Her face was drawn with pain. She was very nervous when she hobbled up to the witness chair. Her answers were hesitant.

"You are forty-nine years old?"

"Yes."

"You are divorced?"

"Yes."

"You never remarried?"

"No."

"How many jobs have you had in the past five years?" Alicia's lawyer objected. The objection was overruled.

"Three."

"Were you fired?"

"No."

"I have here a report from your last employer that says you are a "difficult person.""

"I don't know about that. I was in pain from my leg and couldn't walk."

Her lawyer again objected and was overruled.

"Well, you couldn't get along with your husband or your employers but you say you're not a difficult person?"

The judge sustained the objection and instructed the jury to disregard the question. "The plaintiff's personality is not in issue," he told the jury. But, of course, they had heard the question.

Alicia's previous accidents were presented to the jury. She was subjected to a merciless cross examination.

"You are accident prone, aren't you, Alicia?"

"No."

"Well, you've been involved in three accidents in two years, haven't you?"

"Yes, but—"

"That's all. You've answered the question. And in each case you sued, didn't you?"

"Yes."

"And now you want money from Dr. X., don't you?"

"Yes."

"Are you working now?"

"No."

"Why not?"

"Because my job required me to stand on my feet all day and I can no longer do that."

"You are a high school graduate aren't you?"

"Yes."

"There is other work you could do, such as a receptionist or a phone operator, where you sit, isn't that true?"

"I believe so. But I haven't been able to find such a job."

"You'd rather Dr. X. would pay you to stay home and relax for the rest of your life wouldn't you?"

After two hours of such questioning Alicia was in tears.

Dr. X. was a distinguished-looking, silver-haired man. It took more than a half hour for him to detail his credentials, the schools he had attended, the honors he had been awarded, the learned papers he had written. Seven of his colleagues testified as to his competence and brilliance.

Alicia's lawyer was prevented from proving the six malpractice cases that had been brought against him and settled, because the records in those cases were sealed. His incompetence had not been proved.

The jury returned a verdict for the doctor.

With hindsight Alicia wished she had taken the substantial settlement the insurance company offered. She was so sure that her case was meritorious, *and it was,* that she ignored her lawyer's advice. He, like all experienced lawyers, knew what a grueling ordeal cross-examination is for all litigants. Alicia did not know what she was up against: a doctor fighting for his professional life with the best lawyer money could obtain. She was only an average woman. Even though she had a very good lawyer, she was no match for the suave and desperate doctor. Before you ignore advice and turn down an offer of settlement, ask yourself if you can undergo the kind of cross-examination Alicia was subjected to. If you are like most women who shrink from nasty personal attacks, a settlement may be more advantageous to you than a trial. But, if you can endure what Anita Hill went through and keep your composure, then don't settle. Fight!

When the Facts Are Not in Dispute

Vera is a divorcée with three young children. She is a registered nurse who has been employed at a leading hospital for ten years. When the house Vera had rented was sold, she looked for an apartment. Her requirements were very specific. It must be within walking distance of the children's school. It had to have some place where they could play. It had to be near public transportation so she could get to work easily without a car, a luxury she could not afford because her husband was two years behind on his child support payments.

Vera found a garden apartment that met all her requirements and was within her budget. When she came to sign the lease, the manager asked Vera if she had children. She told him she did.

"This is a very quiet apartment complex with only adults. We don't want any noisy children here," he told her.

Vera sued. The court ordered the apartment owner to rent her an apartment and to pay her court costs and a reasonable counsel fee. She and the children have been living contentedly in the apartment for five years.

This was a case in which the defendant admitted the charges but claimed that the law did not require him to admit children. The case was tried on what is called "a case stated." That is, there was no testimony. The lawyers agreed to the facts and the judge decided the case on the law without hearing any testimony. Vera did not have to undergo a trial. All she risked was the lawyer's fee and court costs. The likelihood of winning was good and she wanted the apartment badly enough to risk $1,000.

The Trauma of Child Abuse Cases

The most painful court experiences a woman undergoes are custody and rape cases. In both these kinds of cases the woman is really on trial. As we have seen in the previous chapters, the husband does not have to prove that the mother of his children is unfit. She has to prove that she is the better parent.

In rape cases often the woman has to prove not that the man had intercourse with her but that she did not consent. He has the benefit of the presumption of innocence. There is no legal presumption that favors her.

When a father is accused of sexual abuse of his child, this is one of the most difficult cases to prove. Most adults, both male and female, unless they have had such an experience themselves, recoil from the charges. Like Sigmund Freud, they prefer to believe that the charges are a figment of a child's imagination or the suggestion of a vengeful ex-wife. Unfortunately, many of these charges are true. It is estimated that as many as a half million children are sexually abused each year. The vast majority are girls.

Child abuse is one of the most difficult facts to prove. A trial on this issue takes a terrible toll on the mother and the child who makes the allegations. If you honestly believe your ex-husband has abused your daughter or your son then you must insist upon obtaining custody, no matter what the cost.

The most common incidents of child abuse are not by baby-sitters or operators of day care centers, although these have received enormous media attention and have been the subject of lengthy trials, but within the family. At least 75 percent to 85 percent of all reported cases are father–daughter and stepfather–stepdaughter. This is a crime that knows no economic, educational, or social characteristics. It occurs throughout the entire spectrum of society. Child abusers are wealthy, educated professional leaders of their communities, and poor, ignorant slum dwellers, and everyone in between. The effect on the girl victim is incalculable and long lasting. Many prostitutes report that they were sexually abused as little children. After that experience they were never able to achieve a sense of self-respect.

Nothing can be more painful for a woman than to watch her child undergoing the ordeal of cross-examination in a child sexual abuse case. As a judge who presided over many criminal prosecutions for rape, incest, and indecent assault by fathers, stepfathers, grandfathers and other family members on children, I believe that every effort should be made to avoid subjecting a child to what I can only describe as a form of legal torture, unless that is the only way to stop the continued abuse of the child.

As we have seen in previous chapters, it is advisable in divorce cases to separate the issue of child custody from the financial considerations. You and your legal advisor should work out an agreement with your husband *before* the divorce. If, as is usually the case, he wants a quick divorce and custody is important to you and your children, then he will most likely be willing to concede the custody issue in return for your consent to the divorce. You can fight over the money later when your custody of the children is secure.

When You Are a Crime Victim

Women appear in criminal court as witnesses, often the prosecuting witness, and also as defendants charged with crime. If you are the victim of a crime, your immediate response is to call the police and make a complaint. You do this to protect yourself and to protect society. The legal system cannot apprehend, try, and convict offenders if the victims do not notify the police.

If your car is stolen, your home is burglarized, or your purse is snatched, you naturally call the police in the hope that the thief will be apprehended and you will get your property back. If you are physically attacked or raped that is also your natural response.

But you should realize that as a crime victim you are not a party to the prosecution. You are only a witness. You have no control over the case. The prosecuting attorney for the state or the federal government is in charge.

You will be summoned to court to testify. If you do not appear you can be held in jail for contempt of court, without the right to be released on bail while the defendant is free on bail. You cannot withdraw the charges without the consent of the prosecutor. The prosecutor, however, can enter into a plea bargain with the defendant without your consent and without even notifying you.

You will probably not be permitted to be in the courtroom during the trial except for your own testimony. And you will have no way of knowing during the trial what lies the defendant and other witnesses may have told.

As a witness you will be paid a fee of approximately $10.00 per day, depending on the jurisdiction, plus the cost of public transportation to and from the court. If your stolen property is found, you will most likely get it back. If it is not recovered, you will probably not receive any monetary compensation, although there are crime victim compensation laws in most states. Under these statutes you must make a claim to get compensation; it will not be awarded automatically.

If the case goes to trial and the accused is convicted, in some states you are permitted to file a victim impact statement before sentencing, or in some jurisdictions appear and address the court at sentencing. The court does not have to take into account either your recommendations for a prison sentence or for lenience.

Prosecuting a Rape Case

Rape cases, like child sexual abuse cases, are the most difficult to prove and the most painful for the victim. This is still true, even though most states have enacted legislation designed to make it easier for rape victims. The law no longer requires a corroborating witness, a legal rule that made it almost impossible to convict a rapist. It is a rare case in which a rape occurs in the presence of a neutral third party. In addition, the victim's prior sexual history can no longer be inquired into unless the defendant claims that there was consent as was the case in the rape charge against William Kennedy Smith. He was acquitted.

The rape victim, like all crime victims, cannot retain her own counsel. She must accept the assigned prosecuting attorney no matter how incompetent or unsympathetic that lawyer may be. The defendant, of course, can choose his own lawyer, the best he can afford. You, as the victim, must testify. The defendant has the right to remain silent. He can sit through the entire trial, say nothing, and watch the embarrassed victim describe in detail the degrading acts performed upon her.

In a gang rape case tried before me, the alleged victim was a young mother, a divorcée. She testified as to what two young men did to her. The prosecutor was an inexperienced young man. He obviously had not prepared the victim/witness. She appeared wearing a short skirt and a tight sweater. Defense counsel on cross-examination brought out that she was divorced. The prosecutor made no objection to the question.

The two defendants testified that the complainant had voluntarily gone with them to a dark wooded part of a park and that they asked her if "she wanted some fun."

The complainant had testified that they invited her to go with them for some refreshments. The two defendants corroborated each other. There was no one to corroborate her version of the incident.

It was only after the two defendants were acquitted that I discovered that both were married men. The young prosecutor had neglected to ask them that question. He did not think it was relevant. I believe the jury would have taken a different view of two married men who left their wives alone and went out in the park looking for "some fun." The complainant was devastated by the verdict.

If she had sought help from a woman's organization knowledgeable about the prosecution of rape cases, she would have been advised to wear different attire; she would have told the story to a rape counselor who might have been able to persuade the prosecutor to bring out evidence favorable to the victim.

Kimberly was seventeen, a graduate of the local high school in a small town. She had never been away from home except for summers at a Girl Scout camp before she went to a large university in a metropolitan city. She knew no one there other than the girls in her dormitory.

Their main topic of conversation was the fraternities. Campus life centered around the fraternities and their parties. Kimberly was a good student. She wanted to excel academically and she also wanted to be part of campus life. Her parents were both graduates of this university and had met at a fraternity party.

When Everett invited her to go to a party at his fraternity house Kimberly was delighted. She had been introduced to Everett by a girl in her dorm, who had attended the same high school as Everett.

He was looking for a girl, any nice-looking girl he could bring to his fraternity house and show off to the "brothers." Everett was a sophomore, a poor student who had spent an unhappy, aimless first year at the university. He had just been pledged to a fraternity. This was the most important event in his uneventful life.

Everett and Kimberly went to the fraternity house on a warm Friday evening. The house was filled with young people. Music blared from boom boxes. Young men and women were drinking beer on the porch, the lawn, and all over the house. People upstairs called down and greeted them cheerily.

Everett asked Kimberly if she wanted a beer. She said she'd prefer a Coke. He brought her a plastic cup with some liquid that he said was the fraternity's special punch. Kimberly didn't like the taste but she was hot and thirsty. She drank one glass and then another. Everett asked her to come to his room and see his high school year book. They walked upstairs with other couples. Kimberly saw students sitting in all the bedrooms laughing and talking. When they entered Everett's room he immediately pushed Kimberly down on the bed.

"Now we'll have sex," he declared.

"No, we won't," Kimberly replied. "I'm leaving."

He pushed her back on the bed. Everett was six feet tall and weighed 200 pounds. Kimberly was five feet two and weighed 110 pounds. Kimberly pushed and struggled but he succeeded in having intercourse with her. When Everett got up she vomited and cried. She was bleeding and in pain. When he left the room she tried to clean herself and comb her hair so she could leave the fraternity house inconspicuously.

Before she was finished five fraternity brothers came into the room. One by one they had sex with her while she cried and protested. One young man said this was her initiation into campus life.

When Kimberly was finally able to make her escape she ran back to her dormitory where she cried herself to sleep.

In the morning Kimberly saw Jessica in the bathroom.

"What's the matter. You look awful! Are you sick?"

Here was a friend, the only one Kimberly had in this strange place. She wept and told Jessica what had happened. Jessica was an upper class woman, the person assigned by the dormitory as Kimberly's mentor.

"That's rape, gang rape," Jessica declared. "This is outrageous. It happens too often. I belong to the woman's rights group on campus. We have to report this and protest."

"But I don't want anyone to know. I'm ashamed. If my parents find out I'll have to leave school. It will be the end of my life."

"It's not your fault. You've got to report this or rapes on campus will continue. You don't want this to happen to anyone else, do you? You have to assert your rights! We'll support you."

And so, reluctantly, Kimberly went with Jessica to the woman in charge of student life and made a report. She was immediately taken to the infirmary where she was kept for several days. The doctors told her she was not pregnant and that she had not contracted a disease. She was suffering from drug withdrawal symptoms.

Apparently *the punch had been spiked.*

When she was released from the infirmary Kimberly returned to her classes. But wherever she went there were whispers. She was pointed out as "that woman." Meanwhile the university had not taken any action against Everett and his fraternity brothers.

The women's organizations held campus vigils. They marched on the office of the president. The fraternities and their wealthy alumni pressured the president to quiet the campus.

"Boys will be boys," they said. "The girl has not been injured. If the boys are charged with rape, their lives will be ruined. They won't get into law or medical school."

The alumni were big contributors to the university. Not all the women supported Kimberly. Many alumnae were interviewed by the press.

They said, "She should have known better than to get drunk and go to a boy's bedroom. Nothing like that ever happened to me and I was on this campus for four years."

And so the controversy raged while Kimberly tried to hide. Later she told me she could have coped with her feelings of revulsion and self-hatred if she had been let alone. But the atmosphere on campus was menacing. None of the fraternity brothers had been charged with any crimes. It appeared that she was the accused, not the victim.

In despair Kimberly dropped out of school and went home. Her parents could not understand how this had happened. They did not know that even way back in 1982 it was reported that more than 23 percent of all college women had been raped. *The number of reported rapes is much higher now.*

Kimberly's parents were angry and ashamed. They spoke with the university president, who deplored and lamented but took no action.

Kimberly refused to talk to her parents. She avoided her

friends. Finally her parents took her to a psychiatrist. She was in therapy for three years.

After more pressure from the women's campus organizations, the fraternity was suspended for six months. But no one was charged with a crime. The fraternity brothers graduated from the university with unblemished records. Kimberly's record was marked, "Dropped for psychiatric problems."

Neither Kimberly nor her parents knew about the prevalence of violence against women on college campuses. It is a well-kept secret. The administrators of colleges and universities do not want the facts to become known because they would discourage potential applicants for admission. They would also discourage big donors.

Rape is a terrible, violent crime. It should be prosecuted by the government. If you are a rape victim and your assailant is a fellow worker or a fellow student, do not go to the company or the university with your complaint. They will try to protect their institution. *Go to the public prosecutor.* It is the job of that office to prosecute crimes.

Most authorities now recognize that rape has nothing to do with the behavior or appearance of the victim. It is not a "crime of passion" but an act of hatred performed to degrade the woman. However, many judges and jurors do not recognize this fact. Defense counsel will inevitably attempt to portray the victim as sexually provocative or a liar.

If you are a victim of a crime of physical violence, there are now in most communities organizations of women that will help you during the pretrial procedures and the trial. And a number of judges have been sensitized to the problem. Many males, however, still believe the lie that there cannot be a rape without some evidence of physical injury or trauma, and many prosecutors fail to inform the jury of this fact.

Violence Against Women

Like child abuse, physical violence against women is most often not the act of a stranger but of spouse or lover. Violence against females should be stopped wherever it occurs: on the streets; on campuses; and in the home.

As we have seen in the chapter on "Before You Decide to Divorce," many women are ashamed to admit to their families and friends that they are being physically abused.

Belinda and Johnny were in love. They planned to marry. But when Johnny was angry about even the most trivial matter, his response was to strike out with his fists. He was a big man. (As a child he had frequently been beaten by his father.) It was a life-long pattern. After each episode Johnny was contrite. He wept and promised that it would not happen again. And Belinda believed him for months, despite black eyes, cut lips, and bruises. These injuries were always explained as accidents. When Johnny broke her arm and took her to the emergency room of the hospital, X-rays showed a number of healed fractures and several bruises.

The attending physician told Belinda that if she did not file a complaint he would and that the next episode might leave her permanently injured. And so she filed a complaint. The case was prosecuted and Johnny was convicted. However, his attorney at sentencing presented a psychiatric expert who urged that Johnny be sentenced to therapy, not prison. Within two weeks he returned to Belinda's apartment and beat her so severely that she was again hospitalized.

This time the judge imposed a prison sentence. Johnny has been a model prisoner. He is up for parole. And Belinda lives in fear of what he will do on his release.

Shorty is a violent man. His favorite weapon is a sawed-off cue stick. When I convicted him on charges of aggravated assault against a woman, I discovered that this was his third conviction. The victim was a former girlfriend. His present girlfriend, Leota, was seated in the front row of the courtroom.

Shorty's lawyer promptly stated that he would take an immediate appeal. He asked that Shorty be released on bail pending appeal. This was his right. In my jurisdiction the practice is to post 10 percent of the bail in cash and to sign a note for the balance, which will be owing only if the defendant does not appear for the next hearing.

When I set bail at $50,000, Leota opened her pocketbook and began to count out the money. I quickly stated, "Not ten percent bail, good bail for the entire amount."

Shorty was so enraged that he turned around and knocked Leota to the ground. It took three sheriffs to subdue him. After Shorty was taken to a cell on charges of contempt of court, I spoke to Leota.

"He is a violent, dangerous man," I told her. "If you go back to him you may be seriously injured."

"That's what my mother says," Leota cried. "But I love him."

"This is not love but masochism," I told her.

A wise old court officer who has seen much of the sordidness of this world commented, "She'll go back to him. You might as well save your breath. Some women never learn."

If you are a victim of a crime of violence, remember the new Commandments. The First Commandment is **Protect thyself.** If your assailant is a person with whom you have an intimate ongoing relationship, the best way to protect yourself is to have him locked up for as long as possible.

The Second Commandment is **Anticipate disaster.** Despite his protestations of reform, he almost certainly will revert to his old brutal ways. Do not be fooled by expressions of remorse or promises to reform. A crime has been committed and the courts exist for the purpose of isolating such dangerous individuals.

The Third Commandment is **Act on your own best judgment.**

Do not be persuaded by family members to hush the matter, to give him a second chance, or to protect the family honor. It is you who are in danger and who has been violated, not they.

These same rules and admonitions apply if your child has been raped by a family member.

If your assailant is a total stranger, someone who grabs you on the street and abducts you, then the chances that he will be convicted and that your privacy will be protected are reasonably good.

However, if you are the victim of assault by an acquaintance, what is commonly known as date rape, then you must think carefully and decide what is in *your* best interest. Although everyone who commits a crime should be prosecuted, the cost to you may be more than you can bear. Weigh the factors pro and con. What are the chances for success if you turn to the law? What will be the result to you even if you are successful? What will be the result to you if you fail? Are you strong enough—emotionally and financially—and is your support system strong enough to help you?

Female crime victims of all ages are often victimized three times: first by their assailants; second by the publicity; and third by the legal system to which they turn for protection.

Before you go to court, whether as plaintiff or defendant in a civil suit or as prosecutrix in a criminal case, remember the Five Commandments.

Although everyone wants to see that justice is done, that people live up to their civil obligations, that they pay for harm they have negligently caused, and that criminals are prosecuted and convicted, the legal process may not be beneficial to you as a woman.

The First Commandment, *Protect thyself,* is important. The law may not protect you. The emotional costs, the time spent in court, and the wear and tear may weigh more heavily than the possible benefits to you.

If you are a litigant in a civil suit, either plaintiff or defendant, remember the Second Commandment. *Anticipate disaster.* What will be the result to you if you lose the case? Often, a settlement, though less than what you think you are entitled to is the better part of wisdom. If you are a plaintiff, you have the recovery at once and do not have to wait for an appeal that you might lose. If you are a defendant, at least you know what the cost is to you. At trial, the plaintiff might recover more. Of course, if the case involves matters of principle and you can afford the costs of trial and appeal, be resolute.

At all times, remember the Third Commandment. *Act on your own judgment.* Your lawyer and your friends may urge you to go to trial for vindication. Your lawyer wants to win the case.

Your friends believe in your cause. But it is *you* who will have to bear the strain and costs of trial and appeal.

The recommendation of the Fifth Commandment is crucial. *Discuss money.* In a civil case your most important recovery will be money. Ask your lawyer for a professional judgment as to the best and the worst scenarios. How much can you likely recover? How much can you possibly lose? Then act on your own judgment in *your* interest. In a criminal case, find out whether you can recover your lost property, whether you can recover from the Victims' Compensation Fund. Weigh the costs to you of the trial, the time spent waiting for the case to be called, the time in court, the emotional stress, and decide what is in *your* interest.

The words "Equal Justice Under Law" are engraved on the marble portico of the U.S. Supreme Court building. It is a noble sentiment, the ideal toward which the American legal system aspires. But, unfortunately for many women, that ideal is often betrayed by legal precedents that are based on male perceptions and by a legal system dominated by men.

These are important facts you should consider *before* you go to court.

BEFORE YOU GO TO COURT

Before you decide to go to court make four lists in parallel columns. In the first column are "The Questions You Should Ask Yourself." In the second column are "Some Possible Answers." In the third column are "The Best Results You Can Hope for in Your Lawsuit." In the fourth column are "The Worst Results That Could Occur."

Questions You Should Ask Yourself	Some Possible Answers. (You may have others.)	The Best Results You Can Hope for in Your Lawsuit	The Worst Results That Could Occur
1 Do I want vindication?	Satisfaction, a verdict that says I am right, or an apology, or an acknowledgment that the other party was wrong.	Acknowledgment of wrong done; public retraction of a libel; apology for harassment or other misconduct.	Decision that the defendant was right and you have no valid claim.

Questions You Should Ask Yourself	Some Possible Answers. (You may have others.)	The Best Results You Can Hope for in Your Lawsuit	The Worst Results That Could Occur
2 Do I want to change an inequity in the law?	A decision that will change what you think is an improper waiting period before getting an abortion, or a decision that deadbeat dads can pay more support for second families than for their children by the first wife.	A court decision upholding your position that will change the law for all similarly situated women.	The decision will set back the law.
3 Do I want monetary damages, and if so how much?	How much money do you want? Out-of-pocket expenses; wage losses; damages for physical pain and suffering; damages for emotional harms; punitive damages to hurt the defendant; or all of them?	List the largest sum of money you can reasonably expect for each of the items of monetary damages that you claim.	You will not receive any monetary damages and costs and counsel fees will be charged against you.
4 Do I want job reinstatement, promotion, or some other award?	Job reinstatement, promotion, promise to be put on the fast track, or some other job related benefit?	Reinstatement in your job with back wages; promotion; promise you will be on the fast track; better working conditions; vacation; pension rights; sick benefits; and other job benefits you believe have wrongfully been denied you.	No job reinstatement, advancement, or other benefits.
5 What do I really want?	All of the above.	Any other benefits you want.	All of the above.

Now compare columns three and four. Get a realistic assessment of the likelihood of success or failure from your lawyer, including the probable time it will take before the case goes to verdict and is appealed and the amount of costs and counsel fees you must pay if you lose.

Then ask yourself whether you can afford the action financially and whether you have the physical and emotional strength to undergo a proceeding of this length.

PART III

WORK
AND
MONEY

12

Before You Take a Job

You may tempt the upper classes
With your villainous demitasses
But Heaven will protect the Working Girl . . .

EDGAR SMITH

Almost every woman in the United States will at some time in her life seek employment outside the home. This chapter will tell you the dangers to look for, the most common pitfalls that await the unwary female who looks for a job. Whether you work on an assembly line, behind a counter or before a computer, in an operating room or a board room, you will encounter problems. Some will be the same problems that your male coworkers face. But you, as a woman, will confront many problems that your male colleagues do not.

When you seek a job bear in mind these four principles:

1. You are working for money.
2. Your work is not an act of charity.
3. Your work is not a hobby.
4. As an employee you have rights.

Whether you are an heiress or a penniless student in debt, whether you have a Ph.D or are a high school drop-out, you may encounter many of the same problems in the work place. Whether you are a pretty teenager, or a former homemaker returning to the workplace, or a woman joining the workforce for the first time, you will have to be alert and knowledgeable to assure that you are adequately paid for the work that you do and that you are treated fairly.

Some years ago I was a guest of a young woman who was graduating from an exclusive girls' prep school. Margaret Mead, who gave the baccalaureate address, said to the graduating class:

"Young ladies, you will now go to college for four years. You will probably marry and raise two children. Your life expectancy is almost eighty years. When your children leave home you will be in your mid-forties. What are you going to do with the rest of your lives?"

Probably the graduating women did not listen or pay attention to this chilling prognostication. But as I looked around the auditorium filled with well-dressed, attractive women in their forties I saw a sea of stricken female faces. The mothers exclaimed, "Why didn't someone tell me that *before* . . .?"

Irrespective of your ability, training, and experience, you will encounter difficulties in getting a job because you are a woman and even more difficulties in getting advancement and compensation commensurate with your qualifications. A survey of professional and managerial women in Philadelphia revealed that 90 percent of them said that they face more career obstacles than men.

Depending upon your work, you may encounter problems simply because you are a woman. If you choose well-paid nontraditional employment such as becoming an electrician, plumber, mechanic, assembly line worker, or police officer, your male colleagues may resent you; may feel that you are taking a job that belongs to a man. Others may be hostile and try to make your life miserable by trying to give you the hardest, dirtiest work assignments.

A male police officer testified before me in a case involving the arrest by a female officer of an armed robber at 3 A.M. in a notoriously dangerous area. She was walking the beat alone. He was in a police car with another officer.

When defense counsel questioned why the female had this assignment, the male officer replied,

"She wanted equal treatment. She got it."

Many male coworkers who know women only as mothers, wives, daughters, and girlfriends have difficulty in adjusting to a woman who does not have such a personal relationship with them. Older men sometimes try to be fatherly. Many men see all women as potential girlfriends despite the fact that they themselves are married and their female coworker is also married.

In all kinds of work some men will expect you to cater to their whims and wishes as their mothers and wives do. Even if you are a professional, a lawyer, a doctor, or an engineer, a male colleague may expect you to sew on a missing button or get him a cup of coffee or to submit to his sexual advances.

When these inappropriate requests or advances are made, remember the Fourth Commandment. *Have a velvet glove in an iron hand.* Speak softly, but firmly. Establish at the first encounter that you are a working colleague, nothing more and nothing less.

This chapter tells you some ways of avoiding this endemic bias against women in the workplace.

When you take a job outside the home, it is essential to remember the First Commandment: *Protect thyself.* You will have to protect yourself not only on the job but at home. Most women work what is called the "second shift," a full day's work after they come home from their paid jobs.

You will be doing the same work as your male colleagues on the job, *and* you will also have all the unpaid work in the home that you had before you took the job, unless you act wisely *before* . . .

If you are married be sure your family understands that you no longer can be at their beck and call. You cannot be an unpaid chauffeur, laundress, gourmet cook, meticulous housekeeper, hostess at dinner parties, *and* a full-time employee or self-employed worker. You cannot do your own work and your children's homework. You cannot be the unpaid nurse/companion to your elderly parents and parents-in-law and also do a day's work outside the home. Other members of the family will have to assume some of these chores.

If you are single and are not a highly paid individual you undoubtedly have household tasks: shopping; marketing; cleaning; and other chores that wives do. Only you do not have a wife, so you must do these tasks for yourself.

Remember these rules before you take a job!

Work Should Be Compensated for in Money

Do not let your employer pay you a lower wage simply because you do not *need* more money. Find out what other employees doing similar work are being paid. Find out the going wage for your type of job in your community and insist on being paid at that rate *before* you accept the job. It will be more difficult later to get a raise that brings you up to that level.

A star reporter on a Philadelphia newspaper was hired in 1980 by a New York newspaper. She worked there for ten years and was considered a first-class reporter. In 1990 she became engaged to another reporter who had been working for that paper less than one year. Imagine her dismay when she learned that he was being paid $11,000 a year more than she for doing the same work. When she complained, she was given a merit raise of $3,500 a year, still $7,500 less than her male counterpart was being paid.

Before you accept a managerial, paraprofessional, or professional position, find out how many women are employed by that company in such positions, whether they are as well paid as their male colleagues, and whether they have been promoted to top jobs.

You can simply ask the person who is interviewing you how many women are employed in comparable jobs and how many women have high-level positions. If these questions evoke hostility or evasion, that should be a red flag, a warning that the employer is not receptive to female employees.

A less obtrusive way of finding out is to use the ladies' room. Talk to the women you see in there and find out from them what they think of their employer.

Most communities have women's networking groups. Get in touch with one or more of them if you have any doubts about the company's attitude toward women, and find out from them what that firm's attitude is. Your best information will probably come from whomever told you about the job opening and referred you.

If the record of this prospective employer as to women is not good, you may want to look elsewhere. Before you accept a job with any employer, have a frank discussion about salary and your advancement prospects. You will know his or her attitude and that person will know that you expect to work hard and advance.

Here are some of the basic questions you should ask:

- ◆ the salary scale for your type of work
- ◆ advancement policies
- ◆ in-service training and promotions
- ◆ additional education (If you take courses at a school or university will that enhance your career? And will the employer finance that?)
- ◆ sick leave, family leave, vacation
- ◆ health benefits
- ◆ pension and retirement benefits

These questions indicate that you are a serious employee, one who sees this position not simply as a dead-end job but as a step in a career. If the employer is looking for a permanent employee who will be an asset to the organization, you will be the kind of person who is wanted. If, however, the employer is simply looking for a pair of hands to do a routine job for a limited period of time with no security and no future then you will not be the type of person wanted and this will not be the kind of job you should want.

Work Is Not Charity

Your work is not an act of charity. It is to be hoped that you, like more fortunate men, will enjoy your work. Some work is satisfying in itself. Some work may be drudgery, but it gives the worker a sense of self-worth. Still other work, which may not be exciting, may be socially useful. To some people, the knowledge that they are doing worthwhile work compensates in some measure for tedium and toil, but that is not a substitute for pay.

Employee Versus Independent Contractor

Charlotte is a highly skilled marriage counselor. She has a master's degree. She gives courses in marriage counseling. She worked many years for a respected nonprofit organization. When she took the job, the director of the agency said to her,

"Charlotte, your husband is a successful doctor. You don't need health insurance and other benefits. These are very costly to the agency. Why don't we hire you as an independent contractor? You'll get the equivalent hourly pay of an employee and you'll have the freedom to work fewer hours if you wish."

Charlotte had been on the board of the agency and knew its financial problems. She believed deeply in the value and importance of the work it was doing. His suggestion seemed to her to promote the welfare of the agency. And so she worked for the agency for almost twenty years as an independent contractor. During all this time she never asked for a raise because she believed she did not need the money. She thought it was undignified for a woman in her position to ask for a raise. And the agency, as always, was short of funds.

Then her husband decided he wanted a new, younger wife. When she came to me to represent her in the divorce proceedings she learned to her dismay that because she was not a regular employee she had no pension rights. She also discovered that no Social Security payments had been made on her behalf. Also, she would have no health benefits. Because she had not been on the payroll she was not covered by the agency's insurance policy.

As a divorcée she would not be entitled to remain on her husband's medical insurance. That would cover his new wife. She also learned that while she was being paid an hourly rate that was fair twenty years ago, her younger colleagues, even those who had been hired within the past five years, were earning more than twice the rate she was being paid. If she applied for a job at another agency, her low compensation would indicate that she was not a very valuable employee.

She is another women who wailed, "Why didn't I know all this *before* . . . ?"

Charlotte, like many married women, ignored four vital economic principles that all working women should be concerned with. *She did not bear in mind that she was working for money.* Money includes not only salary or hourly wages but also fringe benefits. Even though Charlotte did not need the health benefits at the time, she was certainly entitled to pension benefits, Social Security, and vacation pay. She unthinkingly gave up all these rights that were worth a great deal of money.

She treated her employment as an act of charity. Even though she was deeply committed to the good purposes of her agency, there was no reason for her to make a nondeductible contribution of her fringe benefits. If she wanted to help the organization, she could have given it a cash contribution equivalent to the value of her fringe benefits. The organization would have been in the same cash position; she would have had a deductible contribution; and she would have had all the benefits to which she, like all the other employees, was entitled. When the unanticipated end of her marriage came, she would have had 1. health benefits; 2. Social Security; 3. pension rights; and 4. a salary comparable to those of her coworkers.

Charlotte treated her work as a hobby because at the time she did not need the salary or the benefits. Consequently, she was treated not as an employee but as a volunteer, even though she was receiving an hourly wage.

Not only was she entitled to the fringe benefits that went with the position, she was also entitled to the raises in pay that the other employees received at regular intervals. Because she did not insist upon her rights, the organization did not provide them.

Work Is Not a Hobby

Do not treat your job as a hobby. Treat it as a career. No one knows how long she will need to work or want to work. Think of what your situation will be a year from now or five years from now. Will you still be in the same dead-end job? Will you have improved your skills so that you can get a better job, if that is what you want or need then?

STEADY EMPLOYMENT VERSUS FREE-LANCE WORK

When Mary Jane graduated from nursing school she was offered a number of jobs in hospitals. The pay was good, but she could make almost twice as much on an hourly basis as a private-duty nurse and work only when she felt like it. She thought that in a few years she would marry a rich doctor and then lead a life of leisure.

The good-looking young doctors she met were interested in the female doctors or were already married to their childhood sweethearts. The older doctors were interested in Mary Jane but not in marriage.

She married her childhood sweetheart, a nice young man who had a job in a factory. When he was laid off and Mary Jane became pregnant with serious complications, she discovered that she had no medical insurance, she had no unemployment rights, no sick leave. She and her husband had been earning big money. They had bought a house. Now they could not make the mortgage payments. They had to move in with her parents.

After the baby was born and they were more than $5,000 in debt, Mary Jane went back to her nursing school and asked for help in getting a steady hospital job. She had to accept entry-level pay even though she had more than seven years experience. Many of her classmates had well-paying supervisory hospital jobs.

Mary Jane knew she was working for money, that nursing was not an act of charity or a hobby. But she ignored the fact that employees have rights. Today most employees, except those who work in fast food restaurants or other low-paid jobs, have rights. They have sick leave, health benefits, and pensions. These benefits are worth money. If Mary Jane had calculated the value of these benefits and compared them with the hourly rate she earned as a free-lance private duty nurse, she would have seen that the advantages in pay were not that great. Also, she gave up the opportunities for advancement that she would have had as an employee.

Mary Jane ignored the First Commandment. *She did not protect herself.* She ignored the Second Commandment. *She did not anticipate disaster.* No woman can or should count on finding a rich husband. Even if she does, the marriage may not be for a lifetime. Every woman should recognize that illness may befall her. She may be in an accident. Health care is extremely costly. Therefore, it is essential either to purchase health insurance, which is also very expensive, or to be covered by health insurance as part of her employment.

Look to the Future

Heather graduated from an Ivy League college in 1980 with a Phi Beta Kappa key. She was pretty, popular, and talented. She had many job offers but she wanted freedom and excitement. For ten years she had a series of temporary assignments writing speeches for high-paid executives of Fortune 500 corporations. She went to high-powered meetings with these executives. She made lots of money and went on junkets to Asia and Africa. She had friends all over Europe.

And then—the recession hit. Comptrollers looked with a jaundiced eye on payments of $40,000 for a speech. One man who had employed her to write four speeches a year was forced to take early retirement. Others who used her for one or two speeches a year were writing their own speeches and worried about their own jobs.

Heather went to a headhunter, one who had found her more assignments than she wanted. He was discouraging.

"There's no more big money out there for free-lance writers," she was told. "But give me your portfolio and I'll see what I can do."

Heather realized that her name was not on any of the speeches. She had no portfolio.

"What about a teaching job in a business college? I know more about big business than most people."

"You don't even have an M.B.A. There's no place in academe for you."

"How about an editorial job?"

"You don't have experience on a newspaper, a magazine, or at a publishing house."

Finally Heather found a job that pays $30,000, writing for a business journal. She is ten years older than her colleagues and the prospects of advancement are dim. Her classmates are editors of national magazines and executives. She is another unhappy woman who says, "Why didn't I know *before?* . . .

Heather, like many bright young women, lived for the day and gave little thought to the future. She thought that because she was bright and gifted that she would always be able to make big money, that it was unnecessary to establish a career.

Aesop's fable of the grasshopper and the ant points up a moral that has been valid for more than two and a half millenia: It is all well and good to play in the sunshine and enjoy oneself, but the winter inevitably comes. I do not suggest that you ignore the pleasures and excitements that are available and drudge in anticipation of a rainy day. But, as in all things, a median position is desirable. *Enjoy today but do not ignore the future.*

Heather expected to work and have a career. But she did nothing to prepare herself for a permanent job. She ignored the First Commandment. *She did not protect herself.* If she had insisted, she could have been credited with the work she did so that she would have a portfolio, a record of her writings. She ignored the Second Commandment. *She did not anticipate disaster.* No one can count on boom times lasting forever. In every industry there are good times and bad. The workers are not responsible for these fluctuations and can do nothing to prevent them. But, the best security in times of economic recession is a marketable skill and, in the world of today, academic credentials. Heather had job skills but they were not marketable because she had no record of her achievements. She had no personal credentials. She was in the same position as a new college graduate except that she was ten years older. And that is a disadvantage. Her contemporaries had advanced far ahead of her on the career ladder.

Heather disregarded the fundamental principle that work is not something she could do at her convenience, and consequently, she missed the opportunity to develop a satisfactory career.

Employees Have Rights

Although you may want a job desperately, you should bear in mind that employees have rights. Some employers expect their secretaries to balance their family checkbooks, chauffeur their children, and even type the children's school papers. White collar workers who are not unionized and who have a one-to-one relationship with the boss are often subject to petty, unconscious forms of tyranny.

Domestic workers, women who are accustomed to toiling hard for low pay, make very clear to their employers when they are hired exactly what tasks they will and will not perform. Most domestic dayworkers tell their employers *before* they start work, "I don't wash windows."

Ask your prospective employer what tasks you will be expected to perform. If you are a secretary, a law clerk, a doctor's assistant, a researcher, or have any other job in which you have a one-to-one relationship with your boss, ask for a job description outlining just what your duties are.

If your boss is a woman, treat her with the same respect and formality that you would accord a male boss. And demand in return dignity and respect for your private life.

If you are a professional or a paraprofessional, you are not a file clerk, a switchboard operator, or a secretary. When my female law clerks completed their stints with me and were hired by private law firms, I warned them, "Don't let your next boss know that you can type or you will find that you are also doing the work of a secretary."

What Track Are You On?

Josephine is an experienced lawyer. When she worked for the federal government, she was in charge of a section of her agency.

She was the boss of twenty-five lawyers. She had years of trial experience. She was an expert in writing appellate briefs.

A leading law firm in another city lured her away from the government with the offer of a substantially higher salary. Private law firms have a much higher pay scale than government agencies. Josephine was delighted. Although moving was a chore and she would miss her friends, she was ready for a change and she could use the money.

The first few months were fine. The work was challenging and interesting. Then a senior partner told her the firm was instituting an appellate section and asked her to head it. She was in charge of a group of young associates who were assigned to write briefs for cases that had been appealed. Many of the issues involved novel points of law. Josephine liked being on the cutting edge.

All went well for a year. Then she discovered that two of the young men she had been supervising were made partners. She went to the head of the firm and asked why she was not made a partner.

"You are not on the partnership track," she was told.

"Why not?"

"That wasn't our agreement with you. However, we are pleased with your work and we'll give you a $5,000 raise."

"And next year, will I be on the partnership track?" she asked.

"No. We want you in this position."

Because other women lawyers had been made partners, a gender-discrimination lawsuit would probably not have been successful. It would have been costly, unpleasant, and taken at least two years of her life to prosecute. Josephine quit. At considerable expense and inconvenience she packed her belongings and went back to the government.

Josephine is an intelligent woman and a very able lawyer. But she did not anticipate the gender bias in that law firm. The firm came to her with a job offer, so she blithely assumed that they wanted a woman. But, in her interview she did not ask how many women partners the firm had or what her opportunities for advancement were. If she had asked these questions, she would have discovered that there were few women partners and they were all relatives of clients. She would have learned that the managing partner disliked women and that she was replacing a woman who had been refused a partnership. At that point she could have told the firm that she would not accept the position unless she was on a partnership track.

If the firm really wanted her, it would have promised her a partnership within a certain number of years provided her work was satisfactory. If the firm had refused to give her a partnership-track position, she could have rejected their offer, kept her position with the government, *and* sued the firm for gender discrimination.

If she had sued, the firm would probably have made a substantial settlement with her. But even if it did not, she would have saved herself the expense and inconvenience of moving and the frustration of the experience.

When you are interviewed for a position, remember the list of subjects we mentioned at the beginning of this chapter that you should discuss *before* accepting a job.

Sexual Harassment

Mildred and Estelle work for an insurance company. They both began as file clerks. Because they were smart and hardworking they slowly advanced to midlevel jobs. With the raise in status and salary they came under the direct supervision of Tom, a good-looking executive.

Tom is married to the daughter of a wealthy executive in the company. They have several children and live a busy social life. Tom fancies himself irresistible to women. He thinks his cadre of female subordinates compose his own private harem, paid for by the company. As each new woman comes under his supervision he makes advances to her.

All the women, except his long-suffering, unattractive secretary, secretly detest him. She adores him. He overworks her shamelessly but ignores her as a woman. When Mildred and Estelle came into his section, Tom followed his usual routine with attractive female employees. First he gave them special assignments where they would have to work closely with him. Then, there were business lunches in his office and then in quiet little bistros. In due course Tom suggested working at night.

Mildred was uncomfortable but agreed to come in at eight P.M. The office was empty at that time. And Tom made his usual advances.

"You're a very pretty girl. I see a great future for you here."

"That's nice. I like my job," she said.

"And I like you very much," Tom murmured in his most seductive, practiced manner.

A kiss was soon followed by a struggle in which Tom ripped Mildred's blouse. She slapped his face and rushed out of the office.

It was soon obvious that Mildred was on Tom's shit list. Her evaluation was marked "unsatisfactory." She was described as "uncooperative." At the end of the year Mildred did not get a raise.

Mildred consulted a lawyer to see about bringing a sex harassment action.

"In order to sue the company, you will have to prove that Tom's supervisors knew of his advances to female employees and condoned them," she was told. "What evidence do you have that he behaved this way to other women?"

Mildred talked to her colleagues, but none was willing to testify for her.

"You shouldn't have gone to his office at night," they told her. "You knew what he wanted."

"I'm sympathetic," one woman told her. "But, I need my job. I don't want to get involved."

The lawyer told Mildred that she could sue Tom individually. But, since he had little money of his own, that did not seem to be a useful course of action.

"Tom assaulted me. Isn't that a crime?" Mildred asked her lawyer.

"Of course, it's a crime. You can file a criminal complaint with the prosecuting attorney. That office may or may not choose to prosecute. You weren't raped; you weren't injured. With all the serious crimes in this city it's unlikely that they will pay much attention to your complaint. And if they did prosecute what good would that do you?"

"Wouldn't I collect damages?"

"No. In a criminal case, the victim doesn't get any damages," she explained to Mildred. "The crime victims' bureau might award you something if you could show them that you had medical expenses or lost wages."

"What would happen to Tom?"

"He would probably demand a jury trial. His lawyer would ask you all kinds of embarrassing questions about your relations with men. Hadn't you had men friends before? Did you ever go to a man's office or apartment in the evening? That sort of thing. It is very uncomfortable to be a prosecuting witness."

"Would I have to testify in public?"

"Yes. If you file a complaint, you can be subpoenaed. If you don't appear you can be jailed for contempt of court. But Tom, as the defendant, doesn't have to take the stand. He can just sit back and say nothing. He is presumed to be innocent.

"Well, the criminal law won't do me any good. How about a civil suit?"

"It's expensive. Much as I sympathize with you, since the likelihood of your recovering anything other than nominal damages is very remote, I could not take the case on a contingent fee basis. My fee would be $100 an hour, plus costs: the filing fees; the subpoena fees; expert witness fees; and so on.

"That's out of the question. I don't have any money except my salary. Would they fire me if I sued?"

"It's possible. You could always then sue for wrongful discharge. But, it would be almost a year until the case came to trial. If you won, the company would appeal. That might take another two years and more fees."

Mildred needed her job. The prospects of finding another one if she were fired were uncertain.

Mildred asked the lawyer, "I don't say your fees aren't proper. But since I can't afford a lawyer, how about Legal Aid? Don't they provide counsel for poor people?"

"How much do you earn?"

"About $27,000 after taxes."

"And how many people do you support?"

"My mother's a widow. I help her a little."

"Is she your legal dependent? Do you take her as a deduction on your taxes?"

"No."

"Then she doesn't count."

"I also help pay for my niece's therapy. She's a handicapped child."

"But she isn't legally your dependent?"

"No."

"Then you are in the position of lots of Americans—too poor to afford private counsel and too rich to qualify for legal aid."

"But I thought under the Constitution we were entitled to legal counsel."

"Only if you are accused of crime. And in a few civil matters to assert constitutional rights. But suing for damages isn't considered that kind of a right. If I thought you had even a reasonable chance of recovering enough damages to pay for costs and cover my time, I'd take the case on a contingent fee basis because I think you were wronged. But I can't imagine you could recover more than a few thousand dollars and more likely you would lose. I have to support myself, too."

"Doesn't the civil law protect me?"

"Only if you can afford it."

Mildred, too, sighed, "Why didn't I know this *before* . . . ?"

Sexual harassment is a subject that every woman has read about and most women have experienced at some time, either in school or in the workplace. For years they endured these unwelcome advances in silence knowing there was little they could do to obtain legal protection. With the long overdue developments in the law, many women now believe that they can have meaningful redress when this sort of unwanted behavior occurs. *Unfortunately, the law promises more than it delivers.*

As Mildred's lawyer correctly advised her: *A sexual harassment suit is difficult and expensive.* A complaint to your supervisor will often be ignored. Or worse, you will be treated as a troublemaker. In many businesses and even in government agencies, there is an "old boy" network. The supervisors, who are predominantly male, combine to protect one of their own.

In the chapter "Before You Go to Court," we discuss the difficulties of winning sexual harassment suits. The best way to be free of this obnoxious behavior is to head it off at the outset. This is what Estelle, Mildred's coworker, did.

When Tom began the same routine with Estelle, she always had an appointment with the doctor or the dentist at lunchtime. When Tom suggested working in the evening, she told him that her boyfriend would not approve. In fact, Estelle did not have a steady boyfriend, but Tom decided it would not be wise to rouse the ire of a jealous male. As a compromise, Estelle told Tom she would be happy to come in on Saturday if they could not finish the work by six or seven in the evening. She knew that Tom's golf game was more important to him than his sex games.

Estelle rebuffed Tom without embarrassing either of them. Her evaluation was "satisfactory." She applied for and received a transfer to a different section. Her new boss appreciated Estelle's work and she soon received a raise.

When a fellow worker or boss makes unwelcome sexual advances, that is not a sign of love or passion but a matter of power. He is trying to show dominance, not love. Sexual harassment is not a new phenomenon. What is new is that more women are reporting these incidents; 40 percent of federal female employees have reported such episodes.

Today no woman has to put up with unwanted sexual attentions in order to keep her job or to get a promotion. Many businesses and educational institutions now have an employee relations program for dealing with this widespread problem. If your employer has such a program, by all means, speak to the person in charge. If that individual is dismissive or not sympathetic, suggest a transfer in lieu of making a formal complaint. Few employers want to go through the expense and trouble of hearing such a complaint in-house or having to defend a complaint before a government agency or court.

If the person who is harassing you is the head of the company or organization, the problem is more difficult. He will not be pleased with a complaint against him personally. This is a time when it is desirable to consult a lawyer. Often the threat of a lawsuit will suffice to stop the behavior or get you a transfer. It may, however, have detrimental consequences to your career. Be sure your lawyer gets a written agreement that if you leave you will receive a good reference.

However, if you succumb to the boss's blandishments and then later attempt to refuse, you will find that the law may not protect you. If you, like Mildred, accede to improper demands by reporting late in the evening to an isolated office, as she did, remember that the likelihood of getting adequate redress through the law is remote and the cost may be more than you can pay. It is wiser to be like Estelle and avoid compromising situations *before* . . .

Work can bring you not only financial security over a lifetime but it can also bring you independence and intellectual and personal satisfaction. You will achieve these goals only if you have a clear understanding of your rights, duties, and chances for advancement *before* . . .

BEFORE YOU TAKE A JOB
TRAPS FOR THE UNWARY WOMAN

1 When a prospective employer tells you, "We don't have a union. We take care of our employees," remember that a union is an employee's protection against unfair labor practices—*not an employer's!*

2 When a prospective employer suggests that you become a consultant or independent contractor, this is not for your benefit but a way for the employer to avoid paying benefits: vacations; health insurance; sick leave; and pension.

3 When you are offered an employment contract that is satisfactory with respect to compensation and benefits but is silent as to promotions, this may be a warning about the future.

4 When you are offered a position where you will be working as an assistant to a particular individual—private secretary, administrative

assistant—and you are told, "You will be my girl Friday, we'll work together," this may mean you'll be doing the boss's work and the family errands as well as your own work. Explore this to make sure these assignments are not part of the job.

POSITIVE DEFENSES

1 Ask for a contract and see that it covers these items:

- ◆ length of the contract
- ◆ health benefits, sick leave, pension, maternity leave
- ◆ salary—is it the prevailing rate in that community?
- ◆ severance pay
- ◆ an advancement plan

Ask if the company has a grievance procedure.

2 If you are an independent contractor, be sure that the compensation is sufficient to cover the cost of benefits you would get if you were an employee.

3 Ask about promotions. Are you in a track leading to a managerial position or a partnership?

4 Tell your prospective employer you want to know exactly what your duties are so that you can be sure you know what is expected of you.

13

BEFORE YOU REACH A DEAD END AT WORK

What a bore it is waking up in the morning always the same person . . .
LOGAN PEARSALL SMITH

All gainful work requires some repetitious boredom. But if your work is mostly boring, if you dread going to work and look for excuses to stay away, if your work makes you feel tired and without hope, then you should think seriously about another job or a different career.

If you are in your twenties or early thirties, you may have been lured into the business world, law, or engineering because those occupations were newly opened to women and seemed to be glamorous and well paid. But such a career may not be what you really want. No matter what your age or condition in life, you can and should explore other possibilities if you are dissatisfied with your present work situation.

It is usually easier to change jobs than to change husbands. However, giving up a job can sometimes be as catastrophic as dissolving a marriage. You *must* examine your options with similar care and foresight. And you must be mindful of the Five Commandments.

It takes determination and daring to give up the security of an established career. If you want to make a change in your occupation, you must consider the positive and negative factors. You have a vested interest in your employment. You have rights, benefits and entitlements that you may be relinquishing and you may be unable to obtain a similar level of benefits at a new job.

A hundred years of blood, sweat, and toil have been expanded in the struggle to protect working people in the United States. Labor organizers have been beaten and even killed in behalf of American workers' rights.

This struggle came to fruition over a period of years in a series of laws that many younger workers take for granted: the right to join a union; the right to strike; minimum wage and hour laws; child labor laws; laws that protect women from hazardous employment; workers' compensation laws; pension rights; health benefits; occupational safety laws; antidiscrimination laws; as well as Social Security, Medicare, and Medicaid.

But, many of these gains have been eroded by loss of union jobs, judicial decisions denying women special protections, and changing markets. Skilled blue-collar jobs have been moved to other countries that do not have these protections, thus enabling manufacturers to reduce their costs. Low-paying, nonunion jobs in the service industries remain. Pay and working conditions for all Americans have deteriorated, but especially for women and children.

In recent years, catastrophes at work have occurred with alarming frequency, not only in mines but in chicken processing plants and other workplaces. And many of the victims have been women.

After the elimination of piecework in factories for jobs with regular wages, it is ironic that women are now working at home, without supervision or oversight, doing what is essentially piecework. And children are also illegally working in the home, helping their overworked, underpaid mothers.

This trend has been accelerated by the practice of hiring women to do computer data processing at home, essentially on a piecework basis. While the pay may appear to be good, few of these home workers have job security or benefits.

When you are offered a job selling door-to-door on commission, or working at home on a piecework basis, ask yourself what protections and benefits these jobs offer? What rights do you have in the event the employer absconds or does not live up to the agreement? While the promises of better pay may be rosy, read the fine print before you give up a good job. *A lawsuit for misrepresentation is not an asset. It will not pay the rent.* And you may be spending money you cannot afford on lawyers and court costs.

If you have a position or job that you do not like but that has protections and benefits, you should *think carefully before giving up perquisites that you may not need now but might need in the future.* Again, it is helpful to list them on a sheet of paper so that you can review and evaluate them before making a decision.

Here are five important points to consider when you contemplate a career or job change. Write them down. They are:

- ◆ Pleasure in the work itself—Do you truly enjoy what you do?
- ◆ Pleasure in the workplace—Are you happy with your colleagues, the physical surroundings, and your contacts with other people?
- ◆ Compensation—Are you being paid as much as your co-workers? As much as you reasonably think you are worth? As much as similar workers in other companies?
- ◆ Opportunities for advancement—Is this a dead-end job? Do you foresee a future without improvement?
- ◆ Benefits—vacations, sick leave, family leave, health insurance, pension. Are you provided all these benefits as part of your employment? Are they adequate? Will you get comparable benefits in a new position?

These factors are all significant. But they are not all of equal value to all people. You must assign a percentage value based on the importance to *you* of each factor. The total values must equal 100 percent.

In making your job satisfaction chart, assign a percentage value to each of the five factors. Be sure they add up to exactly 100. Then assign a percentage of satisfaction you have in your present work to each factor.

For example, let us assign 30 percent to pleasure in one's

work, 10 percent to the satisfactoriness of the workplace, 40 percent to benefits, 15 percent to compensation, and 5 percent to advancement opportunities. The maximum value one can assign to each factor is 100 and the minimum is one. Then multiply the percentage of the importance of each factor by the percentage of satisfaction.

The chart will look like this:

Work Satisfaction Analysis

Factor	Importance	Satisfaction	Value
1	30	40	12
2	10	20	2
3	40	75	30
4	15	25	2.5
5	5	25	1.25
Total	100		47.75

In this example, the individual has less than 50 percent satisfaction out of a possible 100. Her benefits are very important to her and 75 percent satisfaction for benefits is good. But pleasure in her work is next in importance to her and that factor she rates as only 30 percent satisfactory. Probably she should look for a different kind of work that she would find more interesting. None of the other factors has an acceptable satisfaction rating. But unless she can find another job with adequate benefits she should not make a change.

Let us see what we mean by each of these factors. Pleasure in work is often overlooked in the quest for higher compensation and better benefits. But if you spend a good part of your waking hours at work, then the pleasure you derive from that work or the lack of satisfaction can determine whether or not you are a reasonably fulfilled individual.

What makes one woman satisfied can drive another to distraction. One of the happiest people I ever knew spent her entire working life deciphering and translating ancient clay tablets. Many people would have considered that intolerably tedious and boring. But she said, "If I weren't paid for doing this, I would pay for the privilege of doing it." She died at ninety-three, still happily reading her tablets, unfazed by world catastrophes and family problems. But such a life is not for everyone.

A good test for measuring happiness with your work is to ask yourself, "Would I want to do this work even if I weren't paid (and didn't need the money)?"

If your income is not essential for the support of your family, and if you are young and in good health and do not seem immediately to need your medical, pension, and other perquisites, then pleasure in your work should receive a very high percentage value, perhaps 75 or 80 percent. But, before you assign a percentage value, consider how important the other factors are to you.

If you do not work at home, then the ambience of the workplace affects your happiness. Is it a light, airy, pleasant place, or is it noisy, crowded, and dingy? Do you like your colleagues? Is your boss a tyrant or an understanding person?

Eileen is a competent secretary. She works in an office with three other women. They are all friendly and compatible. She has more than a dozen friends in the same company. She lunches with a different friend every day. Her office is across the street from a department store and several boutiques as well as an excellent food market. She can do her shopping at lunch or after work without wasting much time. The work, although not intellectually challenging, is varied. Eileen is not bored. She is satisfied with an unpressured, pleasant workplace and a fair but modest salary. Her marriage is not happy but she stays with her husband because of the children, whom they both love. She told me she probably would not have been able to hold the marriage together if she weren't so happy during the working day. She comes home feeling good and that enables her to cope with the disagreements and problems at home. The ambience of the workplace is the most significant factor for Eileen.

Compensation is an important factor for two reasons: money and status. Unless you are independently wealthy, you can probably use more money. But even if money is not a decisive factor for you, in our society people are all too often judged by their earnings. If you are paid less than other people in similar occupations, then despite your ability and competence, you will be considered a less valuable individual.

Martha is thirty-two years old. She has two small children. Her former husband has left the state and rarely pays support. The children are in day care, which is costly. If one child gets sick, she must hire a sitter to care for the child at home. Money is always a problem for Martha. She is an intelligent woman who left college to get married. She hopes to go to night school when the children are older and become qualified for a better job. Her present job is pressured; she works in a small cubicle in a large noisy room. But she earns $950 a week, which is more than she could get in any other job for which she is qualified. Compensation is her *most* important consideration.

Advancement, like job satisfaction, is a meaningful consideration for many people. How important it is to you depends on your situation and your personal desires. If you are in your thirties and single or without children, then opportunities for advancement are of major significance, counting for perhaps 50 percent. If your job is only a temporary stopgap, then opportunity for advancement is less important to you. If you are in your late fifties and have no exceptional skills or training, then job advancement is probably less important to you than a pension.

Benefits are included as part of many jobs. These usually consist of health insurance, paid holidays, sick leave, and pension rights. Think carefully about the benefits you will be giving up if you leave your job.

If you are a single mother, then health insurance, parental leave, and paid vacations are crucial. If you have aged, dependent parents, family leave may be important to you. If you have no independent means or substantial savings and you are approaching fifty, a pension may be the most important factor for you.

Andrea, like Eileen, works for a large company. She and her

husband have two children in elementary school. Andrea's husband recently left his job in an accounting firm and is doing free-lance accounting. He is making an adequate income but he cannot afford health insurance. He expects within a few years to have his own firm and that it will be able to provide benefits. In the meantime, the family has health insurance through Andrea's job. Andrea does not want to work any longer than necessary. She hopes to return to free-lance commercial art. However, until her husband's business can provide health benefits, that is the most important job consideration for her.

Many single mothers who are on welfare would like to work and be self-supporting. But the jobs that are open to them do not provide security or health benefits. They cannot afford to leave welfare that includes Medicaid for themselves and their children.

Renee is a successful public relations person. She has breast cancer that is in remission. Her medical expenses were paid under her company's health insurance plan. A rival company offered Renee a comparable job at almost double her salary. She told the personnel chief of her medical problems and was assured that the company health plan was as good as the one she was under. Renee accepted the job offer with delight.

Six months later, after a bad earnings quarter, the company decided to downsize the work force. Renee as the last hired was the first fired.

"You knew my health condition," she told the personnel manager. "What can I do now?"

"Your contract is not for a specific number of months or years. It is a contract at will. Unless you are fired for an impermissible reason such as race discrimination, the company has a right to fire you."

At her former job, Renee was one of the older employees and would not have been let go in a time of financial crunch. Renee consulted a lawyer. She wanted to sue the company for breach of contract and misrepresentation. Then she discovered that she had no contract; she was an employee at will. And there was no misrepresentation. The company insurance policy was just what they had told her. But it does not cover "former employees." She discovered she had no legal rights.

Renee asked me, "Why didn't I know this *before* . . . ?"

The lessons learned by the following women will guide you in deciding whether or not a job or career change is right for you and your circumstances.

When Satisfaction Is Worth More Than Money

Mildred was head buyer for a big, successful women's wear chain of retail stores. She was fifty years old, had never married, and was without dependents. She had a busy high-pressure job and she loved it. Her contacts with suppliers, colleagues, and people in the fashion industry comprised most of her social life. She had a six-figure salary and many perquisites and benefits. She was content.

A rival company offered her a position as CEO at almost twice the salary. She would have to move to their headquarters in another city where she had no friends. Mildred discussed this offer with her lawyer, her stockbroker, and her boss. These three men advised her to take the offer.

"We'll miss you," her boss said. "But you have reached the top of the ladder here. I won't stand in your way to get this great advancement."

"You'll never get anything that good again. A plum has fallen into your lap. Grab it," the lawyer and broker advised.

The new company gave her a deadline. The last day she called and accepted the offer. While Mildred was not beautiful, she had style and a lively vibrancy. She was fun to be with. I saw her six months after she took her new job. She looked worn and old.

"What's the matter?" I exclaimed in alarm.

"I hate this job. I have nothing to do with fashion, which is my real love. My work here is all finance. The only people I see are men who are interested in money. I want to go back to the fashion world where I deal with lots of artistic women and men.

"I've asked friends in the trade about a job as a buyer, what I really like to do.

"'You're overqualified,' they tell me. 'No one will hire a person who previously has been the head of a company.'"

As many lawyers, architects, engineers, and accountants discover in their fifties, it is difficult to make a lateral transfer, to go to a comparable position in a rival company. And it is almost impossible to get a decent job at a lower grade. *The time to make a change is before you get to the top.* People tend to think that there is something wrong with a person who does not want power and money.

Money and power are often more important to men than to women. Men get satisfaction out of being the "boss." So do some women. But many women find the nature of their work more important than power. For a woman like Mildred who had neither a husband nor children, work was not just a job. It was the most significant part of her life. It was what gave her happiness. Her business associates were her friends and substitute family. Her male advisors did not understand this.

Mildred violated the Second and Third Commandments. *She did not anticipate disaster,* the possibility that she might not enjoy the new position and the difficulty of finding another when she was at that level in her occupation. *She did not act on her own best judgment;* instead she took the well meant advice of men whose needs were very different from hers.

Although there are laws prohibiting age and gender discrimination, an older woman usually finds it more difficult to obtain a mid- or high-level job than does a man of the same age. If his hair is gray, he looks distinguished. If her hair is gray, she looks old.

Age discrimination cases are hard to prove at higher job levels, particularly when an older woman is seeking a new job and there are, as always, other qualified applicants.

If Mildred had constructed the work satisfaction chart suggested in this chapter she would immediately have seen that pleasure in her work and the ambience of the workplace were of greatest importance to her. In those, her level of satisfaction was very high. Money, benefits, and advancement were much less important to her.

Mildred is another unhappy woman who says, "If only I had known *before* . . . "

The Importance of Job Benefits

Alicia's life circumstances were very different from Mildred's. She was a school teacher married to a sick man. They had one son, who was attending graduate school on scholarship. He had a bright future. Alicia's husband was unable to hold a regular job but worked at home as a free-lance writer. He made a modest income but had no benefits. The family relied on Alicia's health insurance, which was part of her employment benefits. She also had a generous pension plan. When there was a teachers' strike, Alicia was one of the leaders of the movement. She made speeches; she rallied her colleagues. For the first time in her life she received recognition for the leadership qualities she had. Alicia was fired by an irate school board.

She then got a job as executive director of a small nonprofit organization devoted to improving education. She loved the work, which consisted of traveling around the country, organizing groups, and making speeches. But the pay was very low and there were no job benefits. Many nonprofit organizations believe their employees should work for the good of the organization and they consequently offer low pay and few benefits. The satisfaction of doing good is supposed to compensate for low pay and no benefits.

A few years after the strike, the teachers' union lawyers negotiated a settlement with the school board. Alicia and the other teachers who had been fired were offered their old jobs and given credit on their pension rights for the years they had been illegally deprived of their jobs. Alicia proudly and indignantly refused to return to the classroom.

Within three years the organization where she was working ceased operations. It had no funds. At age fifty-two Alicia was unemployed. Her husband's condition had deteriorated. They had no health insurance, no savings, and no pensions. Their son helped a little but he had married and now had his own family to support.

Alicia had to sell her home and move to a tiny apartment. With the proceeds from the house and a series of temporary jobs she managed to survive until she reached her sixties and began to receive her meager Social Security. When she had a serious illness, her medical bills were covered by Medicare but her friends had to pay for her nursing care and household help.

She enviously watches her former colleagues, who have retired on comfortable pensions, take interesting trips, and live carefree, happy lives.

Many women, like Alicia, see their work primarily as an opportunity for self-fulfillment, not as a means of earning a livelihood. They value the job for what it does for their ego and for the excitement and stimulus lacking in their personal lives. They forget the four principles set forth, in the preceding chapter:

◆ You are working for money.
◆ Work is not an act of charity.
◆ Work is not a hobby.
◆ As an employee you have rights.

Nonprofit agencies in some states are exempt from many laws that protect workers. For many years they could not be sued for negligent injuries. Often they do not provide health and pension benefits.

Alicia moans, "If only I had known *before* . . . "

When Fulfilling Your Own Needs Is Right

Dorothy is a happy, mature woman. She is not extraordinarily bright or pretty. But she is warm, loving, and enjoys life. She has been a good wife, a good mother, and also good to herself. Her husband said at their fiftieth wedding anniversary,

"If I had it to do over again I would."

She returned the compliment.

Dorothy was a social worker when she married Abe. He was a struggling young architect and her salary kept them going for the first few years. When her first child was born Dorothy quit work and stayed home with the baby. When the youngest child entered elementary school Dorothy went back to college and got a master's degree in communications.

Abe's partners' wives were disapproving.

"Your job is to care for your children and entertain Abe's clients the way we do."

But Dorothy knew that such a life was not for her. She talked it over with Abe.

"If you want to get out of the house and go back to work," he said, "why don't you go back to social work? You were very successful."

"Social work is too depressing," Dorothy told Abe. "We don't need the money or the benefits. You have a pension and health insurance."

She went to school, got her degree, and then found a job as public affairs programmer at a local TV station. Her children always said their mom was the most interesting person they knew. She brought exciting people home for dinner. Conversation sparkled.

Dorothy and Abe are now happily retired. They look back on fulfilled lives without regrets.

Dorothy obeyed the First Commandment. *She protected herself.* She achieved the life she wanted and in doing so she made herself and her family happy.

If you reach a dead end in your present work, you have many options.

- ◆ You can change your job.
- ◆ You can change your career.
- ◆ You can start your own business.
- ◆ If you are a professional and associated with a firm, you can establish your own firm or practice. If you are a teacher, you can start your own school.

If you are unhappy or see no possibility for advancement in your present job, look for another one. Do it now! *It is easier to find a job while you are still employed than when you are unemployed.*

If you don't like what you are doing, think of other occupations. There are many opportunities for women in what are called nontraditional jobs; a woman can be an electrician, plumber, carpenter, in the building trades, police officer, fire fighter, corrections officer, and maintenance worker, for example. These are all well-paid fields that were formerly closed to women.

Very few of such positions require great physical strength. They do require skills. But you can go to a trade school and become qualified for a new career that pays well.

For many women the rewards of having their own business outweigh the risk and the work. This situation provides one of the few opportunities most women have to be in charge. When you were a girl, you probably had to live according to your parents' rules and ideas. When you marry, even today, you have to accommodate yourself to some extent to your husband's wishes and desires. When you are an employee, you may be subject to gender discrimination and sexual harassment. Even in an ideal workplace, you will have to follow the boss's dictates. But when you own your own business, you can be in charge. You can express your ideas and desires. And you can have the thrill of creating an enterprise and seeing it flourish. Since this country began, owning one's own business has been an integral part of the American dream of self-sufficiency.

Whether you should embark on such an enterprise is a question you must ponder carefully.

Consult your friends and family, your lawyer and your accountant, and people in the line of work you want to go into. Learn all you can from them, but make up your own mind.

There are countless reasons for not going into a business of your own. Any new enterprise is risky. If you have a job that you are giving up, you must figure the difference between what you will make initially in your own business and what you have been earning, and treat the difference as a part of your new business costs. Market analysts may tell you that this is not the optimum time for starting a business. Either the market is inflated or it is depressed. There is a recession or there is inflation. To economists, the right time never seems to come. You must decide what is *the right time in your life* to take this momentous step.

Wise old heads will discourage you by saying,

"Mary Jane, you have never operated a business. What makes you think you can do so successfully when all about you experienced financiers and manufacturers are failing?"

There are many answers. If you have run a household on a budget, you already have some of the skills needed to operate a business. You probably have had one or more employees. You have had to juggle too many tasks for the limited number of hours in a day. You know how to set your priorities. You know how to shop and make a fixed amount of money go very far.

If you have been an employee, you learned some job skills and also have seen how an enterprise really operated from the inside. If you had special academic training in the field in which you want to start a business, you already have an advantage over those who simply learn by doing.

The decade of the 1990s is a particularly propitious time for women to begin their own businesses. A study by the National Foundation for Women Business Owners found that in 1990, 28 percent of U.S. businesses, including large corporations, are owned by women. These businesses employed close to 11 million workers. It is predicted that in 1992 the number of workers in businesses owned by women will equal the total number of workers employed by the Fortune 500 companies. In 1987, 30 percent of small businesses were owned by women. The study also found that women owned businesses tended to be more stable than nonfemale owned businesses.

Not only are women succeeding in business in record numbers, but they can no longer be discriminated against in obtaining loans, mortgages, and other types of financing; nor can you be denied credit because you are a woman. You can get a loan from the Small Business Administration if you meet its qualifications. You are classified as a "minority" and are entitled to special help in getting loans and in getting government contracts. Your mother and grandmothers did not have these rights and opportunities.

If you think you would like to have your own business here

are some of the questions you should ask yourself thoughtfully
before . . .

First, *make an honest evaluation of yourself—your strengths
and weaknesses.*

◆ **Are you willing to work hard?** Or is this going to be a hobby,
something you can drop when you want to go on a vacation or
feel tired or become bored with the enterprise? If you have never
worked or haven't had a job for some years, perhaps you should
try working for six months to see if you really *want* to work hard.

◆ **What are your personal capabilities?** Do you have an ex-
pertise in any field? Your friends and family may think you are
a gourmet cook, a green-thumbed gardener, or a talented dress-
maker, but are you really knowledgeable? If not, then perhaps
you should take some courses to improve your skills *before* you
start your own business.

◆ **What do you know about the kind of business you want
to start?** It is usually advisable to work as an employee in a
similar business before you try to run one of your own. If you
are thinking of opening a beauty parlor, work in one for a few
months and see the problems from the inside.

◆ **What is your personality?** As owner of a business you will
have to get along with many people. Are you easy to get along
with? Or do you have frequent serious disagreements with your
friends and relatives? When you are running a business you will
have to deal with your customers, employees, and associates. Do
you have to be the boss in order to play or can you cooperate
and take criticism? Can you assume leadership and responsibility
or do you need someone to tell you what to do?

Second, *do you have an idea for a business? Do you see an
unmet need or are you simply planning to replicate someone else's
business?* Some of the most successful businesses have been built
on a simple idea, to meet an evident need.

◆ A twelve-year-old Italian immigrant boy was working sweeping out saloons at the turn of the century. He noticed that most of the trash he swept up consisted of peanut shells. With his meager earnings he began buying peanuts in bulk and selling them to saloons. When Mr. Obici died he was a multimillionaire, the owner of Planter's Peanuts.

◆ The collapsible baby stroller was invented by a man who watched his wife attempt to board a trolley with her baby in one hand and a stroller in the other. If you see a need that is not being met, then there is clearly an opening for a new business. If you are not an inventor, then take your idea to a trustworthy lawyer and hire the engineering skills needed to start your enterprise.

Your idea need not be original, or one that never was thought of before. Ben and Jerry, the makers of the famous, delicious ice cream, recognized that there was a market for a better, richer, and more expensive ice cream than was generally being sold. Even though Häagen Dazs made a similar rich, expensive ice cream, Ben and Jerry believed that there was a market for a second high-quality brand. In the unlikely rural area of Vermont, they began their extraordinarily successful business.

◆ The owners of many of those thriving computer businesses in Silicon Valley did not invent the computer. They saw its possibilities and seized the opportunity that was available to anyone.

◆ Many women of color have built thriving businesses on the need for cosmetics and hair preparations designed for black women. They have also established nationally known beauty salons, naileries, and other shops that cater to the particular cosmetic needs of black women. They did not invent the products. But they saw the need and the opportunity and had the courage to try.

Third, *what capital do you need?*

◆ Can you run your contemplated business out of your home or will you have to rent or buy a place? How much will it cost?

- ◆ How many employees will you need? What salaries and benefits will you have to pay them?
- ◆ What equipment and supplies will you need?
- ◆ Have you made a budget?
- ◆ How much money can you afford to put into the business?
- ◆ If you need more, where will you get it?
- ◆ How long can you survive on your savings and other income before you must begin to make money from the business?

I have not mentioned demographic surveys or marketing surveys. These are expensive and not always helpful. Ford Motor Company paid enormous sums to survey the market before launching its ill-fated Edsel. But there are certain common-sense surveys you can make for yourself. If you are planning to open a retail store or restaurant, or bed and breakfast, look at the neighborhood. Is it attractive? Stand on the corner for a day and count the number of people who pass your location. Are they likely to walk into your place? Are they the kinds of people who will buy your product or services? Is there a well-established competitor a few doors away? What can you do to be more attractive than the competitor?

Whether you plan to open a knitting shop, a bagel shop, a factory, or a professional office, there are many legal problems you will face. It is better to get advice *before* . . .

Here is a partial list of things to ask your lawyer:

1. Is my proposed enterprise permitted under the zoning laws? If not, can I get a variance?

2. Do I need a license for this kind of business? If you plan to run a day care center, a center for older people, or some similar activity, you will probably need a state or city license. You may also have to meet certain qualifications of education and experience. You may also need a license, for example, to be a cosmetologist.

3. Do the premises I own or plan to rent meet the local inspection laws for this kind of activity?

4. How much insurance do I need? And what kinds of insurance? You will probably need fire insurance, public liability insurance, business interruption insurance, and if you are a professional, malpractice insurance.

5. Should I incorporate? There are advantages and disadvantages to incorporation that you should consider. Among the factors are taxes, personal liability, and control of the enterprise.

6. Do I need a patent or copyright for my product? Will it violate some existing patent or copyright?

7. If I have one or more partners, what rights and obligations will each of us have? Do I need a written agreement? No matter how well you know your prospective partner, it is advisable to have your agreement in writing to avoid future problems. President Reagan in negotiating with Khruschev used to say, "Trust but verify." A better motto might be, "Trust but have it in writing."

Thousands of women are now starting their own businesses. Judging from past experience, many will be successful. They will make money; they will provide jobs in their communities, they will have the satisfaction of creating an enterprise and seeing it grow and flourish. And they will have the incomparable joy of being their own boss.

You can make a change in your occupation if you are not happy with what you do. But before you give up your job weigh carefully the security and benefits that you will be losing. Remember that as an employee, especially in a unionized company, you have many protections. However, there is no assurance that your employer will always continue to operate that company or that you will continue to be employed. Companies are bought out; they merge; they are taken over by conglomerates; they downsize. Even the best employees are terminated for economic reasons.

If you own your own business or professional firm, you cannot be fired; your job cannot be eliminated; you will not be sexually harassed. But, you can fail and lose not only the business but your life savings.

Remember that when you quit your employment for a new position, if you have any ongoing medical problem, you will probably not be covered for medical expenses during the first six months on your new job.

In your present position you may have started with two weeks vacation a year and have worked your way up to four weeks. What will you have at a new job? Will you start at the bottom of the vacation ladder again?

And what are the terms of your new employment? A CEO who has plunged his company into debt retires with a "golden parachute." What security will you have in a new job? Probably none, unless you insist on a written contract for a term of years. Otherwise, like Renee, despite your ability you may be fired for no fault of your own. And you will have no redress.

The time for careful assessment, evaluation, and consideration of a change in your working life is *before* . . .

BEFORE YOU REACH A DEAD END AT WORK

Here is a checklist to help you in deciding whether or not to leave your present work:

1 Do you enjoy what you do most of the time?

2 Are you happy in the workplace?

3 Is your compensation adequate to meet your needs and is it the prevailing rate for your skills?

4 Are your benefits adequate?

5 Do you have an opportunity for advancement?

After you answer these questions, make a work satisfaction chart. If your satisfaction is less than 60 percent, look for another position or occupation. Before you leave make a projected job satisfaction chart for your new work. If it is not substantially higher than your present work, continue your search before you leave.

14

BEFORE YOU JOIN AN ORGANIZATION: STOP, LOOK, AND LISTEN!

Americans are a sociable people. We join all kinds of civic and nonprofit organizations for companionship and to help our neighbors and fellow citizens. In our complex, technological world one individual can't do much alone to advance a good cause. But through organizations we can make our voices heard.

Some organizations, however, have a hidden agenda that carries a buried message. In our computer-driven society once your name is on a list you may experience unforseen and embarrassing consequences. Many a politician who joined a local "whites only" club has lived to regret this casual decision.

Even if you are a purely private citizen who has no political aspirations, membership in a seemingly innocuous organization may sometimes have unpleasant, unexpected, and costly consequences.

One way to avoid such unanticipated embarrassments is to look for semiotic danger signals. Semiotics is a philosophy of understanding signs. It is a fancy, academic word for a common phenomenon. All of us recognize that signs have meaning. We know that a red flag is a warning. When we see a red flag on the highway we stop, look, and listen, and hopefully avoid danger. Bells and sirens are also warnings. Sensible people heed these common signs. Those who do not pay attention get into trouble—often serious—that could have been avoided.

Many danger signals are artfully camouflaged to mislead the unwary. They are buzzwords, benign-sounding words and phrases that seem appealing but that have a particular hidden meaning understood by the initiate, but misunderstood by many of the rest of us.

These buzzwords are cleverly designed to trap naive, well-meaning individuals into supporting ideologies or programs that are not in their best interests, projects that most individuals would shun if they knew the real meaning concealed under neutral verbiage.

Law and order, for example, is a phrase that includes two words symbolizing beliefs that most Americans cherish. All of us believe in law. All of us also want to live in an orderly community. But the phrase *law and order* carries a hidden meaning. As a buzzword, it has come to connote harsh, repressive measures; power over the rights of others, particularly over dissidents and minority persons; and a denigration of the protections of due process of law. The phrase is a semiotic danger signal for both women and men.

In this chapter we shall examine other catchwords and phrases addressed primarily to women. They sound neutral and benign. But their real purpose is to persuade women to support organizations and programs that you would probably not endorse if you understood the hidden meaning. Once your name is on a list, it is probably available to countless people. Your name may be in the computer of individuals and causes that you do not approve of. This can bring you not only embarrassment but can also cost you money and be detrimental to you and your family.

Politicians, idealogues of all views, and countless groups seeking either public support or money are now focusing their appeals on women. Women constitute the majority of the population; they vote in increasingly large numbers; they are sympathetic to calls for help. Consequently, women are the targets of those who have a hidden agenda.

When you are asked to lend your name, sign a petition or

document, or pay even nominal dues to any group, look beyond the pleasant phrases. Look for the hidden semiotic signals *before* . . .

Family values is a phrase used by many individuals and organizations who seek your support for purposes that may not accord with your beliefs. The concept of family values has a special appeal to women. Every woman, like every man, is a member of a family. We all have or had parents. Many of us have siblings and children, aunts, uncles, and cousins. Most women cherish their families. They derive comfort from those who are near and dear to them. Most women want to help and protect their families. They want to improve schools, provide good affordable day care for young children, good nursing care and homes for the elderly, and health care for all members of the family.

When you are asked to support an individual or organization that claims to promote family values, your first impulse may well be to say yes. However, many who trumpet forth *family values* have a different agenda. They oppose day care, parental leave, and women in the workplace.

Often these persons have in mind not your family, but the family depicted in the Dick and Jane readers that were popular forty or fifty years ago. Women who are old enough probably remember the little books with brightly colored pictures of a suburban house, father going to work in a business suit, carrying a briefcase; mother wearing an apron and caged behind a neat picket fence while Dick and Jane walk to the neighborhood school accompanied by their dog Spot. Spot is the only member of the household who is not lily white.

But in the 1990s, families come in many different forms. The nuclear family, consisting of mother, father, and children who live together, is no longer the norm in the United States.

In 1990, 24.7 percent of American children lived in single parent families. The number is growing. In 1990, 23.3 percent of children in the United States were born to unwed mothers.

More than half the mothers of young children are in the workforce. Many of these children live with their mothers, without fathers in the home. Others live with grandmothers or other relatives. In 1992, 48,924 children in New York City alone were living in foster care. Almost 60,000 children were incarcerated in some form of juvenile correctional institution.

In addition to the nuclear family and the single parent family, there is the extended family, in which grandparents, parents, children, aunts, and uncles live together. There are also homosexual or lesbian couples who live with the child or children of one of the pair, or adopted children. Many of those organizations that raise the cry of *family values* do not have in mind these varied types of families. Rarely are they concerned with helping single mothers. Nor are they concerned with helping elderly persons remain in their own homes. For many who loudly proclaim *family values,* this cry is a smokescreen or camouflage to conceal a hidden agenda to relegate women to the role of childbearing and housekeeping. It is often a sign to mask a regressive war against women. Often, groups that use the phrase hope to convince female voters that they are truly interested in helping women. The words are honeyed but the meaning is often barbed.

Communitarian is another word popular with certain academics and some members of the media. Like *family community,* it is a warm, pleasant word redolent of small town life and neighbors helping each other.

Most Americans belong to many communities. We feel a tie to our geographical community whether it is a rural area, a suburb, a small town, or a section of a metropolitan city. Many women feel strong ties to their churches or temples. Countless women also maintain close ties with their schools or colleges, which constitute another community. In some occupations, such as teaching, medicine, and law, we belong to our professional communities. Many of us also have strong ties to our ethnic communities, the roots from which our parents and grandparents came.

All these communities are overlapping and nonexclusive. Involvement with one group does not detract from one's ties to another group. In pluralist America we can be good members of many communities.

But *communitarian values,* like *family values* carries a hidden message. Those who espouse communitarian values as a philosophy of jurisprudence elevate customs and practices of these various communities to a preferred legal standing, a legal position that predominates over the rights of the individual.

This communitarian view contradicts the constitutional principles on which our government is based. All the major documents of American polity speak of the rights of the individual, not the family or the community. Each individual is promised life, liberty, and the pursuit of happiness. The First Amendment to the Constitution guarantees to each individual the right of free speech, freedom of the press, and religious liberty. The Fourteenth Amendment guarantees to each individual due process of law and equal protection of the laws. They are the source of every woman's right to life, liberty, property, and privacy.

Many who espouse communitarian values give precedence to the rights, privileges, and immunities *guaranteed to the community rather than the individual.* This is a novel and dangerous departure from traditional American jurisprudence.

Unfortunately the traditions and practices of some ethnic, religious, and social groups are predicated on a patriarchal social order in which women are second-class citizens. To permit the customs of these various groups to determine the rights of Americans would erode the broad guarantees of freedom intended to protect all Americans. Emphasis on community, like emphasis on the family, derogates the rights of the individual and most particularly the rights of women.

Pornography is another word that must be scrutinized by women with extreme care. Very few women like to attend burlesque shows, watch "blue" movies, or see portrayals of females in brutal or degrading situations. Some women feel demeaned by such films and pictures, and songs and books describing such acts. Many women, however, recognize that literary and artistic merit and a deeper understanding of human nature can be found in books, pictures, songs, and movies.

Legislation banning pornography as an assault on females appeals to some women who fail to consider the dangers to free speech implicit in such legislation and the semiotic signals concealed under the benign banner of protecting females. They ignore the fact that women, even more than men, need the protections of the First Amendment. The economically and politically dominant group in any society has access to the media to get its views expressed. Minorities and less powerful groups can easily be silenced under benign-sounding justifications, such as obscenity, pornography, and protection of children. Authority to censor expression is a dangerous threat to the freedom of everyone. Again, it is women who are most apt to suffer when expression is regulated or censored by government.

Some women have forgotten the prosecution of Margaret Sanger, who, under the banner of decency, was denied her First Amendment rights to discuss birth control. And they disregard the fact that despite legislation designed to give women and minorities access to the airwaves, few women actually control TV and radio stations.

The print media are also male dominated. While many talented and able women are editors of magazines, columnists in the daily press, and editors of books, the publications are predominantly male owned. These men determine whose voices shall be heard and what messages will be disseminated.

The principal bulwark of protection for the rest of the population, and particularly women, guaranteeing a woman the right to have her ideas printed and aired and to hear all points of view, is the First Amendment to the Constitution. Women who fought for suffrage, for birth control, for child labor laws, and countless other pieces of legislation that we now take for granted had great difficulty in getting their messages to the public.

There is a long history of efforts to restrict freedom of speech and of the press. We know that Stalin and Hitler banned what they called "degenerate art." Book burning by zealots from Savonarola to the Ayatollah has been advocated and actually accomplished. In the United States books by Mark Twain, James Joyce, and J.D. Salinger have been "purged" from libraries in the guise of protecting women and children. The Constitution protects your right and your children's right to read, to see, and to hear what you want and also your right to decline to read, view, or listen to what you dislike. Do not relinquish these precious rights under a specious claim that you will be protected from baneful influences.

Those who promote laws to ban pornography as an attack on women forget that in proper Victorian England, when words like *limbs* were used rather than the vulgar forthright word *legs*, in order to protect delicate female sensibilities, and when even piano legs were modestly concealed under skirts, prostitution flourished and women and children toiled long hours under inhuman and cruel conditions.

Movements to "protect females" are all too often a *cover for a hidden agenda to relegate women to second class status.*

Another common phrase that carries a hidden meaning is *pro-life.* Women are by nature of their biology the creators of life and in most instances the nurturers of life. *They care for the young, the elderly, and the ailing.* Every woman who bears a child puts her life and health at some risk. The human species would not have survived for these countless millenia if women were not committed to creating and protecting life.

Throughout history wars have been almost exclusively the province of men. The female Amazon warriors of legend are a rarity in the long record of taking life, which has been perpetrated by men—whether using rocks and clubs, bows and arrows, or nuclear missiles. Thus, when the term *pro-life* is used by politicians and demagogues, intelligent women should recognize it is a semiotic danger signal and look for the hidden agenda, which often is to relegate women to second-class citizenship, consisting of unwanted perpetual childbearing, and a Hitlerian view of woman's place as being *Kinder, Kirche,* and *Kuche*—children, church, kitchen.

There are many popular words and phrases that carry a hidden meaning. Despite their superficial appeal, such slogans should alert you to danger. They are a warning to "Stop, look, and listen!" before you act. It is unnecessary to list all these semiotic danger signals. No list can be complete. Clever public relations personnel will undoubtedly continue to misuse common words for the hidden purposes of their employers. You must be alert, cautious, and investigate an organization thoroughly before you join.

The experiences of the women described in this chapter should suffice to warn you to look for the hidden agendas of many organizations and individuals who seek your support.

Saviors Can Be Destroyers

Jane is an intelligent college graduate. She is married and has a responsible job. Her hobby is breeding dogs. She loves animals. She shelters injured birds and stray cats. She works diligently for the local zoo and contributes generously to organizations to save endangered species. When she received a beautifully illustrated brochure from a group interested in the humane treatment of animals, even though she did not recognize any names of the sponsors, she gave generously. Soon she was asked to serve on the board of directors. The pleasant voice that called her assured Jane that she would only be asked to attend two meetings a year and continue her financial support. And she consented.

A few months later to her horror she read in the morning paper that members of this organization had broken into a university biology laboratory, released the research animals, and destroyed millions of dollars worth of genetic research studies on Alzheimer's disease. She is now a defendant in a suit against the organization for $3,500,000 compensation for the damages caused by the raid on the laboratories. She is also concerned that the animals released may spread disease.

Jane has no insurance to protect her against the lawsuit. She has had to retain her own counsel because the attorney for the organization is representing the individuals who planned and participated in the raid on the laboratory. She is one of many women who say, "If only I had known *before* . . .

You May Want to Help; Others May Want to Hurt

Virginia is a devout Catholic, a mother of four. She is a good, law-abiding citizen who is opposed to war, violence, and racism. She has been active in her church and her neighborhood, working for safe streets, drug treatment centers, and interracial understanding.

When she was asked to join a pro-life group she did so. Virginia's husband works hard and earns a modest living. Their budget is stretched almost to the breaking point to educate four children and care for her elderly mother. Virginia gave a small contribution. She was touched by the plight of young, pregnant, unwed girls and wanted to help provide them with prenatal and obstetrical care and find good homes for unwanted babies.

Virginia was asked to go with her group to the local offices of Planned Parenthood to persuade young women not to have abortions. After the three older children left for school, Virginia took her baby and joined her friends. She was standing on the sidewalk opposite the clinic holding a banner in one hand and her baby in her other arm when she saw several young men leave her group, cross the street, and assault a young woman who was about to enter the clinic. The men knocked the woman to the ground, dragged her along the street while shouting at her, "Murderer!"

The police were there and so were the TV cameras. The young woman, who was injured, was taken to a hospital. The men who had assaulted her and all the persons holding signs, including Virginia, were arrested. She and her baby were taken to the police station. Virginia had only $5.00 in her pocketbook. She called her husband, who had to leave his work and come and post bail for her.

That night Virginia's picture was shown on the TV news as she and the baby were being shoved into a police van. Her older children and her husband were watching the news. She was humiliated and ashamed. Her husband was furious.

"Why can't you mind your own business?" he shouted. "You cost me money we can't afford and time from work. You embarrass me."

"I only wanted to help," Virginia wept. "I had no idea there would be violence."

Virginia's next-door neighbor, a social worker, who is employed at a shelter for teenage pregnant girls, told Virginia that their friendship could not continue.

A few days later Virginia found that she would have to retain two lawyers: one to defend her in the criminal trial for conspiracy and assault; the other to defend her in a civil action brought by the woman, who had suffered serious injuries while she was being dragged along the street.

Virginia and her husband had to get a bank loan to pay counsel fees. She has been to court three times. She fears to watch the evening news lest she see herself again.

"Why," she asks, "didn't I know *before* . . . ?

Joining Is Not a Job Requirement

Juanita has an executive position in a bank. She is the highest-ranking black female in the bank. She obtained this position by intelligence and hard work. Juanita's first job in the bank was as a low-paid key punch operator. She took all the in-service training available and was promoted. She also went to night school and obtained a bachelor's degree after six years of working days and attending school at night while supporting her children.

Juanita has had little time for socializing and has few friends at the bank. She was pleased when an officer invited her to a party at his home. On arriving at his spacious, suburban house she was astonished to discover that she had not been invited to a social gathering but to a meeting to obtain members for a group devoted to backing political candidates who espouse family values.

A number of other bank employees were present. A young male officer hoping for a promotion promptly signed the membership application and paid the $25.00 fee.

Juanita did not want to offend her host, who was also her boss, but she wanted to know more about the organization.

"I believe in family values," she told him. "But I'd like to know the candidates you have supported in the past."

In a few days she received a list. All the candidates were white. All but one were male. The female who had been elected had voted against a day care bill and voted to cut welfare for women who had another child while on welfare. One candidate was opposed to affirmative action.

When the officer stopped at Juanita's desk in the bank and asked her for her membership application, she was very uneasy.

"I cannot support some of these candidates," she told him. He walked away in high dudgeon.

At the end of the year, when the employees received their annual bonuses, for the first time Juanita did not get one. Her job ratings, as always, had been excellent. She made discreet inquiries and learned that her coworkers had all received bonuses. Juanita consulted a lawyer. She told Juanita that she could file a complaint with the local Human Relations Commission alleging both race and gender discrimination. The lawyer investigated that organization and discovered that despite its professed charitable nature, it had made illegal political campaign contributions. She suggested notifying the Internal Revenue Service and the Fair Election Practices Commission.

She also suggested that Juanita give the bank officer an opportunity to rectify the matter without taking action. Armed with this information, Juanita called for a conference with the bank officer. He met her with a show of camaraderie.

"You're looking very well," he said.

"Thank you. But I'm not feeling very happy," she replied. "There is an important matter I'd like to discuss with you. You don't mind if I tape record our conversations, just to make sure there are no misunderstandings?"

Somewhat discomfited, he muttered, "All right."

Juanita set her tape recorder on the desk and proceeded. "I did not receive my usual bonus this year. Can you tell me why?"

"That depends upon your efficiency ratings. I have nothing to do with them."

"Good. Here is a copy of my ratings. As you will see they are all excellent."

He looked at the report and blushed.

"Could the withholding of my bonus have anything to do with my refusal to join your family values organization?"

"What makes you ask that?"

"It is the only explanation that I can think of. Have you another?"

"Well, we do want cooperative employees, employees who contribute to the community."

"I contribute to the United Way, to the Red Cross, Cancer Drive, and countless *bona fide* charities," Juanita replied.

"What do you mean, 'bona fide'?"

"I investigated your family values organization and I find that it made illegal political campaign contributions. Would you like me to go to the Internal Revenue Service? I also believe that I, a black woman, am the only employee who did not receive a bonus. The Human Relations Commission would probably find that of concern."

"Now, Juanita. Let's not be precipitate. I'm sure there was some mistake in the payroll office and that I can get it straightened out for you."

"I'm sure you can. How long do you think it will take?"

"Just a few days, not long."

"I'll wait a week," she said firmly.

Within three days Juanita received her bonus with a little note saying there had been an unfortunate computer error.

Community Values Can Violate Individual Rights

Rebecca and her family are members of a strictly religious sect in rural Pennsylvania. Her father has a large, successful farm with acres of crops and more than one hundred cattle. She was a happy girl in elementary school, the first in her class when she graduated from eighth grade. Rebecca loved to read. She was good in math. She dreamed of being a scientist. She wanted to go to high school and the university.

Her father forbade her to go to high school.

"It is unnecessary. You know how to read and figure. That's all a woman needs to know. You will stay home on the farm and help your mother."

Rebecca's teacher tried to talk to her parents. Rebecca's mother was sympathetic but her father was adamant. And his word was law.

The teacher told Rebecca that the state law requires all children to attend school until the age of seventeen. When Rebecca consulted a local lawyer she learned that there was a special act of Congress exempting children of her family's faith from attending high school because it violated their religious tenets and communitarian values.

"School doesn't violate my religious beliefs," Rebecca cried. "I am a good Christian. But I also want to learn."

Rebecca is now twenty. She refused to marry the nice young farmer her father had selected and ran away from home. Without a high school diploma there are few jobs for her. She is working in a fast food restaurant and going to school at night. It is a lonely life. She is estranged from her family.

"Why doesn't the Constitution protect me?" she asked me. "I have read the Bible again and again. I can't find anything in the Scriptures that prohibits higher education."

But communitarian values have been placed above the rights of the individual to the detriment of some girls like Rebecca.

Sally New Moon also discovered that the communitarian values of her husband's tribe deprived her of the constitutional rights guaranteed to other Americans. I met Sally at an Indian reservation in New Mexico. She had grown up in California. Like many Native Americans and members of minority groups, she was seeking her roots. She met a Native American from New Mexico at a government school run by the Bureau of Indian Affairs. They fell in love, married, and moved to his reservation. They had two children. Life there was hard and conditions more primitive than those she was accustomed to. But Sally was committed to her husband and to living with him and his family in the home and community that he loved.

Sally organized the women of the tribe to demand running water, better schools for the children, and better medical care. The women loved Sally and worked with her. They nominated her to serve on the tribal council. Then she learned that under tribal law women could not be on the council. When she wanted to take her children to California so they could get a better education, she discovered that her children belonged to the tribe. She was forbidden to take them away.

Unless she can persuade her husband to leave the reservation,

Sally is faced with a terrible dilemma, a Sophie's choice. Her husband will let her go to California with her daughter but not with her son.

A popular book and later a movie, *Not Without My Daughter,* graphically describes the problems of an American woman who married an Iranian and went to live with him in Iran. She discovered that under Iranian law and custom, a mother does not have the right to custody of her children. The father does.

That was true under English law for centuries. It is true today in many countries where women are second-class citizens. By custom and law women's rights are not recognized. Before you decide to live in another country or in a close-knit community in the United States, one that does not recognize or tolerate differences, examine carefully the rights that you as an American citizen will be surrendering.

Wherever you live, when you are asked to support an organization that espouses *communitarian values,* stop, look, investigate, and be sure you know whose values you will be supporting. The law did not help Sally, as it did not help Rebecca, because communitarian values prevailed. Even if the community you contemplate joining is not recognized by law as having special rights and privileges, remember that if you seek to assert your rights, the judges who preside in the local courts *are probably chosen from the community and share its values. If you demand a jury trial, the members of the jury will be chosen from that community.* You will have a long, expensive, and unequal legal struggle in attempting to secure your rights.

One day when I was presiding in felony court, I heard the case of Willie, who had brutally beaten his ten-year-old son. The neighbors who heard the boy's screams had called the police, who took the youngster to the hospital. The doctor in the emergency room testified. He presented X-rays showing more than a dozen healed fractures and pictures of the raw lesions on the boy's body from a leather belt with which he had been lashed.

Willie's defense was that he was "disciplining" his son. Willie's mother testified that she had "whupped" Willie when he was a boy and that her mother had "whupped" her. Willie's lawyer argued that in their culture parents were expected to beat their children. I ruled that the child was protected by the Constitution and convicted Willie of aggravated assault. I was accused of being insensitive to minority cultures and communitarian practices.

Many Hispanic and Asian women who are beaten by their husbands are afraid to complain to the police. If they do so they will be ostracized by their communities. And when on a rare occasion the police prefer charges, the husband's defense is *communitarian* practices.

When you are asked to support an organization devoted to communitarian values, investigate. Find out whether those values and practices will preserve your rights or abrogate them. Ask questions; demand full and complete answers; and act forthrightly.

The history of Anglo-American law makes shocking reading for women. For centuries the laws were made by male legislators, administered by male public officials, and interpreted by male judges. Only in the last half century have women had any significant role in the American legal system. A woman's rights to vote, to hold public office, to obtain a divorce, to have custody of her children, to have control of her own money, property, and earnings, and to attend institutions of higher learning and become a licensed professional, were won only after long and arduous struggles on the streets, in the legislatures, and in the courts. There are many men and some women who would turn the clock back and deny you those rights. They can do so only by obtaining the support and the votes of women.

Here are some things you should know *before* you join any group . . .

- ◆ Who are the key figures in the organization? Get the letterhead and see if you recognize the names. If it is an organization, look the people up in *Who's Who*. If it is a local group, inquire about it among community leaders.
- ◆ Has the organization supported any political candidates?
- ◆ Who are those candidates? Do you agree with their platforms? What legislation have they endorsed?

- ◆ To what *groups has the organization given money?*
- ◆ Does it have a brochure setting forth its goals and policies? If so, get a copy and read it carefully.
- ◆ Is the organization recognized by the Internal Revenue Service as a bona fide charity? If not, your contribution is not tax deductible. If it is recognized and it makes political contributions, you may be in trouble for improperly taking a tax deduction.
- ◆ If you are not satisfied with the answers, go to the public library and consult the various registers of charitable organizations.

Think carefully when you are asked to give your name or your money to any organization, group, or political candidate. Look for the semiotic danger signals *before* . . .

BEFORE YOU JOIN

Here is a summary of items every woman should review before she joins an organization:

1 Read the printed brochures or other literature. If there is no literature, this is a red flag! Investigate further.

2 Who are the officers and board members? Do you know them? Are they people you respect? If you have never heard of any of these people, check them out.

3 What has the organization done in the past?

4 If it is a political organization, what candidates has it supported? What laws?

5 What do you know about the ideas and beliefs of the person who solicited your membership?

15

BEFORE YOU BUY A HOME

*Home is the girl's prison and the
woman's workhouse . . .*
GEORGE BERNARD SHAW

Until the 1970s few banks or mortgage companies would lend money to an unmarried woman to purchase a home. If they did, the interest rates were excessive. Consequently, it is only recently that women have emerged as a significant market for housing. Women without husbands began owning and buying homes. Some of these women are divorcées. Others have never married. Some women purchase homes with a female or a male companion. This pattern of home ownership reflects the changing nature of the family.

Unfortunately, in this area of the law, as in many others, there is a decided lag in the development of rights and protections for the female home owner or buyer.

Originally the tacit premise of the law was that a home was purchased by a couple. In order to protect a wife in the event of the husband's desertion or bankruptcy, she had a vested interest in the dwelling. The husband could not sell or mortgage it without her consent. By law, the home was owned by them jointly. If he died, she succeeded to the ownership. If he had financial reverses, the creditors could not take the home. And if they divorced, she had an interest in the property. This was true even if the husband had furnished the entire amount of the purchase price.

Today, with the prevalence of divorce and with the new laws of equitable distribution of marital property, *ownership of a home is no longer the financial bulwark of security for a wife that it was formerly.*

If you purchase a home with a person to whom you are not married, you have none of the protections of a wife. If you own the property jointly, regardless of which of you contributed the purchase price, and he becomes bankrupt, his creditors can attach his share of the premises. You may have to sell *your* home to pay *his* debts.

If you come to a parting of the ways, your rights depend entirely on the agreement the two of you made. If the property you co-own with a person to whom you are not married is mortgaged and there is a default, even though he promised to make the payments, the mortgagee can foreclose on your home. Similar problems prevail when you purchase a home with a female friend.

In many instances your rights may depend on your status—married or unmarried. Your rights also depend on the kind of ownership you have.

In the past generation there have been many changes in the home market. There are now new kinds of homes and new types of legal relationships. Before making a purchase, you should investigate all these options.

Housing complexes for the wealthy, the middle class, and the poor have become popular in cities, suburbs, and rural areas as the problems of maintaining an individual detached home with garden have increased. Household help and yard help are hard to find and expensive. With so many women in the work force, fewer married women have the time, energy or inclination to do considerable housework or gardening. Accordingly, the more maintenance-free types of dwellings appeal. Many women alone find such homes attractive.

The mobile home or trailer offers home ownership at far less cost than a traditional house or apartment. Renovated factories and lofts also offer space for less money.

Types of home ownership have also expanded. You can still buy an individual house in fee simple, owning the building and the land. But you can also buy a condominium or a cooperative dwelling. In most condominiums, you buy and own a space in a larger dwelling, either an apartment building or a housing complex. The condominium owns the land, the exterior of the building, and the common spaces such as halls and lobbies. You can sell your condominium on the open market and take whatever profit or loss there is. You are subject to many restrictions on the use of the property even though you are the owner.

A cooperative is similar to a condominium except that you are limited in the sale of your cooperative. The purchaser must be approved by the other members. In some cooperatives the property must be sold back to the cooperative and the owner/seller does not get the benefit of a rise in the market. Ownership in many cooperatives entails restrictions on the use of your dwelling.

Mobile parks also impose restrictions on the occupancy of mobile home owners. Some limit occupancy to married couples. Others exclude children. Some restrict the external improvements that the owners can make to their own dwellings.

If you rent a house or an apartment, the landlord has obligations and the law now affords you many protections. The landlord warrants the habitability of the premises. If there is no heat in the winter, if the water is cut off, if the roof leaks, or the plumbing does not work, you, as a tenant, have rights. You can go to court and the law will compel the landlord to provide all these elements of a habitable dwelling even if you are delinquent in the rent. This is usually a lengthy and costly procedure.

Many tenants in large buildings or complexes, including public and subsidized dwellings, have banded together in tenants' associations so that they can more easily sue the landlord. It is a legitimate practice to withhold some or all of the rent if the landlord fails in his obligations.

When you own a home, you have none of these protections. You are responsible for the maintenance of the dwelling, the heat, water, electricity, and all the other necessities of modern living.

In all types of ownership, as contrasted with renting, you are responsible for repairs, maintenance, taxes, and often other charges.

Today home ownership of any type of home is a viable option for every woman who has a steady income or moderate assets, regardless of her marital status. Because a woman now has the same right as a man to purchase every kind of home and theoretically, at least, equal access to financing, every woman who has an income or assets should consider the advantages and disadvantages of home ownership.

In this chapter we shall point out the problems that you will face in purchasing or owning a home depending upon your marital status, the person or persons with whom you purchase the home and the person or persons who live in the dwelling with you.

When you purchase a home of any kind it is essential to remember the old caveat: *Let the buyer beware!*

If the seller makes fraudulent written inducements to get you to buy, you may recover damages in a lawsuit. It is possible in some states to set aside the sale. But you will incur many expenses and a great deal of trouble that you can avoid by careful inspection and investigation *before* . . .

Here is a useful checklist to guide you before you sign an agreement to purchase any kind of dwelling:

- ♦ Have the premises inspected by a competent engineer or architect. Be sure the dwelling is structurally sound, that it does not have termites, that the heating system works, and that the plumbing is in good condition.
- ♦ Have the title checked and get title insurance. If you buy a home that the seller does not own or is subject to mortgages or other liens, you are not protected unless you have title insurance.
- ♦ Check the zoning. Make sure that the property is zoned for the purposes for which you intend to use it.
- ♦ Have the property surveyed unless there is already an up-to-date survey so that you will know exactly what you have bought. Do not rely on the fact that there is a fence, a hedge, or other visible demarcation. It may be on the neighbor's property.

- See if there are any restrictive covenants. Many residential properties are subject to covenants that restrict ownership or residence to Caucasians, Protestants, or single families. Racial and religious covenants are now unconstitutional. But you may be buying a lawsuit with your home.
- Get an appraisal of the property from someone recommended by your realtor or real estate board. Just because you think it is a good buy does not mean that the property has a resale value equivalent to the purchase price. And remember that while home ownership is often thought to be a good financial investment that offers security and tax deductions, in fact, it may turn out to be a financial disaster. While most young couples buy a house with the expectation that their marriage will last and that they will live in the home for many years, they may encounter unanticipated changes in their circumstances and have to sell the property.
- Retain a lawyer. Usually there are three parties to the sale of a home: the seller; the realtor; and the buyer. The realtor may be your friend. He or she may be very knowledgeable and helpful. But the realtor's interest is not the same as yours. The realtor is paid a commission on the sale. It is in the realtor's interest to see that you buy the property. But the purchase may not be in your best interest.

There are many times when it is not necessary to retain a lawyer. *Buying a home is not one of them.* If your lawyer fails to check on the title or the zoning or other problems that you may not even be aware of, you can sue your attorney for malpractice. If you are ignorant or negligent, *you* must bear the brunt of your mistakes.

The Five Commandments apply to the purchase of a home. Protect thyself. Anticipate disaster. Discuss money *before* you buy.

Here are true experiences of some women who have been my clients or appeared in court before me. Their stories should help you anticipate some of the most common problems that occur when a woman buys a home.

Check the Zoning Laws

Many women, especially when they have young children and cannot afford good day care, believe that they can earn a living and care for their children by working at home. Marlene was one of these caring, hard-working women.

Zoning laws in most residential areas restrict the uses to which a home can be put. There are many things you can do legally in your own home. You can do secretarial work, freelance writing or art work, computer data processing, sewing, and piecework for manufacturers. But there are many occupations and trades that women follow that are prohibited. If you contemplate operating a beauty parlor or a school in your home or even having a professional office in your home, have a lawyer check the zoning laws *before* . . .

Marlene bought a large old house with a big back yard, intending to operate a day care center for preschool children. She told the owner of the house her plans. After Marlene moved in and began operating the center, the neighbors went to court and got an injunction to prevent operation of the center. The zoning laws prohibited this commercial activity. Marlene sued the former owner of the property. Marlene lost.

Ethel is a divorcée with three sons. She wanted a house in the country where her boys could play ball and live an outdoors life. She found just the place she wanted. It was in a good neighborhood. But the house was in poor condition and needed a lot of repairs. It had three acres of ground that Beth did not need or want.

"I can sell two acres and with the proceeds pay to renovate the house," she told the realtor.

And so Ethel happily bought the property. When she put two acres of land up for sale, she discovered to her dismay that the area was zoned for three-acre homes. She cannot sell the land unless she wins a lawsuit to have the zoning declared unconstitutional.

The lawyer she consulted told her that she has a good chance of winning if she is prepared to take the case to the Supreme Court of her state. Similar zoning laws have been held unconstitutional. But even if she wins in the lower court the other property owners will appeal. It will be at least three years until the case is finally decided. Such a lawsuit is expensive and the outcome is far from certain. Ethel has put the property up for sale. Meanwhile she is hard pressed for money. She and the boys are living in a small rented apartment.

Ask About Restrictive Covenants

Women frequently find it desirable to share living quarters with a friend or colleague. Because the incomes of most women are insufficient to support themselves and maintain a household, they must share expenses. This is a problem that middle-class men do not face as often. Also, in many neighborhoods it is unsafe for a woman to live alone.

A woman is also more likely than a man to open her home to a needy student or distant relative or an abandoned child.

These sensible and generous acts often violate restrictive covenants limiting occupancy of a house or apartment to members of a family. This is another of the many gender-neutral laws that in operation bear heavily and unfairly on women.

Sondra is a school teacher. When she and her husband were divorced, they sold their home because she could no longer afford to maintain it. He earns a substantial living as an engineer. With his share of the equitable distribution he bought a posh apartment.

With her share of the distribution Sondra decided to buy another home with a colleague. She could not afford to buy or maintain the home on her salary alone. The house they found was a good buy in a nice residential neighborhood near their school. After Sondra and her friend took title and moved in, they were faced with a lawsuit brought by the neighbors. Then she learned that the houses on that block were subject to a restrictive covenant limiting ownership to a single family.

She was served with interrogatories, questions that must be answered under oath before the case comes to trial. The first question was, "What, if any, is your relationship to the co-owner?"

Sondra answered truthfully, "We are not related."

The lawyer for the neighbors promptly filed a motion for judgment on the pleadings, that is, a court order finding that Sondra's possession of the house was illegal. This order was entered before trial.

At great trouble and expense, Sondra retained a lawyer who defended her on the ground that the covenant was illegal. The purpose of the covenant, the lawyer argued, was to prevent the single-family homes from being used as boarding houses.

When the case came before me, counsel for the neighbors admitted that the two women were not running a boarding house. But, he argued, each of these women has an automobile. That increases traffic and is undesirable.

"Would you have any objection if the two women were sisters?" I asked.

"No, your honor," he replied. "They would be a family."

"If they were sisters, each one might own her own automobile," I pointed out. "Do you claim you have the right to demand the birth certificates or marriage licenses of any persons who buy a house on this block?"

His answer was "Yes."

I held the restrictive covenant unconstitutional as applied to these two women because it invaded their right of privacy. Other courts have reached different decisions.

When Unmarried Couples Buy a Home

If you buy a residence with a person to whom you are not married you will face many problems in the event that you come to a parting of the ways. You will also have problems if you lease a residence with an individual to whom you are not married.

These legal questions are novel and the law is still being developed. In grandma's day, most landlords refused to rent to an unmarried couple. Some condominiums and cooperatives still have such restrictions and so do many retirement complexes.

Similar difficulties arise in connection with the leasing of rent-controlled properties occupied by unmarried couples. In the event of death, does the survivor of an unmarried couple have the right to occupy the apartment? Can the landlord take back the premises? Can the family of the deceased? These are questions you should investigate *before* . . .

Jessie and Bert are elderly divorcées who do not wish to re-marry. Both have children to whom they wish to leave their money. Jessie's divorce settlement provides for adequate support until she remarries. If she marries Bert, she will have to spend all her capital on living expenses and she will have nothing for her children. Bert is living on a small pension. He cannot afford to support himself and Jessie.

When Jessie divorced, she took her cash settlement and bought an apartment in a retirement complex. She and Bert thought that they could enjoy their remaining years together if he moved into Jessie's apartment. The management of the retirement institution, however, will not permit unmarried persons to share an apartment. If Jessie sells her apartment she will lose a substantial sum of money and will be unable to purchase another apartment.

The fine print in the agreement of purchase clearly specifies that only single persons and married couples are eligible to live in the complex. Her lawyer has advised her that a lawsuit would be expensive and probably unsuccessful.

If you, like Jessie, under your divorce agreement lose your alimony if you remarry, then you should carefully investigate the restrictions on occupancy by unmarried couples in any dwelling you contemplate buying.

Divorcées of every age do fall in love again. They want to share their lives with a compatible person. Even when you divorce and romance is far from your thoughts, it is a contingency that you should not rule out. Although some divorced wives pay alimony to their former husbands, it is women who are most often hurt by this standard provision in many divorce agreements.

When you consider investing in the purchase of a home, be sure you can live in it as you wish and with the person or persons of your choice before you buy.

Getting a Mortgage

Clara is a single mother who has a responsible job and makes a good income. Her credit rating is excellent. When her daughter was six years old, Clara decided to buy a house in a suburb where the schools were reputed to be very good. She found a house within her means and signed an agreement of sale contingent on getting a mortgage.

When she applied to the local bank, she was refused. The loan officer of the bank, she discovered, lived in that neighborhood and was, as he put it, determined to keep up the neighborhood. An unwed mother, he thought, would lower property values.

The realtor was sympathetic and suggested that she look elsewhere. Clara was outraged. "This is gender discrimination," she told him. "I am going to sue you and the bank."

Six months later Clara did sue. Two years later she won. But meanwhile the house was sold to another purchaser, a married couple. If Clara had filed suit at once, it would have acted as a lien on the property and it is unlikely that a prospective purchaser would have bought the house knowing that he could lose it. Clara did recover sufficient damages to pay for a more expensive home.

Sue and Steve had been married for fifteen years. They bought their expensive house five years ago at the top of the market when Steve was making lots of money. They assumed the mortgage of the previous owner.

Steve ran into troubled times. He could not sell the house except at a substantial loss. He was having marital difficulties with Sue. He wanted to reduce the marital assets in anticipation of a divorce. His solution was to obtain a large second mortgage. This would give him substantial ready cash and reduce the value of the marital property and the amount he would have to pay Sue when he got his no fault divorce.

Sue was unaware that Steve was contemplating a divorce. She knew he was short tempered and testy but attributed his irritability to his money problems. One evening Steve came to her with a sheaf of papers, each marked with a red X on a signature line and asked her to sign them.

"What are they?"

"Business papers for me to get a loan."

"If the money is for your business, why should I sign?"

"Because you are my wife."

And so she signed what turned out to be a note for $100,000 and a second mortgage on the house.

Sue did not discover what she had signed until she retained a lawyer to represent her in the divorce action that Steve brought.

Her efforts to set aside the second mortgage failed.

Whenever your husband asks you to sign legal papers, *beware!* That should be a warning that you are giving up rights that you have under the law. Otherwise your signature would not be required.

A home owned by a married couple belongs in part to the wife. If you are married and own a home or stocks or other securities jointly, your husband cannot sell or encumber the property without your consent. But, if you do sign, even in ignorance, the law will assume that you gave consent unless you are feeble-minded or have been declared incompetent. The persons who rely on those documents have a right to assume that you signed knowingly and intelligently. The law will protect *them*, not *you*.

Watch Out for Termites

Beth is a single woman. She loves dogs and gardening. For years she wanted a house in the country. When she received an unexpected inheritance from an aged aunt, she determined to buy the house of her dreams. After a long search she found just what she wanted, an old colonial house with beautiful grounds and a little stream. It was her dream come true.

She bought it, moved in and lovingly furnished the place with antiques. All went well for a year. And then she noticed that the front porch was sagging perilously. She called in a contractor who told her that the place was riddled with termites. It would cost her thousands of dollars to shore up the sagging foundations and get rid of the termites.

Beth went to the nice realtor who had found the house for her. "You told me it was in good condition," she said.

"I didn't make any warranties. You could have had the place inspected. You could have gotten insurance. You knew it was an old house. Why didn't you?"

"I trusted you," Beth said.

When Beth consulted a lawyer, she told Beth that she should have retained counsel before she made the purchase. It was too late to recover either from the realtor or the previous owner.

All too many women assume that the professionals they deal with are honest and have their interests at heart, especially women who have not been in the business world. During most of their lives they have relied on their fathers and then their husbands. Many women go through life without consulting a lawyer. They know not to trust a used car dealer who says the car was owned by a little old lady who never drove it, but they assume that realtors, insurance agents, brokers, and other licensed people with whom they deal can be relied on. What they do not recognize is that these individuals are in business and their primary purpose is to make a sale on which they get a commission, not to protect *you*.

When you make a large or important purchase, you should have someone who has *your* interest as his or her primary concern. When you retain a lawyer, he or she is obligated by law and by professional ethics to represent you. Standard agreements of sale are usually drawn to represent the seller, whether it is the sale of a house, an automobile, a work of art, or any other thing of value. Unless you are particularly knowledgeable, you should have someone examine these documents and see that the oral representations made to you are contained in the deed or agreement of sale.

A Wise Purchase

Monica is a forty-five-year-old journalist. She writes a column for the local daily and she also does free-lance journalism. When she got a well-paid assignment from a magazine, she decided to buy a house.

"Why should I continue to spend a good part of my salary on rent? I have no equity, no security, and I don't even like my apartment. I'm going to buy a house," she told her colleagues.

Everyone discouraged her. It would be a constant expense, repairs, maintenance. The house would be vandalized while she was away on a long assignment. What did she need it for anyway?

Monica persevered. She found an old, large house that was structurally sound. She retained an imaginative young architect who drew up plans to establish an apartment on the first floor as a rental, and a bright, airy apartment for Monica on the second floor. She consulted a realtor who advised her that she would have no problem getting a tenant at a substantial rental. She retained a lawyer who got her a zoning variance to renovate the building into two apartments, and she hired a reliable builder.

She got a loan from the bank at the going rate of interest. Six months later Monica moved into her new home. It has everything she has always wanted—a fireplace, a deck with a garden, a study, a country kitchen. Her tenant is a colleague, who pays the rent promptly.

Monica lives the way she wants to and with the income from the rental apartment spends less than she did when she was renting. Real estate has appreciated. She has a substantial asset, a form of security that is better than money in the bank because it gives her enjoyment.

There have been unexpected pluses. Monica belongs to the local neighborhood organization, where she has found many new friends. Because she has a large living room, she can entertain. She can also have meetings for the many causes in which she is interested.

It was a wise, relatively trouble-free decision because Monica remembered the commandments.

She protected herself by retaining competent professionals for every one of the problems that a home buyer faces.

She anticipated disaster by getting a zoning variance before she bought the property and by taking out building insurance.

She acted on her own judgment and not the advice of her friends.

Monica is a happy homeowner.

No one can ensure her happiness with a home. Princess Di is reportedly miserable living in a palace. But if you want to buy a home, whether it is a big house in the country, a small apartment in the city, or a mobile home, you can do so whether you are single, married, or divorced. You can get credit on the same terms as a man or a married couple. You cannot be denied a home because you are a woman or unmarried.

Many of the problems you will face in purchasing a home are the same as those that couples encounter. But because home ownership by a woman on her own is a fairly new phenomenon for average-income women, you must exercise careful precautions so that you receive all the protections that the law allows.

Home ownership can be a wise decision if you investigate the advantages and disadvantages of your available options and the financial benefits and detriments *before* . . .

PART IV

THE
SECOND
HALF

16

BEFORE YOU MAKE A WILL

Thou makest a testament
As worldlings do, giving the sum of more
To that which had too much . . .
WILLIAM SHAKESPEARE

Sophisticated men of property do not wait until they reach old age to have their wills drawn. They know that airplanes crash, automobiles collide, people become ill. All these unpleasant vicissitudes of life can befall the young as well as the old. They prepare in advance so that in the event of some unfortunate incident their wishes will be carried out and their property will not be dissipated in costly and divisive litigation.

When a man gets a good job, starts his professional career, or marries, his friends and family usually advise him to make a will. If he buys life insurance, the salesperson will also probably suggest that he make a will.

Women are seldom given this advice unless they are wealthy. It is usually assumed that a woman has little property or that she will marry and want to leave everything to her husband as the law provides.

Now that the majority of women are or will be in the workforce at some time in their lives and when marriages are far from permanent, women also need to have wills. Every woman from age eighteen onward, regardless of her economic status, has the right to such legal protection. If you do not avail yourself of it, you have no one to blame but yourself.

These documents offer a simple, inexpensive way of obeying the Five Commandments: You will protect yourself. You will anticipate disaster. You will have acted on your own best judgment. You will also have the force of law to carry out your wishes and not have to rely on the good intentions of your husband or other relatives. But you must not wait for an emergency to arise. You must act *before* . . .

You may think that if you have no property and very little money that you do not need a will. However, almost everyone who has ever held a job has had Social Security payments deducted from her salary. These payments are your assets. You have the right to decide who will receive them and any other property you may have or acquire.

Even though you are young and healthy today, accidents can befall anyone. You may fall into a coma and become unable to give consent or instructions as to your wishes. You also may have the misfortune to be in a permanent vegetative state after an injury or illness. Unless you execute a living will, the doctors and hospital will be compelled to keep you alive indefinitely even though you are brain dead.

You may not be old or wealthy, but whatever property you have is undoubtedly important to you. You have friends and relatives that you would like to help or remember and you may have relatives who do not need your property or toward whom you do not feel kindly disposed. If you die intestate these unloved, undeserving relatives may receive your property instead of those you love and want to help.

Unless you make provisions, a distant relative or unknown lawyer or banker may be in charge of disposing of your assets. Ask yourself who will carry out your wishes. Will it be someone you do not know or trust? You can choose a person you do trust who will deal honestly and fairly and also intelligently with your hard earned savings and precious keepsakes.

You should make a will even if you are only eighteen years old. In most jurisdictions, eighteen is the legal age of maturity when without parental consent you can enter into contracts, join the armed forces, buy property, have an abortion or other medical procedure, and make a will.

Every woman should consider executing three documents. They are:

1. A will disposing of her property and, if she has minor children or dependents, appointing a guardian for them
2. Power of attorney
3. A living will

Many women find the thought of death so painful that they refuse to prepare for the inevitable. There is nothing ghoulish or gruesome about taking sensible precautions to guard against accidents. Prudent people have life insurance, health insurance, and insurance on their property. We hope to live long, healthy lives and never need this protection. We hope our property will not be burned, stolen, or vandalized. But we insure against these contingencies for peace of mind and to avoid catastrophic consequences.

We also have annual medical checkups, mammograms, and innoculations, not because we think we are in imminent danger of serious illness or death, but wisely to take preventive measures to ward off illness.

Providing at an early age for disposition of one's property is common sense. If nothing untoward happens to you, you have lost nothing but a little time and a small legal fee. In return you will have peace of mind and as much assurance as the law can provide.

If you have children, you will want to protect them as best you can in case of your death or disability. You can designate a guardian for your children. That person will decide where they are to go to school, their religious education, and all the personal decisions you would make if you were able to do so.

If you do not designate a guardian for your children, the law will appoint your husband. Even if you are divorced, your former husband, if he is the father of your children, will be their guardian and have control of the property they inherit from you. *Is this what you want?*

If you and your children's father are both deceased, the law will probably appoint your parents or his parents guardian of the children and their property. Are these the persons you want to have rear your children and control their property? If not, then execute a will appointing the persons you want to have these powers. You can appoint one person to be guardian of their persons and someone else to be guardian of their property, a person you trust to manage money wisely. You can also appoint coguardians.

If you have a lover (male or female), that person under the law is not your heir and has no rights to care for you or to receive your estate unless you make a will giving that person those rights. Some wealthy men, like Douglas Cooper, the great art collector, provide for an intimate friend by adoption. This gives the adoptee the rights of a child to inherit and to make decisions for the adopting parent. You can make a similar provision if you wish and if you act *before* . . .

If you do not have much money or property and you are not interested in minimizing taxes, you may not need a lawyer to draw your will. In most communities your local bar association will give you forms for a simple legally valid will that permits you to designate the persons you want to receive your property and estate. However, if there are any complications it is desirable to retain a lawyer. The wishes of many testators have been thwarted because their wills were inexpertly drawn or failed to comply with state law. This is a time when being penny wise is pound foolish.

A will not only ensures that your wishes will be carried out, it also saves your heirs the considerable trouble and expense that is required to transfer property if you die intestate.

If you are ill, temporarily disabled, or out of the country and unable to manage your affairs, *a power of attorney* giving authority to a trusted relative or friend is a wise precaution. This document authorizes the person you designate to take control of your medical treatment, authorize expenditure of funds for your care, and execute legal documents on your behalf.

See the Appendix for a form of power of attorney.

A *living will* is essential in today's world of medical marvels. Doctors can keep a body legally alive, even when a person's brain is dead and she is in a permanent vegetative state. Doctors and hospitals are required by law to keep patients alive even when there is no chance of recovery. Many people believe that a living death imposes extreme emotional hardship on one's family and friends as well as exorbitant expenses.

Most bar associations will provide you with a form for a living will. Many states by statute now recognize the validity of living wills. Some states, like Pennsylvania, however, will not honor the living will of a pregnant woman. Even if your state does not have a law recognizing living wills, if you have one it can help your loved ones to deal with the problems that may arise if you should become permanently and totally disabled.

There are certain defining events in every woman's life when she should think about making a legal testament, a living will, and a power of attorney. These are usually:

- ◆ The legal date of majority in the state of your residence
- ◆ Your first steady job that carries benefits (pension, Social Security, insurance)
- ◆ Purchase of a home or expensive property such as an automobile, work of art, musical instrument, or other valuable thing
- ◆ Taking a trip
- ◆ Joining the military forces
- ◆ Marriage or the beginning of a long-term relationship
- ◆ Motherhood (to protect either a biological or an adopted child)
- ◆ Any surgical procedure
- ◆ Divorce
- ◆ Remarriage
- ◆ Widowhood

- ◆ A substantial change in your economic status
- ◆ When your children become adults
- ◆ When you become a grandmother (either biologically or through adoption)
- ◆ When you enter a nursing home or retirement residence

Any of these events is an occasion for you to reexamine your will and make appropriate changes to conform to these changed conditions.

All these documents should be given to your lawyer, if you have one. If you do not have a lawyer, you should keep the documents in a safe, secure place and notify your relatives and close friends that you have executed these documents and where they are. If you execute a living will you should give a copy to your physician.

The women whose experiences I am about to recount were intelligent and thoughtful. But under the pressure of daily life they neglected to make proper provision for the future. Their experiences should make you realize the importance of acting wisely *now*.

Jenny was nineteen years old when the company car in which she was a passenger was involved in a head-on collision. Jenny was in a coma for several weeks. For months she was unable to speak. Eventually after two years of intensive therapy she recovered. She is now back at work but will need skilled, expensive, medical care for some time.

The accident occurred when Jenny had been on her first real job for only a few months. Her parents had divorced when Jenny was ten years old. Her mother had legal custody of Jenny, who lived with her until she got this job and rented her own apartment. Her parents were not on friendly terms. Although both her mother and father loved Jenny and were deeply concerned about her welfare, the financial and medical problems arising out of the accident caused further hostilities and threatened Jenny's care.

Both her mother and father wanted to be in charge of Jenny's medical treatment and her legal claims against her employer and the driver of the other car. Jenny was legally an adult. She had no will and no power of attorney. Her parents went to court, each claiming to be her natural guardian. The doctors and hospital needed someone to sign consent forms for the necessary surgery. There were numerous decisions to be made with respect to her treatment since all the options involved risk. Jenny's mother was satisfied with the doctors at the hospital to which Jenny was taken by the police. Her father wanted Jenny moved to the hospital where his doctor was on the staff.

The insurance companies offered settlements. It was clear that Jenny as the passenger was not negligent and was entitled to recover damages. But her mother and father could not agree as to accepting the settlements. Jenny's mother thought that they should take the substantial offer so that Jenny could have extra care and treatment that was not covered under her employer's health benefit plan. Her father believed that she could get considerably more money if they litigated her claims.

Jenny's mother suspected her ex-husband and his present wife of being more interested in Jenny's money if she did not recover than in providing for her immediate care. Jenny's father believed that Jenny might be unemployable and would need a very substantial amount of money for her future.

Both parents retained counsel. They spent a great deal of money litigating their rights to control Jenny's treatment and legal claims. The hostility between the parents escalated.

The court appointed Jenny's father her guardian because he was a successful businessman and was presumed to be more knowledgeable than her mother who was a school teacher.

When Jenny recovered sufficiently to take charge of her treatment, she wanted to leave the nursing home where her father had placed her and live with her mother. She had to retain a lawyer to have her father removed from her guardianship.

These conflicts could have been avoided if Jenny had executed a power of attorney appointing either her mother or her father to act on her behalf. A will designating the persons to receive her estate would also have avoided the suspicions and recriminations concerning the settlement of her claims.

Carol Cruzen and Karen Quinlan, two young women whose cases were much in the news, were in their twenties when they suffered accidents that left each in a permanent vegetative state. Because they had not executed living wills or powers of attorney, their families were forced to endure years of emotional agony and undergo costly and difficult litigation to terminate medical procedures that could not possibly restore these unfortunate young women to any form of sentience.

You can spare yourself such indignities and save your families if you execute a living will and a power of attorney *before* . . .

Your Legal Heir May Not Be Your Beneficiary of Choice

Miranda was a successful businesswoman. She was the CEO of a small corporation she founded and nurtured. It is now on a stock exchange and Miranda toward the end of her life had only a minority interest. For fifteen years Christie, a young protégé, lived with Miranda. Christie was bright and had a good position with the company. But Miranda knew that when she retired or died, Christie would probably lose her job. Many people resented her and her relationship with Miranda.

Miranda had been divorced for many years. She had one son, a successful doctor who lived half a continent away. She saw him and his family only on special occasions or when she took them on a vacation. Her son's wife did not turn out to be the loving daughter Miranda had hoped for.

Like many busy people, Miranda put off making her will. She was only sixty-four and in good health. The future appeared to stretch ahead as secure as the past. Then—Miranda was in an accident. She suffered internal and head injuries. The doctor told her that an operation was necessary to save her life but that it was risky and she might not survive.

Christie was at the hospital with her. Miranda told her to get her long-time friend and trusted lawyer at once. "I must make my will before the surgery," Miranda said.

The lawyer came promptly and drew a will in which she left substantial sums to several women's charitable organizations in which she was deeply involved. She established trust funds for her grandchildren. She gave her valuable art collection to her son. And she left her home and furnishings, her jewelry, and all the rest of her property to Christie. She named her lawyer executor of her will. She also executed a living will in which she gave Christie power of attorney to decide on her medical treatment. The doctor and two nurses witnessed the will just before Miranda was wheeled into the operating room.

Two days later Miranda's son arrived. Miranda was in a coma. Her son examined her medical charts and consulted with her surgeon. The doctor recommended a second operation to relieve the swelling and pressure on the brain. If that operation was successful, Miranda might make a complete recovery, but there was only a fifty percent chance of success.

"Does my mother have a living will?" her son asked.

He was told that she did.

"Well, then," he said, "I oppose the surgery."

He was shown the living will in which Christie was given the power of attorney. She ordered the operation to proceed.

Miranda regained consciousness after the surgery. But three weeks later she died of pneumonia and other complications.

Miranda's lawyer called her son, Christie, and representatives of the chartities to his office for a reading of the will. Her son was furious and promptly moved to set it aside, charging Christie with undue influence and alleging that his mother was incompetent when she made the will. If the will was set aside, the son would receive all her property and neither Christie nor the charities would get anything.

The litigation was bitter, protracted, and expensive. The son made many accusations against Christie. Some employees and officers of the corporation testified for the son and against Christie. She quit her job in dismay over the venomous attacks on her.

Seven expert medical witnesses testified, in addition to Miranda's doctor, who had witnessed the will. The case dragged on for months with charges and countercharges.

When Miranda's executor was presented with a bill from the hospital for more than $100,000 for the three weeks she was hospitalized after the surgery, the son obtained an injunction barring the executor from paying the bill. He claimed that since Christie had ordered the unsuccessful surgery, it was her obligation to pay.

After more than a year and legal fees of tens of thousands of dollars that Christie could not afford, she implored her lawyers to settle. She just wanted to leave town and get away from the hostility that was poisoning her life.

The charities relinquished their claims because, under the law, a bequest to charity made less than a month before death is voidable. Miranda's son agreed to let Christie have the house and furnishings. He got the jewelry and money as well as the art collection. Miranda's attorney was dismayed. As executor he could have carried on the fight, but Christie begged him not to.

He discussed the case with me before he agreed to the settlement. "I consider this a travesty," he said. "This is precisely what Miranda did not want. She was as competent as you or I. But Christie is near a nervous breakdown. I don't want to endanger her health."

Deathbed wills are difficult to uphold in the face of determined opposition by the next of kin. The only way to avoid such hostility and protracted litigation is to act *before* . . .

A Dying Mother and Her Children

Marlene was thirty-five when she first noticed a lump on her breast. She was a happy, pretty woman who had always enjoyed good health. She was married to her childhood sweetheart. They had two sons aged ten and twelve.

Marlene and her husband rushed to their family physician, who examined her and told them it was simply a benign cyst, nothing to worry about. Delighted they went home and tried to put the frightening thought out of their minds. Marlene bought a book on breast cancer and regularly did self-examination. Six months later she felt another lump. They went back to the doctor, who again examined her and gave the same reassuring diagnosis.

When she felt another lump, Marlene talked to her best friend, who urged her to go to a specialist. This doctor immediately performed a biopsy. Marlene then learned that she had a malignancy and a mastectomy was performed. Unfortunately by this time it was too late. The malignancy had spread. She was told that she had six months to a year to live.

Marlene suffered a severe depression. Her friend advised that she see a psychologist to help her deal with these last difficult months. She also urged her to see a lawyer.

I saw Marlene, her husband, and her sons in court. She was the plaintiff in a malpractice suit against the family doctor. She was grossly fat and unattractive. Her husband was hostile, withdrawn; the children bewildered.

The psychologist testified in the presence of the lawyers but, at their suggestion, out of the presence of Marlene, the boys, and her husband. The psychologist showed a picture of Marlene before the operation. She was slim, vibrant, and attractive. She also presented to the court the letters that Marlene had written to her sons to be given them on certain occasions: bar mitzvah, high school graduation, college graduation, marriage, the birth of a grandchild whom Marlene would never see.

These heartrending letters that were Marlene's attempt to retain contact with her sons from the grave also revealed that she was aware that her husband had a new girlfriend whom he expected to marry after Marlene's death. She expressed concern that the boys should use any money she recovered from the malpractice suit to pay for their college education.

Both Marlene and her husband were represented in the malpractice action by the lawyer her husband had retained. It is customary for the same attorney to represent both the injured persons and his or her spouse because the spouse has a legal right to sue for loss of consortium (her companionship). When the couple is happily married this presents no problem. In Marlene's case it did.

Marlene was naturally distraught. She was unable to argue with her husband about the choice of a lawyer, the disposition of the proceeds of the trial, or even the care of the children. She wept. And he made the decisions.

After two days of testimony the insurance carrier for the physician made a substantial offer of settlement to be paid in one lump sum for Marlene and her husband in whatever proportions they wished.

The lawyer was in an unenviable position. He knew, as I did, that Marlene's husband intended to remarry. He also knew that Marlene wanted all her property to go to her children. Her only assets were her engagement ring and the settlement from this lawsuit.

I indicated my concern for the welfare of the children. The amount of the recovery allocable to her medical expenses would go by law to her husband even though he had not paid them because they were covered by insurance. He was also entitled to recover for loss of consortium.

By dint of persuasion and shame, the lawyer obtained the husband's consent to place all the money received in the settlement in trust for the sons. Had Marlene's husband refused, the lawyer would have been obliged to tell either Marlene or her husband to retain other counsel so that Marlene's interests could be adequately represented. The settlement might not have proceeded in face of such complications. Marlene would have had to go through the remainder of the trial and take the risk that the jury might award her less than the offer of settlement.

I, the judge, was restricted in what I could do for her. I had no control over the settlement although I could express an opinion, when asked, as to whether it was fair and reasonable. I could not compel the husband to forego his rights. And I could not order Marlene to obtain separate counsel.

If Marlene had earlier executed a power of attorney appointing a friend or relative, that person would have retained separate counsel for Marlene, and the children's interests would have been protected. If Marlene had made a will she would have left all her estate to her children. Her husband could have taken against the will. But he would have been obliged to go to court to do so. He would have received one-third of her estate and her sons two-thirds.

Who Will Be Guardian of Your Child?

Sybil and Wilbur were in their thirties when they were killed in an automobile accident. Their car was struck head-on by a drunk driver who had crossed the median strip. They had been married ten years and had one daughter Belinda whom they dearly loved. Neither Sybil nor Wilbur had a will. They had no property except their automobile. But Wilbur as part of his employment benefits had a life insurance policy for $300,000.

Under the law, since Sybil was younger, it was presumed that Wilbur had predeceased her. Sybil's mother was dead. Her father as her legal next of kin became the guardian of Belinda.

Sybil and her father had not agreed on anything. He was opposed to higher education for women. Sybil had left home and worked her way through college. She had often talked of her daughter's future. She wanted her to go to college.

But Sybil's father had control of the proceeds of the insurance policy and was appointed guardian of Belinda. Had Sybil executed a will, she would have appointed her sister-in-law guardian of Belinda and trustee of her estate because the sister-in-law and she had the same views and values.

When Belinda was graduated from high school at age seventeen, her father refused her permission to go to college and refused to give her any of the money from the insurance. When she was eighteen, Belinda went to court to obtain control of her property so that she could go to college.

It took more than a year for the court to reach a decision. The father maintained that Belinda was incompetent and irresponsible because she refused to live in Sybil's home (into which the father had moved). Instead she was living with a friend in cramped quarters, which were all these two young women could afford.

The father called witnesses, including a psychologist. The court compelled Belinda to undergo a psychiatric evaluation. Belinda had no money to retain an expert witness. She had had to save for a year to pay a lawyer who was so outraged by the situation that she took the case for a minimal fee. She called Belinda's high school counselor who agreed to testify without fee. This kindly woman brought all Belinda's school records and proved to the court that Belinda was not only a good student but a responsible person. There was some difficulty in qualifying the guidance counselor as an expert witness. The father's lawyer contended that because she did not have a degree in psychology she could not testify. Belinda's lawyer managed to persuade the judge that a counselor was an expert on young people.

When Belinda was almost twenty, she finally obtained control of her money. There was then only $170,000. The father claimed he had spent $130,000 in supporting and caring for Belinda. Belinda had missed two years when she should have been in college but instead was working as a waitress. She can never regain those two years of her life but she is trying to make up the lost time by going to summer school and taking extra courses.

Belinda replicated Sybil's difficult girlhood, precisely what Sybil did not want to have happen to her beloved daughter. Had Sybil made a will appointing her sister-in-law executrix and guardian of Belinda, all this would have been avoided.

Even if you are young and healthy, as Sybil was, you should make a will *now* to ensure that your wishes will be carried out in the event of an unfortunate accident.

Choose Your Own Lawyer

Naomi and Zeke had been married for more than thirty years. They had no children. They owned a small house and had almost $100,000 in savings. Zeke invested in CDs at a local branch bank.

When he became ill, his niece Clarissa visited them. She suggested that Zeke make a will. She took them to her lawyer, who drew wills for both Zeke and Naomi. Zeke left everything to Naomi and she left everything to him. Both left any remainder to charity.

Clarissa suggested that they make her executrix of their wills. Naomi reluctantly agreed.

When Zeke died ten years later, the lawyer got in touch with Clarissa and the estate was probated. Since all the securities were in the names of both Zeke and Naomi, as the lawyer had instructed them to do, there were almost no taxes to pay and minimal fees. Clarissa, as executrix, knew exactly how much money Zeke and Naomi had and where it was.

After Zeke's death, the neighbors came to pay the usual condolence calls and met Clarissa.

A few weeks later a friend came to visit Naomi. No one was at home. She peered in the window thinking that perhaps Naomi had not heard the doorbell. To her amazement she saw that there was new furniture in the living room. She stopped at Naomi's next-door neighbor's home and asked how Naomi was. The neighbor replied that she had not seen Naomi for some time but that Clarissa was apparently living with Naomi. Yes, she had seen furniture being moved in and the old furniture being moved out. Clarissa had a son who was also living there.

The friend came back a few days later and this time spoke to Clarissa.

"Where is Naomi?" she asked.

"Oh, she's in a nursing home. She's really very ill and I decided that was the best thing for her."

Clarissa refused to tell her the name or address of the nursing home.

Much concerned, the friend went back to the neighbor, who called together all the friends on the block. They then discovered that no one had seen Naomi for several weeks and that the last time they had seen her she was in good health. She had remarked to someone that she was not happy having Clarissa in the house, that Clarissa was doing the shopping and was buying things Naomi did not want.

The neighbors went in a delegation to see Clarissa but could not get any information. In alarm, they retained an attorney. He discovered that Clarissa had taken Naomi's bankbooks to the bank and removed almost all the money in her savings account. She had also cashed a number of CDs. They also noted that Clarissa had a brand new automobile, which was parked in front of Naomi's house. The dealer's name was on the car.

The attorney went to the dealer and discovered that Clarissa had bought the car with cash, not a check. The dealer remembered it clearly because it was such an unusual transaction.

I saw Clarissa, the neighbors, the car dealer, and the bank officials in court. The neighbors had brought a suit on Naomi's behalf, demanding the return of the money from her bank account and the CDs, and the eviction of Clarissa and her son from Naomi's house. Clarissa's lawyer moved to have the case thrown out of court. These people had no standing to represent Naomi, he alleged.

"Where is Naomi?" I asked. I ordered Clarissa to tell me the name and address of the nursing home and issued an order that she be brought to court.

Clarissa's lawyer objected on the ground that Naomi was too ill to come to court. He presented a doctor's affidavit to that effect. I appointed a physician to examine Naomi. He reported that she was extremely distraught but that her appearance in court would not be deleterious to her health.

The following week she appeared in court. She testified that Clarissa had taken her bankbooks and CDs without Naomi's permission. When Naomi questioned her, Clarissa became very angry. The next day she said that she would take Naomi to the bank and show her that everything was all right. Instead, she took Naomi to the nursing home and left. Naomi had no money with her to take a taxi from the nursing home. The nursing home refused to let her make any phone calls.

The proprietor of the nursing home was also in court demanding payment for Naomi's care. She testified that Clarissa had brought Naomi there saying that Naomi was deranged and was not to have contact with anyone. The proprietor also testified that she couldn't see anything wrong with Naomi.

A tearful Naomi went home with her neighbors. But the case was far from over. She promptly asked the lawyer whom the neighbors had retained to sue Clarissa and the bank. He also got an order impounding the car.

The nursing home proprietor was advised to sue Clarissa. Naomi's lawyer also failed a complaint with the local prosecutor.

Eventually Naomi recovered all her money from the bank, which took possession of the car. The bank is now suing Clarissa who, when I last saw her, was out on bail pending trial on fraud and embezzlement.

Naomi told me that she never liked Clarissa. She would have preferred choosing her own lawyer. She did not want Clarissa to be her executrix but the lawyer assured her that Clarissa was a competent person who would take good care of everything. When Zeke and Naomi told the lawyer they intended to leave their money to charity, not to their relatives, Naomi had noted that Clarissa was upset.

This sad story has a happy ending only because of the concern and initiative of Naomi's neighbors. They are poor, unsophisticated people. None of them even knew a lawyer. But they called the bar association, which referred them to a bright young attorney who was just beginning practice and had the time and energy to devote to a most unpromising case.

Had Naomi gone to an attorney who was not Clarissa's friend, he or she would never have suggested that Clarissa be the executrix. If Clarissa had not been the executrix, she would not have been privy to the information regarding Naomi's estate and would have been unable to take advantage of Naomi. Be aware that not all relatives can be trusted.

Your attorney should be your agent and not have a divided loyalty. You can ensure that by making your own selection of counsel. If your attorney reveals information about your will or your estate to anyone, including your relatives, that is malpractice for which he or she can be sued.

When you make your will, be sure that you choose your lawyer carefully. Select as your executrix a neutral, trustworthy individual, not someone who hopes to be a beneficiary of your estate. If you have misgivings about the lawyer or the executor or trustee, get a second opinion. When you contemplate surgery, you are told to get a second opinion. When you are making provisions for your future, you should also be very cautious.

A Husband Also Needs a Living Will

Claire's husband Donald suffered a stroke at the age of forty-seven. For the past three years he has been in a coma, kept alive by intravenous feedings. He is in a hospital tended by nurses around the clock. Donald was an official in the state government. His stroke occurred at a conference with state legislators. Legally this was a work-connected injury for which he was entitled to payment for his medical care for a maximum of three years.

Although Donald had been instrumental in preparing legislation authorizing recognition of living wills in his state, he had neglected to make such a will. When the legislation was enacted, Claire had suggested that she and Donald see their lawyer and execute living wills. Both Claire and Donald were in good health. There seemed to be no urgency about the matter. Claire brought the subject up several times but Donald procrastinated. She was reluctant to discuss a subject that he obviously found uncomfortable.

They have two teenaged children. Their only assets are their mortgaged house, a five-year-old car, and Donald's state benefits. Claire has gone back to work full time but her salary is not adequate to support her and the children, and pay for Donald's costly care once his benefits run out.

Claire is neither a wife nor a widow. The children suffer terrible anxiety. They vacillate between believing that their father will miraculously recover and recognizing that he won't. The older child, who was an A student, is not doing well in school. He will need a scholarship to go to college but if his schoolwork does not improve he will not receive one. The younger child clings to her mother and resents the fact that her mother has no time for her between her job and going to the hospital to see Donald.

A man Claire met at work takes her out occasionally and this provokes hostility from the children.

"Dad is still alive. How can you date another man?" they say belligerently. They accuse her of wishing Donald's death. Claire does not know what she wants. She simply struggles to get through each day and fears what will happen when Donald's health benefits run out. Until he reaches the age of sixty-five he is not eligible for his substantial pension. But by then it will be too late to pay for the children's college tuition.

Claire could not have prevented Donald's tragic illness. But she could have avoided the financial and emotional problems she and the children are suffering if she had obeyed the Five Commandments. She did not protect herself. She did not anticipate disaster. She did not wear a velvet glove over an iron hand and insist that she and Donald execute living wills. And she did not discuss money with her husband.

You must discuss your future and that of your children with

your husband before tragedy overtakes you. If he is reluctant to make a will, tell him you are going to make a will and a living will and urge him to go to an attorney with you. When he sees that you are trying to protect him in the event of some tragedy befalling you, he will probably realize that he should make the same provisions for you. It is better to have a few unpleasant hours of discussion about possible disasters than to spend a lifetime of misery as the result of failing to take these simple protective measures.

The Comfort of Wise Precautions

Josephine is fifty-two, a computer programmer who earns a very good salary and has substantial savings. She is unmarried and childless. Josephine has a beloved sister who is divorced and has three children she supports. Her brother who lives in another state is married and has one child. He is very successful. His wife and Josephine are not friendly.

Josephine wanted her property to go to her sister and the sister's children. Sensibly she went to a lawyer and explained the family situation and her wishes.

"What will happen if I don't make a will?" she asked.

"Your property will be divided equally between your brother and sister. If either one predeceases you that sibling's share will go to his or her offspring."

"My sister has three children and my brother only one child," she reminded the lawyer.

"Your brother's child would receive his half. And your sister's three children would share her half."

"That is exactly what I don't want to happen," Josephine exclaimed.

The lawyer drew up a careful will leaving sums to Josephine's alma mater for scholarships for deserving women mathematics students, a few tokens of affection to her brother and his son, and all the rest of her estate to her sister and in the event her sister predeceased her to the sister's children in equal shares.

Josephine was planning a trip to the Orient. The day before she was to leave she called her attorney.

"I want to execute my will today," she told her. "I can't go away for two months, with all the vicissitudes of travel, without taking care of this matter."

On the way to the airport she stopped at the lawyer's office and executed her will and a living will.

Josephine's plane skidded off a wet runway in Burma. She was injured and flown back to the United States for extensive surgery. She told me after she recovered that her greatest comfort during the fright of the accident was the knowledge that she had taken care of her sister and her beloved niece and nephews and that if the brain surgery was not successful that she would not be a living vegetable.

The law zealously protects the wishes of a testator, whether that individual is male or female. You have the same right as a man to designate the persons you wish to receive your property, to administer it, to be guardian of your children, and to act on your behalf if you should become disabled. These are significant rights. But unless you exercise them while you are well and in sound mental condition you will forfeit them, and the law itself will decide these matters for you.

Under the law it is presumed that your husband and children are the natural objects of your bounty. If they are not the persons you wish to benefit, then you must have a will. If you die intestate with minor children, the law will also designate their guardian. You have relinquished your right to choose in a matter that may be of great importance. And if you become ill and unable to make your own decisions, who will make them for you? If you do not make that crucial choice, the law will do it.

On the other hand, if you are of sound mind and foolishly or naively and trustingly give away your property or give control of it to someone else, the law will not protect you. Nor will it save you if you permit others to coerce you into making decisions that are not in your best interest.

The time to make a will, a living will, and designate a power of attorney is *now* when you are well and not in physical or emotional distress and you bear in mind the Five Commandments: *Protect thyself. Anticipate disaster.* You may need your money and property in the future even though you do not need it now. *Act on your own judgment.* Your family and advisors may be well intentioned, but you know what your wishes are. *Wear a velvet glove over an iron hand.* Do not let anyone, including your children, influence you to give away your property or to relinquish control of it. And *discuss money* with your spouse, your children, and your advisors.

Your wishes will be carried out and you will be protected if you act wisely now.

BEFORE YOU MAKE A WILL

As we have seen, every woman needs a will no matter what her financial or marital situation is. When your circumstances change, you should change your will. Here are two lists: the significant events in your life and the provisions your will should contain to reflect those events.

Events	Provisions in Your Will
	What you should include in your will when each of these events takes place
1 Your legal maturity.	Living will, power of attorney, designation of beneficiaries.
2 Acquisition of valuable property or employment rights, Social Security payments.	Review of designation of beneficiaries.
3 Marriage.	Reconsideration of person designated in your living will and of power of attorney. If you do not make a designation or reconfirm your designation after your marriage, your husband may by law be given these powers.

Events	Provisions in Your Will
	What you should include in your will when each of these events takes place

---

4 Birth or adoption of a child.

Designate trustee for the estate of the child and a guardian. If you do not designate someone else, your husband will probably be the guardian and trustee. In the event that you and your husband die in a common accident, the law will probably designate his parents or your parents as guardians and trustees.

---

5 Birth or adoption of additional children.

With the birth or adoption of another child, include this child in your will and review your choice of trustee and guardian.

---

6 Grandchildren by birth or adoption.

Unless you include the grandchildren in your will they will probably not receive anything unless your children predecease them.

---

7 Diagnosis of serious illness.

Appoint an attorney to make your medical decisions, or the law will give this authority to your husband.

---

8 Separation from your husband.

Unless you make other provisions, your husband will have all the legal rights of a husband even though you are separated. You cannot prevent him from taking against the will, but you can make it more difficult for him to do so.

Events	Provisions in Your Will
	What you should include in your will when each of these events takes place
9 Divorce.	Divorce terminates all marital rights. You will need a new will, new executor, administrator, trustee, beneficiaries.
10 Remarriage.	If you do not have a prenuptial agreement, all your property will be part of the marital estate. Your new husband will have a right to take against your will.
11 Entering into a relationship.	When you enter into a relationship you may wish to include this person as a beneficiary or give him or her a power of attorney. If you do not designate this person as a beneficiary in your will, he or she will have no right or claim to any of your property.

17

BEFORE THE AUTUMN YEARS

To every thing there is a season, and a time to every purpose under the heaven . . .

ECCLESIASTES

American women have a life expectancy of almost eighty years, the longest of any demographic group in the world. How will you spend your later years? Think about it *now,* whether you are still in school, a young wife or mother, on a career path, or in your middle years.

The problems most women face as they grow older are different from those that men face. Although the law is, for the most part, gender neutral as to the legal issues that most people face during their later years, *life is not gender neutral.*

Older women are more likely to live alone and in poorer circumstances than men. There are more widows than widowers. Older men are more likely to find a second or third spouse to provide a home for them and nurture them.

Most older men have more money than most older women. Most men earn more money annually than most women. Most men work steadily from the time they enter the workforce until they retire. The vast majority of women interrupt their working careers to have children and care for them or to take care of sick relatives. Consequently, most men have accumulated more money and property and receive larger pensions than most

298

women. Women have fewer means and less security than men as they enter the autumn years, *and* they live longer.

As you approach middle age and beyond, you, as a woman, will probably have to make choices that will drastically affect the rest of your life. Whether those years are secure and comfortable or mean and cramped depends in large part on your wisdom and determination *before* . . .

For these reasons women must be mindful of the Five Commandments when making decisions. In this chapter we shall discuss employment problems, widow's rights, control of one's money and property, illness, life care institutions, and freedom.

Employment Discrimination

For many generations women in the workforce were discriminated against when they reached their middle thirties and forties. Their employers, mostly men, preferred younger and prettier female employees. A silver-haired man is considered distinguished. A gray-haired woman is thought of as old. To obtain and keep their jobs, women often dyed their hair and lied about their age.

Sophia went to work for her company when she was a youthful fifty. On her application she lied and said she was forty. When she reached sixty-five she tried to claim her pension benefits. But the company records have her at age fifty-five. She will have to work an extra ten years that she had not anticipated.

The law now prohibits discrimination in employment on the basis of age. When you apply for a position you cannot be asked your age. Nor can you be asked the year you graduated from school, which would, of course, roughly indicate your age. You no longer have to lie or engage in subterfuge to get employment. If you are denied a job or promotion because of age, that is a violation of the law. You can sue and recover. Airline hostesses have won significant legal battles against restrictions as to age, weight, and pulchritude.

However, female TV personalities have been fired or their contracts not renewed because at age thirty or forty they were considered too old for their jobs. Compare the veneration of the media for the elderly Walter Cronkite and the attitude toward women of the same age. (Have you ever seen an aging anchorwoman being widely promoted on national television?) Some of these cases are now being litigated.

There are many legally valid age restrictions on certain jobs in both the private and the public sector. Under the law an age qualification must be related to the job requirements.

Many public offices and jobs have statutory retirement ages. Retirement at a fixed age is mandatory for police, fire fighters, judges, and a host of other positions. Most of these age restrictions have been upheld by the courts. Age restrictions on some nonpublic employment, such as airline pilots, symphony orchestra musicians, and others have been upheld despite bitter protest. The alternative to an across-the-boards retirement policy is individual testing, a demeaning process for many persons.

Some professionals, such as accountants, have by private contract between the firm and its partners a fixed retirement age. So do many law firms and universities. These fixed retirement ages have withstood court challenges.

Some occupations, like the military and many public school systems, permit retirement after a certain number of years of service. Thus, some workers retire in their late forties or fifties, collect their pensions, and hold down a second job. If you have such early retirement rights, the time to plan for a second career is now. If you fail to take advantage of these early retirement rights, you will be giving up the pension rights you have earned because you cannot receive both a salary and a pension from the same employer.

Despite advances in the law, it is still more difficult for a woman in her middle and later years to obtain and keep employment. As we explained in the chapter, "Before You Reach a Dead End," when you are an employee it is essential to heed the First and Second Commandments: *Protect thyself; anticipate disaster.*

Do not give up a good job with seniority and benefits in pursuit of a more lucrative or promising one unless you strike a good new employment contract before you leave your job to accept the new one.

It is also important to remember the Fourth Commandment: *Wear a velvet glove over an iron hand.* Do not meekly submit to a job termination or a refusal of employment if you suspect that either one is being offered on the grounds of age discrimination. Today no woman has to pretend to be young or try to be beautiful to get a job. Often the threat of a lawsuit is sufficient to make an employer reconsider.

You can be gainfully employed until you reach retirement age.

A Widow's Mite

The law protects a widow. As we noted in the chapter, "Before You Marry Again," a widow has substantial rights to her husband's estate unless she relinquishes them by entering into a prenuptial agreement.

When a married man dies, his property is distributed in accordance with his will. If the wife is not satisfied with what he has left her she can take against the will.

If your husband disposes of his assets before his death, there may be nothing in the estate for you. If he puts your inheritance in a trust fund for you, that money will not be under your control but that of the trustee. You may have to get the consent of the trustee to make expenditures in excess of the annual income of the trust.

Many men believe they are doing their wives a favor by relieving them of financial responsibilities. Some women believe that is being considerate. It is not. Your husband is treating you like a child and depriving you of control of your property.

If you do not have control of the money your late husband left for you, you may find yourself in a difficult and painful situation. You are not being suspicious or untrusting if you insist on knowing what your husband does with the property and assets that have been built up during your marriage. Nor are you being selfish to insist on having the ownership and control of this property during your lifetime.

Care and control of money is burdensome. It requires time

and effort to assure that your investments are wise and safe. But the alternative, to leave your financial future in the hands of other people, even your own children, can be disastrous.

Learn from the examples illustrated by the stories of these loving wives and mothers that follow.

Retain Control of Your Property

Wilhemina and Jasper had been married for thirty happy years. They had two grown sons. Jasper, an astute and successful businessman, was sixty-five and in poor health. Wilhemina was a vigorous woman of fifty-six. As each son was graduated from college, he went into Jason's business, a sole proprietorship.

When Jasper had a severe heart attack, the boys came to him and suggested that he turn the business over to them.

"The doctor says you shouldn't work. We're running the factory. Why don't you give us the business now?" they said. "You won't have to worry about anything."

"What about your mother?" Jason demurred. "This factory is my principal asset."

"Incorporate the business and give us each a third of the stock and put one-third in trust for mother," they replied.

Jason did as they asked. He named his lawyer and the two sons as trustee of Wilhemina's trust fund. Shortly thereafter Jason died. Wilhemina was the beneficiary of his insurance policy and by law owned the house. The automobile belonged to the business.

For a year all went well. The stock paid dividends that enabled Wilhemina to live in the family home and maintain her accustomed lifestyle. Unfortunately, the boys were not the diligent, prudent business men that Jason was. They were more interested in golf and their extramarital affairs than in running the factory.

The lawyer was greatly concerned. He came to Wilhemina and told her that the business was failing but that he had found a purchaser, a large corporation that was willing to buy all the stock for $1,000,000 plus $1,000,000 in the stock of the corporation. This was like manna from heaven.

However, both sons were contemplating divorces. If their stock were sold, their wives would receive a substantial amount of money in the equitable distribution. The stock of Jason's company was not listed on any exchange and would probably not be valued at anything like that sum.

Despite the urging of Wilhemina and the lawyer, the boys refused the offer of sale.

"After our divorces are final, we'll sell the business," they said.

Unfortunately, six months later when both sons were divorced, the corporation was no longer interested in buying the business. Shortly thereafter it went into bankruptcy. Wilhemina's only assets are the proceeds of the insurance policy and the house, which she can no longer afford to maintain.

She is now living in a small apartment and looking for a job. The $100,000 from the insurance policy cannot possibly provide for her for the next twenty or thirty years that she may live.

Wilhemina told the lawyer that she did not know that Jason had given the stock to their sons.

"I would never have agreed if he had told me. I knew the boys could not run the business properly," she told the lawyer. "Why didn't you tell me?"

"You were not my client. Jason was. And I followed his instructions. He wanted to spare you the problems of the business."

Esther's husband Leon also thought he was protecting her. He left his entire estate of almost $2,000,000 to Esther but he established a trust for her so that she would not have the problems of managing the money. He named his attorney and his bank as trustees.

They put two-thirds of the money in a fund operated by the bank. In the boom years, the trustees bought junk bonds. The value of Esther's trust soared to almost $4,000,000. Then came the crash. Her trust was worth less than $1,000,000.

That year Esther received less than $30,000 in income. She consulted a lawyer, not her husband's attorney. Then she discovered that the bank and Leon's attorney had been paying themselves fees based on $4,000,000 and that her money was not insured. They were getting more in fees from Esther's estate than she was receiving in income.

"Why didn't they put at least some of the money in CDs and treasury bills so that it was safe? Isn't a trustee supposed to be prudent?"

Unfortunately for Esther, the trustees under the deed of trust drawn by Leon's attorney had unlimited discretion in making investments. Instead of having a carefree old age, as Leon had intended, Esther is pinching pennies and worrying.

When your husband goes to see his lawyer to have his will drawn, go with him. Ask questions. Ask what the fees for managing the estate will be. *Will they be paid each year on the gross value of the estate or on the income?* Remember it is really your money and your future that are at stake. Even though your husband may have been the sole breadwinner of the family, you are entitled to a share of the marital property and at his death you are entitled to a share. If he takes the control away from you, you are not being protected but deprived of what rightfully belongs to you.

Any woman who can read and do simple arithmetic can understand a will and a balance sheet. Ignorance is not a protection but a recipe for being deceived. This is another time when you must act *before* . . . Do not wait until your husband dies. At that time you will probably be emotionally distraught. You will not be thinking of money. But you will have to decide whether or not to take against his will. If your inheritance is tied up in trusts so that you cannot have control, you may be well advised to take against the will and, perhaps, have less money, but have it in your control.

The less money you have, the more important it is to avoid fees and charges taken by banks and executors. There are many things any woman can do for herself. Some sensible women go to the local community college or an adult course run by the local high school and learn about wills and estates. Attending such a course is another wise precaution to take *before* you are older.

Know What Assets Your Husband Has Before . . .

Rita was Everett's second wife. He had one daughter by his first wife, who died a year before he married Rita. Everett was a successful doctor. He had a good income and many investments. He and Rita lived lavishly. When they were married she signed a prenuptial agreement under which Everett agreed to leave her one-third of his estate.

Rita knew that under the law if she did not sign the agreement and Everett did not leave her money in his will she would be entitled to half his estate. His daughter would be entitled to the other half. Since it was a late marriage and they would not have children of their own, Rita thought the agreement was fair.

When Everett retired from his medical practice, his daughter came to him and suggested that he transfer the bulk of his property, consisting of real estate, securities, and a share in a proprietary hospital to her children.

She explained, "I don't need your money. My husband earns a good living. But we have no real assets. We have nothing to leave to our children who may need help. This way you and I will save substantial inheritance taxes. If you leave your property to me, I will have to pay inheritance taxes and when I leave it to my children, they will have to pay taxes, too."

Everett discussed it with his lawyer who agreed that he would save substantial taxes that way. Neither the lawyer nor Everett thought about Rita. And his daughter, who was not fond of her stepmother, certainly was not concerned about her.

The shares in the hospital, the principal asset that Everett had retained, soon became worthless. A health maintenance organization was established in the vicinity and occupancy declined precipitately. The building was sold. The proceeds barely paid the debts, leaving the shareholders with nothing.

After Everett's estate was probated, Rita discovered that she received one-third of $100,000. His daughter received the remaining two-thirds. The daughter was also the beneficiary of her father's insurance policy, which he had not changed when he married Rita.

"I loved Everett very much and I thought he cared for me,"

Rita told me. "Now my feelings have changed. He has left me impoverished. One-third of almost nothing is not very much."

Rita's lawyer, whom she consulted after the will was probated, told her that she should have had Everett establish an irrevocable trust for her. There is nothing she can do now.

When you contemplate marrying a wealthy man who has children, the law will not help you if he gives away his fortune in his lifetime. You cannot prevent him from doing so, but you should be alert to any major transfers of assets.

Whether yours is a first or subsequent marriage, you *must* discuss money with your husband. Know the extent of your assets, and the incumbrances, if any, on your home. A house worth $1,000,000 that has a mortgage of $900,000 is not a substantial asset. Know what your husband's debts are and talk over your financial plans. If he has a financial adviser, go to the meetings your husband has with him. Being fully informed is every woman's best protection.

The time to protect yourself is *before* . . .

A Worthless Promise

Often children are impatient. They do not want to wait until their parents die to receive money and property. A promise by a child to take care of his mother is difficult to enforce.

Miriam has one son whom she loved dearly. When her husband died, he left all his property to her. Miriam was not in good health. Her son suggested that she place all her property in trust with him as trustee so that she would not have to be bothered with the problems of investments. He also urged her to give him a power of attorney so that he could handle her affairs if she became ill or went on a vacation. The trust also provided that at Miriam's death the principal and accumulated income would go to her son. Since Miriam intended to leave everything to him in her will, she had no objections to this provision.

"This way you will have peace of mind, mom. I'll take care of you," he said.

And so Miriam went with her son to *his* lawyer, who drew

up the papers that she signed transferring everything she owned, about $700,000, to her son. She signed a broad power, not limited to occasions on which she might be incompetent. The son had complete control of her property.

Miriam received monthly checks sufficient for her maintenance. All went well until she fell and broke her hip. Surgery was required. When she was ready to leave the hospital, she was using a walker. She could not maintain herself in her apartment without nurses around the clock.

"Don't worry, mom," her son told her. "I've arranged for you to go to a nursing home."

"But I don't want to go to a nursing home," Miriam protested. "I want to go home where I am comfortable and where my friends are."

"Nurses are very expensive. You will deplete your estate," he said.

"I'm seventy-six and have a bad heart. How long do you think I can live? I don't care if I deplete my estate."

"But I do," he replied. "I hope you will live another twenty years. If you do, you will not have enough money to maintain yourself unless you go to a nursing home."

Suddenly Miriam realized that for all her son's protestations of love and promises to care for her, he would not support her if she was in want. It was a bitter moment of revelation.

"I've canceled the lease for your apartment and arranged for you to go to a nice nursing home in the country, where you'll have fresh air and pleasant surroundings."

"How dare you do that without my permission?" Miriam exclaimed.

"I don't need your permission. I have your power of attorney and I am the trustee of your funds."

The "nice nursing home" in the country was a shabby house far from transportation. Miriam's friends could not visit her. She had to share a room with another woman who snored at night and played the TV all day.

The lawyer whom she consulted in the nursing home assured her that her son had the legal authority to do what he did and that a court might conclude that he was acting as a prudent trustee. He did talk to her son, who reluctantly agreed to pay for Miriam to have a private room. Miriam was unhappy and lonely. After two miserable years in the nursing home, Miriam died.

Her doctor told me that Miriam had no organic ailments other than her chronic heart condition. In his opinion she starved herself to death. Her son inherited the more than $600,000 remaining in her trust fund.

When anyone, even your nearest and dearest and most loving child, comes to you with a proposal regarding money, remember the Five Commandments. *Protect thyself.* Retain your own lawyer, not one whom the relative has chosen, and get your lawyer to explain exactly what you will be giving up and what, if anything, you will be gaining. Do this *before* you sign anything.

Saving Taxes May Be Costly

When an heir tells you how to save money on your estate taxes, remember that he or she is primarily concerned with saving money for him or herself, not *you.* You do not have to live in a place not of your choosing to save your heirs money.

Tax reduction is perfectly legitimate and sensible. But, this is one of the times you must consult a knowledgeable expert. The tax laws are a dangerous thicket for the unwary, who will be scratched and bruised unless an expert shows the way. Before you act on financial or tax advice given by a relative/heir, get advice from someone who is concerned with *your* interests. See an unbiased professional whom you select and you pay.

Millicent was a wealthy widow. She had a son who liked the good life but did not like to work. He advised her to move to Florida to avoid estate taxes. They would diminish his inheritance.

Millicent told him that she didn't want to live in Florida. All her ties were in Pennsylvania. But her son persisted. He made her feel selfish, that she was depriving him of his rightful inheritance because of the taxes. So reluctantly Millicent bought a place in Palm Beach.

She soon discovered that three months in the winter was all

she cared to spend in Florida. The rest of the year she spent at her home in Pennsylvania and the family farm in Vermont.

A few years later Millicent became very ill. She moved to a nursing home. Then she called her lawyer to put her affairs in order.

They went over her stock portfolio, her jewels, and other possessions. Then they came to the real estate.

"I won't have to pay state taxes," she told him, "because now I am a Florida resident. I bought this place in Palm Beach. The real estate market has gone down, but I'll surely save more than the loss of the property."

The lawyer asked Millicent some searching questions.

"How much time do you spend in Florida?"

"Three months a year."

"How much time do you spend in Vermont?"

"Four months or five a year."

"And the rest of the time?"

"In Pennsylvania, where I have a rented apartment."

"Where do you vote?"

"In Pennsylvania."

"What are your principal activities in each state?"

"I really don't do anything in Florida. I'm on the board of the orchestra and the art museum in Pennsylvania. And in Vermont I'm on the board of the hospital, the library, and a council of freeholders in our little town."

The lawyer regretfully told Millicent that she was certainly a resident of Pennsylvania and might also be considered a resident of Vermont. Because she spent as much time in Vermont as Pennsylvania and had as many attachments to that state as to Pennsylvania, Vermont could claim that she was domiciled there. Before she bought the Florida property, the overwhelming portion of her year was spent in Pennsylvania. Her estate may have to pay taxes in both Pennsylvania and Vermont. The purchase of the Florida property was a costly expense.

When Millicent expressed dismay, he said, "Why didn't you consult me *before* . . . ?"

Millicent's medical care is very expensive. She is now frantically trying to sell the Florida property. If she cannot dispose of it, she will have to sell the Vermont farm that she wanted to leave to her grandchildren.

Millicent is another woman who ignored the Five Commandments. She did not protect herself. She did not anticipate her illness. She took the advice of her son instead of acting on her own judgment and she allowed him to override her wishes. She did not discuss money with him. She is another unhappy woman who says, "If only I had known *before* . . ."

When You Are Ill

Both women and men of all ages have accidents, fall ill, and need medical care. Despite the growing numbers of women doctors, the medical profession is still male dominated. Many doctors are inclined to treat their female patients like children; they tell them what treatments to take; they do not explain the available options and give the patient the choice. This is particularly true of their attitude toward older women.

If you are legally an adult (in most jurisdictions this means age eighteen or older) and you have not been legally declared incompetent, you have the right to a full explanation of any proposed medical treatment and the risks and the options. You have the right to make the decisions with respect to your treatment. If you are not given a full explanation *in advance,* and something goes wrong, you have a claim for medical malpractice.

No matter how ill you are, you do not have to go to a hospital, hospice, or nursing home if you do not want to, just because your doctor thinks that is the right place for you. If you are older and living alone, your doctor may tell you to go to a hospital or nursing home. Men, however, are rarely railroaded into a nursing home because most doctors assume that the man's wife or children will take care of him. But when a woman is living alone doctors seldom think of other options. Often the doctor believes that is the right thing for you. But you have the right to make that choice.

A Nursing Home Is Not a Prison

Amanda is an intelligent woman of sixty-five, a retired accountant. She is a divorcée living alone. She has not only medical insurance but ample financial means. She underwent a serious operation. When she was ready to be discharged from the hospital, her doctor told her she should go to a nursing home and made the arrangements for her to go to a place of his choosing.

Amanda called me frantically from the nursing home.

"I want to leave this place and they won't let me. They say I must get a discharge from my doctor, and he says I'm not ready to leave. What can I do?"

Amanda had had serious surgery. When I saw her in the hospital she was recovering nicely. She was ambulatory and she was eating a regular diet. She was frail and certainly needed some help in caring for herself. The hospital had told her that she no longer needed hospital care and would have to leave.

I later learned that her doctor had a financial interest in the home that he recommended and routinely suggested that his patients go there. The home looked pleasant but the services were abominable. The help did not change the sheets regularly. The food was unpalatable. And it was difficult to get any care from the overworked nurses. The fees amounted to more than $1,000 a week.

What provoked Amanda's call was the action of a maid who brought Amanda's dinner tray to the room and set it on the dresser. Amanda asked her to bring it to the bed table so that she could eat the meal while it was hot.

"That's the nurse's job, not mine," the maid told her and stalked out of the room.

The nurse did not come for more than two hours. When Amanda asked that the dinner be heated, she was told that if she wanted that kind of service she should hire a private nurse.

I told Amanda that she could leave whenever she wanted. A nursing home is not a prison. Neither is a hospital. A patient can leave whenever she wishes, with or without the approval of the doctor.

Amanda promptly called an ambulette service and went to a

four-star hotel that has room service around the clock, clean sheets every day, and gourmet food. It costs her less than $4,000 a month. A visiting nurse comes once a day to help her bathe and check her condition.

The doctor was furious when he learned that Amanda had left the nursing home. She promptly discharged him and found another doctor who consults her wishes and gives her the care she needs but does not insist on unnecessary services.

When you are ill, you are still in charge of your own life. You need not accept advice that you think is unnecessary or deleterious to your well-being. You can refuse medication that you do not want. And you cannot be ordered to a hospital, nursing home, hospice, or any other facility unless you choose to go there.

If anyone tries to retain you against your will, the law will protect you. If a hospital or nursing home tells you that you cannot leave without permission of the doctor, *call your lawyer.*

The Blessings of the Autumn Season

A woman's older years may be the only time in her life when she is truly liberated. She can find freedom then if she heeds the New Commandments.

In childhood girls are dependent on their parents. In young adulthood, many women are involved in the often overwhelming tasks of career, marriage, and parenting. During these years we women are expected to be sweet, nurturing, and caring.

When women of any age are employed we must be circumspect about what we say and do lest we endanger our jobs. If we are married, we must think at least twice before we speak lest we embarrass our husbands or endanger their positions. It is only in our later years that we are free to be ourselves, to do what we want and say what we think without having to worry that we will embarrass our husbands or endanger their positions. It is only in the later years that women are free to be themselves, to do what they want and say what they think.

There are many advantages to older age. Here is a comparison of the obligations you have when younger and the freedoms you have when you are older.

Youth	Age
1. Perceived as a sex object; time and money spent on beauty treatment and clothes	1. Perceived as an individual; time and money saved
2. Necessity of being gracious and tactful	2. Freedom to speak one's mind
3. Caring for one's children and family	3. Caring for one's own needs
4. Earning a livelihood or helping the family income	4. Freedom from a job
5. Entertaining your or your husband's business associates and clients	5. Entertaining the people you really like for themselves
6. Pleasing one's boyfriend, husband, and employer	6. Pleasing oneself

A WOMAN'S OBLIGATIONS AND FREEDOMS AT DIFFERENT STAGES OF HER LIFE

Eleanor Roosevelt was the icon of generations of women who saw in her a female who resolutely overcame her shyness and awkwardness, her lack of conventional beauty, and the demands on her as the wife of the President, the leader of the free world, to be her own person. As an individual she made an enormous difference in the lives not only of women but also of the underprivileged and outcast around the globe. But even Eleanor Roosevelt did not find freedom to speak her mind until her older years.

After Franklin Delano Roosevelt's death, she told reporters, "For the first time in my life I can say just what I want. For your information, it is wonderful to be free."

When you are older, you have choices and freedoms that your mother and grandmothers never had. Unless you are very strapped for money or are in extremely poor health, you can make your own decisions.

Remember the Five Commandments. Protect thyself. And protect your money from importuning relatives and friends.

Anticipate disaster. Be prepared for illness and accidents and the fact that your family may be more concerned with their interests than yours.

Act on your own best judgment. When you are urged to do something you don't want to do, *wear a velvet glove over an iron hand* and don't succumb to pressure.

And don't be afraid to *discuss all aspects of money* with your husband and other family members.

If you follow these simple rules, you, like Eleanor Roosevelt, can find that "Freedom is wonderful." This wondrous freedom and joy can be yours if you act wisely *before . . .*

BEFORE THE AUTUMN YEARS

As you approach the autumn years, there are many legal rights and problems every woman should be aware of and take measures to protect herself.

Before you retire, change your lifestyle, or become ill or incapacitated, you should:

1 Make a complete inventory of your assets:
   a. Real estate
   b. Pension rights
   c. Social Security
   d. IRA
   e. Keogh plan
   f. Insurance policies
   g. Securities
   h. Trusts
   i. Household goods
   j. Art, jewelry, and other valuables
   k. Automobiles, boats, and other chattels
   l. Any estates of which you are a beneficiary

2 Make a budget to see whether you can afford to continue your present lifestyle.

3 Consult your lawyer and your accountant before making any decisions as to your lifestyle or disposition of property, including gifts to children, grandchildren, and other family members or friends, giving anyone a power of attorney, or establishing any trusts.

If you retain control of your property, you will be able to make your own decisions so that you can enjoy your autumn years.

PART V

FOR EVERY WOMAN

18

FINAL WORDS

"Women who strive to be equal with men lack ambition" . . .
WORDS STITCHED INTO A SAMPLER

A cross-stitch sampler lovingly embroidered by a friend from the Pennsylvania Dutch country bears the legend above. It hung on the wall in my judicial chambers for more than a dozen years. The responses of the many lawyers who saw it were fascinating. The men started to read smiling and ended looking abashed. The women invariably said, "That's right. Why didn't I realize that truth before?"

I hope this book has made you realize that the aim of women should not be to emulate men, but to be complete, fulfilled human beings, female human beings, persons who enjoy all the rights, privileges, and entitlements of all citizens of this country, and also the very special pleasures of being a woman.

I also hope that this book has fulfilled the promise I made to my women clients and the women litigants who appeared before me in court, that this book will show you and all women readers how to overcome the biases of the law and how to use the legal process so that you will be protected, not prejudiced.

I ask the forgiveness of the women whose lives and unhappy experiences in court as well as their legal victories I have recounted. It was they and their problems that enlightened me and made me aware of the endemic unfairnesses of American law toward women. I hope that their experiences will also enlighten

319

you, and that their failures and solutions will help you to use or to avoid the legal system for your protection and benefit.

Of course, one book cannot encompass all the problems that the heterogeneous population of American women faces. I have not dealt with some obvious difficulties because there are no satisfactory solutions.

Every woman, heterosexual or lesbian, monogamous or promiscuous, is at risk of contracting AIDS, herpes, and other contagious or infectious disease. Until scientists discover a magic bullet, we are all endangered, as are men and children. Every reader knows the common-sense protections she should take. But none is fail-safe. The law cannot help you with these life-threatening problems. It can, however, protect you and your loved ones if you make an appropriate will and a living will. It can also help you if you have a claim against a hospital, doctor, or other medical organization.

Many women are beset by inner demons, arising from an unhappy childhood, sexual abuse, and other misfortunes. I am not a psychiatrist. I have not attempted to give you advice as to how to deal with these problems, to overcome the hurts and to find healing and peace. I cannot even suggest a path to wholeness, forgiveness, and acceptance. Some five millenia of teachings by wise men have not succeeded in putting an end to such mistreatment of females or bringing inner peace or comfort to generations of those who have been tormented. What I have tried to do is to show you how to avoid further abuse by the legal system.

I am not an economist or investment counselor. I have not suggested how you should invest your money or increase the value of your property. I cannot tell you how to become rich. I have only shown you how to use the law to avoid being deprived of your employment rights and to protect your money and property from those, both family and strangers, who would take advantage of your kindness.

I am also not a public relations professional. I cannot tell you how to become famous or popular. I have shown you how to find satisfaction in your work, your home, and in your later years by asserting your rights and avoiding the pitfalls that await unwary women.

I am not a physician. You must find one to treat your medical problems. But, I hope I have shown you how to deal with physicians who ignore your physical problems or attempt to give you nonmedical advice.

Nor am I a sexual therapist. I have not tried to tell you how to enjoy sex once or every time. For such information you must look elsewhere. There are entire libraries of books on these subjects. I have shown you how to use the law and your common sense to protect yourself economically and physically when sexual relationships, whether in or out of wedlock, fail.

If you have more unusual legal difficulties such as accusations of murder or other crimes, libel litigation, Racketeering Influenced and Corrupt Organization (RICO) fraud, or espionage, you need skilled legal counsel. This book is not designed to teach you how to be your own lawyer but to show you how to use a lawyer effectively to promote your own best interests.

My modest goal was to show you ways to meet the practical legal problems of everyday life that most women encounter and in which they are bested by the legal system. In each of the situations you confront from girlhood to old age, there is usually a legal component, a statute or common law doctrine that is male biased and will work to your detriment unless you act wisely *before* . . .

The lives of most women do not follow a single straight path. There are stages or passages, twists and turns that make life richer and more interesting. You can joyfully explore these byways that lead to love, marriage, motherhood, work, sharing, and joining. But unless you obey the Five Commandments throughout your life's journey, you will probably meet disasters, both emotional and financial, that could have been avoided. If you obey the Commandments you can find fulfillment and joy, not simply at the end of the trail, but all along the way.

Emily Dickinson plaintively exclaimed, "I'm nobody." That was not true of her, even in her reclusive home in Amherst. It is not true of you. Every woman is somebody. In the course of your life you will probably play many roles: daughter; wife; mother; worker; retiree; giver; and helper. But through all these many parts that most women play, you are always somebody: *yourself.*

It is that essential self that you must protect and cherish. In your long unending life quest for self, the law can either defeat you or help you. More than a century ago, Oliver Wendell Holmes, Jr., the great justice of the U.S. Supreme Court, wrote, "The life of the law has not been logic but experience." In the 1990s the experiences of women are just beginning to shape the development of American law. This decade will, I hope, mark one of the great turning points in the age-long quest of human beings for bodily integrity, economic security, peace of mind, and freedom.

We look back to Mosaic law, the Code of Hammurabi, the Analects of Confucius, the Koran, and the Magna Carta, as seminal statements that provided rules for decent conduct of life and increased the rights of human beings. Sadly, all these remarkable documents treated women not as intelligent, sentient individuals but like children, as possessions of men, objects to be used or abused, protected or disposed of at the pleasure of men.

Only the Constitution of the United States was gender neutral. It addresses the rights of *persons.* Until 1868 the language of the Constitution, the Bill of Rights, and the other Amendments did not distinguish between males and females. Unfortunately these gender-neutral words were interpreted by male judges to exclude women from basic rights and liberties. That male bias of the law still persists despite the presence of female judges.

You must recognize this unpleasant and demeaning fact. However, the 1990s can still be the best of times for all women who heed the New Commandments given in this book. If you protect yourself, if you anticipate disaster, if you act on your own best judgment, if you are pleasant but firm, and if you discuss money in all your personal, family, and business relationships, you will have opportunities never before available to women.

You can explore the entire universe of learning. You can choose your own husband. You need not submit to a loveless, brutal, or degrading marriage. You can divorce him. You can marry again. You can decide when and whether you wish to become a mother. You can choose the employment you wish *and* be compensated fairly. You can own your own home on fair credit terms. You can dispose of your property as you choose. You can live a very long and happy life. All these options are available to you if you act wisely and follow the Commandments *before* . . .

I hope that in the next century, a book like this will not be needed. But now, in the 1990s, it is an essential guidebook, a survival manual for Everywoman. Use it!

NOTES

P. 4. I served as a judge of the Court of Common Pleas of Philadelphia, a trial court of general jurisdiction from 1971 to 1988. I was appointed by Milton Shapp, Governor of Pennsylvania and elected in a general election in 1973. I presided over major civil cases, major criminal cases (including homicides), and custody matters.

P. 7. For an explanation of the problems of women in court, see Forer, *Unequal Protection: Women, Children and the Elderly in Court.* New York: W.W. Norton & Co., 1991.

P. 8. Deborah L. Rhode, "The 'No-Problem' Problem: Feminist Challenges and Cultural Change," 100 *Yale Law Journal* 1731, 1734, 1991.

P. 10. *Planned Parenthood v. Casey,* 112 Sup. Ct. 2791 (1992). See also *Ohio* v. *Akron Center for Reproductive Health,* 426 U.S. 416 (1983) upholding a requirement of parental consent. See also, *Hodgson v. Minnesota,* 110 Sup. Ct. 2626 (1990), upholding a requirement of parental notification with a provision for a judicial bypass under which a minor female can go to court to obtain an order for an abortion if she cannot obtain parental consent. See also, *Benten v. Kessler,* 112 Sup. Ct. 2929 (1992) in which the Supreme Court refused to vacate the stay on the importation of the contraceptive drug RU486. Justice Stevens, in a dissenting opinion declared that withholding the drug placed an "undue burden" on the pregnant woman who sought to import the drug and subsequently had an abortion. Cf. *Sweatt* v. *Painter,* 339 U.S. 629 (1950), a case involving racial discrimination.

P. 13. *Frontiero* v. *Richardson,* 411 U.S. 677 (1973). Note that Mr. Justice Brennan declared that "classifications based on sex, like all classifications based on race, alienage, and national origin are inherently suspect and must, therefore, be subjected to close judicial scrutiny." In the succeeding two decades, the court has retreated from this position.

P. 17. See *Geduldig* v. *Aiello,* 417 U.S. 483 (1974) holding that pregnancy is not a "gender related" condition.

P. 19. Robert Bly, *Iron John.* Reading, MA: Addison-Wesley, 1990, a popular book exalting allegedly male characteristics of physical violence in contrast to alleged female characteristics.

P. 20. The American Medical Association reports that only 20 percent of subjects in clinical studies of heart attack treatment were women. *Phila-*

delphia Inquirer, 16 September 1992 p. A8. The General Accounting Office of the federal government citicized the Food and Drug Administration for testing new drugs for women in smaller proportions than corresponding to these with the disease. *New York Times,* October 29, 1992, p. A16.

P. 21. See Gloria Steinem, *Revolution From Within.* Boston: Little, Brown & Co. Boston, 1992, urging women to have more self-esteem. See Susan Faludi, *Backlash,* New York: Crown, 1991. Also 9–24 Internal Revenue Code 26 U.S.C. secs. 21 and 275.

CHAPTER 2

P. 27. Because an unprecedented number of women were candidates for the House of Representatives and the Senate, the media coined the expression, "The Year of the Woman." See e.g. Helen E. Fisher, "Mighty Menopause," *New York Times,* October 21, 1992, p. A23 who writes ". . . 'the year of the woman' is here to stay. In fact, it may well be the decade of the woman."

P. 29. Child support for divorced and separated women averaged only $3,268 annually; for unmarried women, $1,888. *Philadelphia Inquirer* 2 August, 1992, p. M4. In 1991 one-fourth of the nation's children under eighteen lived with one parent; 22 percent with the mother, and 3 percent with the father. *New York Times,* 5 October 1992, p. B6.

CHAPTER 3

P. 45. In the musical *My Fair Lady,* based on George Bernard Shaw's *Pygmalion,* the character Henry Higgins sings a song, "Why Can't a Woman Be Like a Man?"

CHAPTER 4

P. 60. See Sara Gauch, "When Mothers Go to Prison." 16 *Human Rights* 33 (April 1989).

P. 66. The problems that arise most often between men and women involve money. They are not the result of miscommunication, as Deborah Tannen argues in *You Just Don't Understand,* New York: Morrow, 1990, but because they do not discuss the question.

CHAPTER 5

P. 83. The Equal Credit Opportunities Act, 15 U.S.C. secs. 1601 *et seq.* prohibits gender discrimination. A female borrower, like a male borrower, must present evidence that she is a good credit risk.

P. 87. *Richette* v. *Ajello* 72 D&C 2d (Pa)1974.

CHAPTER 6

P. 95. In 1990 one in four Americans eighteen years and older had never married. In 1970 the figure was one in six.

P. 101. Wife beating is so widespread that the American Medical Association calls it a "public health problem that has reached epidemic proportions." The association reports that nearly one-fourth of the women in the United States will be abused by a current or former partner at some time in their lives. Carol Lawson, "Violence at Home: They Don't Want Anyone to Know," *New York Times* 6 August 1992, p. C1. See Gary Richard Brown. "Battered Women and the Temporary Restraining Order," 10 *Women's Rights L. Rep* 261 (1988); "Battered Women and the Equal Protection Clause," note 95, *Yale Law Journal* 788.

CHAPTER 7

P. 128. Only 41.6 percent of mothers with children under the age of six are not in the labor force. *New York Times,* 4 October 1992, pp. 1, 32. Obviously, the vast majority of these women are working from necessity, not choice. For the woman who has a choice, there is much evidence of the detrimental effects of motherhood on a woman's career. Better day care, of course, would make the burden easier for both the mother and her children. Other remedies, such as part-time and flex-time work are, in effect in a limited number of work places. Dr. Carl Djerassi, professor of chemistry at Stanford University, proposes five-year subsidies for female scientists to enjoy motherhood without sacrificing their careers. Only four percent of the members of the National Academy of Sciences are women. Fred M. Hechinger, "About Education," *New York Times,* 9 November, 1988, p. B11. Many women pay a price in career advancement when they become mothers. See Meredith K. Wadman, "Mothers who Take Extended Time Off Find their Careers Pay a Heavy Price," *Wall Street Journal,* 16 July 1992, p. B1. See Felice N. Schwartz, "Management Women and the Facts of Life," 67 *Harvard Business Review* 65, popularizing the phrase "the mommy track."

P. 131. For a picture of the treatment of children in England see, Ivy Pinchbeck and Margaret Hewitt, *Children in English Society,* London: Routledge & Kegan Paul, Ltd., 1969. See also Boswell, *The Kindness of Strangers.* New York: Pantheon, 1988, depicting the problems of children in Western Europe.

P. 140. The U.S. government is prosecuting several fertility clinics for overstating their success rates. It costs from $3,000 to $20,000 for in vitro fertilization treatments. *New York Times,* 26 October 1992, p. A15.

P. 145. Tamar Lewin, "Fewer Children Up for Adoption," *New York Times,* 27 February 1992, p. A15.

P. 148. Dr. Herbert J. Cohen reports that up to 40 percent of foster children have some developmental disabilities. Letter, *New York Times,* 1 October 1992, p. A24.

CHAPTER 8

P. 154. See Lenore J. Weitzman, *The Divorce Revolution.* New York: Free Press, 1981; Thomas M. Mulroy, "No-Fault Divorce: Are Women Losing the Battle?" *American Bar Association Journal,* November 1989, p. 76.

P. 168. Report of the Pennsylvania Attorney General's Task Force, "Domestic Violence," 1988. See also "Study of Domestic Violence in Minneapolis by the Police Foundation," *New York Times,* 5 April 1983, p. 4.

P. 179. A small book by Joseph Goldstein, Anna Freud, and Albert J. Solnit, *Beyond the Best Interests of the Child,* New York: Free Press, 1973, is routinely cited by courts as authority to disregard the interests of the mother in custody cases.

CHAPTER 9

P. 186. For a discussion of the pros and cons of alternative procedures in divorce, see T. Grill, "The Mediation Alternative: Process Dangers for Women," 100 *Yale Law Journal* 1545.

CHAPTER 10

P. 215. The Cornell Study is reported in "Personal Briefing," the *Philadelphia Inquirer* 17 August 1992, p. D1.
P. 217. Second marriages are more likely to fail than first marriages. See Randolph E. Schmid, "Grim findings about first and second marriages," *Philadelphia Inquirer*, 13 March 1989, p. 3A.

CHAPTER 11

P. 238. See Arlie Hochschild and Anne Machung, *The Second Shift: Inside the Two-Job Marriage*, New York: Penguin, 1989.
P. 239. The Equal Pay Act of 1963, 29 U.S.C. sec. 206 (d)(1), prohibits pay discrimination on the basis of gender. However, the courts have held that a woman's salary at a previous job is a factor that can be considered in setting her salary. *Kouba* v. *All State Ins. Co.*, 691 F 2d 873 (9th Cir. 1982).
P. 252. Although under the law you are entitled to a workplace free from "abusive" or "hostile environment," in order to win a sexual harassment suit you must prove that the conduct is "sufficiently severe or pervasive to alter the conditions of employment and to create an abusive working environment." *Ellison* v. *Brady*, 924 F2d 872 (9th Cir. 1991). In this case the court adopted a "reasonable woman" standard in deciding whether the environment was abusive. Most courts adhere to a "reasonable person" test, which is based on what a man would consider abusive. Title VII of the Civil Rights Act of 1964, 42 USC sec. 2000 *et seq.* prohibits discrimination in employment based on sex.
P. 258. Sexual harassment is not a matter of sexual attraction but of male dominance and assertion of power. Only 35 percent of women make a formal complaint of sexual harassment on the job. Ninety percent of women who have been sexually harassed would like to leave their jobs but can't afford to do so. "Sexual Harassment: A Matter of Power," *New York Times*, 22 October, 1991, p. C1.

CHAPTER 12

P. 261. Glenn Kaye, "Free of the Law", 94 *Harvard Magazine* No. 3, p. 60. An American Bar Association Study, "The State of the Legal Profession" (1990), revealed that 59 percent of the lawyers who responded to the questionnaire were dissatisfied and that women were much more unhappy than men and were financially worse off. Women hold more than half the nation's accounting jobs but only 4 percent of partnerships. Many women are leaving accounting. Some firms now permit women to work part time in order to retain them. Andrea Knox, "Women succeed in accounting, then drop out," *Philadelphia Inquirer*, 6 January 1989, p. 12A.
P. 277. Advancement is still slow for most women. Despite the gains women have made in employment, they hold only 3 percent of the top jobs. "Study, Women hold 3% of top jobs, *Philadelphia Inquirer*, 6 August 1991, p. 4A. But there is still opportunity for women to advance. Women now hold 40 percent of entry-level and middle-management jobs, double their

share in 1972. Sylvia Nasar, "Women's Progress Stalled? Just Not So," *New York Times,* 18 October 1992, p. 1F.

P. 278. One of the advantages of owning your own business is that you will not be subject to sexual harassment when you are the boss, nor will you be subject to gender bias. Gender bias still pervades the workplace. *Philadelphia Inquirer,* 11 June, 1992, p. C9.

P. 280. The Public Works Employment Act of 1977, 42 USC sec. 6705(f) requires set-asides (a percentage of contracts for minorities and women). But see *Lamprecht* v. *FCC,* 958 F 2d 382 (U.S. Ct. App., D.C. 1992) holding that set-aside credits for minorities and women who seek to obtain a radio station license are unconstitutional.

CHAPTER 14

P. 293. Jane Perlez, "Elite Kenyan Women Avoid a Rite: Marriage," New York *Times,* 3 March 1991, p. 14A describes the attitudes of African society towards women. Similar male chauvinist attitudes prevail in many ethnic groups in the United States.

P. 296. Many self-styled feminists seek to outlaw pornography as demeaning women, without considering the importance to women of freedom of speech. See e.g. Catharine MacKinnon, *Sexual Harassment of Women.* New Haven: Yale University Press, 1979; Andrea Dworkin, *"Pornography.* New York: G. P. Putnam, 1981.

P. 302. None of the federal or state statutes outlawing gender discrimination in employment protects women from this kind of pressure to join.

P. 306. See *Wisconsin* v. *Yoder,* 406 U.S. 205 (1972), in which the U.S. Supreme Court held that parents have the right to withdraw their children from high school because of the parents' religious beliefs, thus denying the children the right to an education.

P. 307. A federal law, 42 U.S.C. sec. 1996 (1978) declares that it is the policy of the United States to protect and preserve American Indians' "inherent right of freedom to believe, express, and exercise traditional religions." Some of these beliefs and exercises are in conflict with the constitutional rights of women.

CHAPTER 15

P. 315. A survey of eighteen lenders reported more unmarried couples buying homes in 1992 than five years earlier. "Home Notes," *Philadelphia Inquirer,* 1 November 1992, p. B17.

P. 319. Racially restrictive covenants were held unconstitutional by the U.S. Supreme Court in *Shelley* v. *Kraemer,* 334 U.S. 1 (1948). Restrictive covenants as to family membership have not yet been invalidated in most jurisdictions.

P. 324. The Equal Credit Opportunity Act, 15 U.S.C. sec. 1601 et seq., prohibits discrimination in mortgages on the basis of sex.

CHAPTER 16

P. 336. See Marc A. Franklin, "Good Names and Bad: A Critique of Libel Law and a Proposal," 18 *San Francisco Law Review,* 1. See also the Proposal of the Annenberg Washington Program of Northwestern University, "A Proposal for the Reform of Libel Law," Washington, 1988.

P. 339. See *Hishon* v. *King and Spaulding,* 467 U.S. 69 (1984), holding that a woman denied a partnership in a law firm that had no female partners had stated a good cause of action.

P. 343. Diana B. Heneiques, "Ms. Siebert Still on the Barricades," *New York Times*, 5 July 1992, p. 15.

P. 350. See *Coy v. Iowa*, 108 Sup. Ct. 2798 (1988), holding that a child rape victim must look her abuser "in the eye" at trial. This meeting with her assailant is often so traumatic that the child is unable to testify. See Edward J. Saunders, "Child Sexual Abuse Cases," 27 *Judges' Journal* 20 (reporting that 2,190 women and children were rape victims in one year in Washington, D.C. *Hilary's Trial*, by Jonathan Groner, New York: Simon & Schuster, 1991, details the long-drawn-out legal fight and concludes that the father was an innocent victim. For a different view of the proceedings see the book by the mother, Elizabeth Morgan, *Custody*; Boston: Little Brown (1986).

P. 351. See Amy Eppler, "Battered Women and the Equal Protection Clause," 95 *Yale Law Journal* 788. She reports that in Milwaukee 89 percent of abused wives asked for the arrest of their husbands but arrests were made in only 14 percent of the cases. But the National Institute of Justice in Washington, D.C., finds that arrest deters violence.

P. 353. See Michael Clay Smith, *Coping With Crime on Campus*, and Peggy Sanday, *Fraternity Gang Rape*. New York: New York University Press, 1990.

P. 364. In *Cox Broadcasting Corp v. Cohn*, 420 U.S. 469 (1975) the U.S. Supreme Court denied recovery to the family of a deceased rape victim whose name was not reported during the trial but was later broadcast. The Court held that the victim was a public figure and had no right to privacy.

CHAPTER 18

P. 378. See the case of Karen Quinlan, whose family was finally permitted to withdraw life-sustaining treatment after she had been in a vegetative state for years. In re Quinlan, 335 A 2d 647 (New Jersey) cert. den. 429 U.S. 992 (1976) For adiscussion of the right to die, see Nancy K. Rhodon, 102 *Harvard Law Review* 375.

CHAPTER 19

P. 400. The Age Discrimination in Employment Act of 1978, 29 U.S.C. secs. 621–34. The upper age limit was abolished by the 1986 amendment to the act. Many older people, however, can be pushed out of their jobs by early retirement incentives. See note 54 *Brooklyn Law Review*, 927.

P. 411. See Kazin, "Nowhere to Go and Chose to Stay," 137 *University of Pennsylvania Law Review* 903.

P. 416. Recent studies show that male physicians interrupt their female patients more frequently than do female physicians and spend less time with them. Female doctors are also more willing to discuss their patients' nongynecological problems. Natalie Angier, "Bedside Manners Improve as More Women Enter Medicine," New York *Times*, 12 June 1992, p. E18.

P. 419. In *Big Town Nursing Home v. Newman* 461 SW 2d 195 (Texas 1970) the court held that an elderly person placed against his will in a nursing home could recover for the tort of false arrest.

APPENDIX

GENERAL POWER OF ATTORNEY

Know all Men by These Presents, that I _____

_____ of _____ City and _____

County in the state of _____ do hereby appoint

_____ _____ and _____ or
either of them my true and lawful attorneys for me and on my
behalf and in my name to perform all such acts as either of them
may deem advisable, in his or her absolute discretion, as fully as
I could do if personally present, including without limitation, any
of the following:

1. To receive all moneys and assets now or hereafter due to
me from any source.

2. To enter and remove property from any safe deposit boxes
rented by me.

3. To endorse all checks and other instruments payable to
me and to deposit the same in any bank accounts in my name or
in the names of either or both of my attorneys-in-fact.

4. To pay any and all bills, accounts, and debts which may
be due by me at any time.

5. To draw and sign checks, withdrawal slips and other orders for the payment of money upon any bank account belonging
to me.

6. To borrow money and to pledge or mortgage any properties owned by me as security therefore.

7. To sell, transfer, manage, maintain, and lease any properties, real and personal, including securities, now or hereafter owned by me.

8. To purchase, rent, or otherwise acquire any properties, real and personal, including securities, for me.

9. To sign, acknowledge, and deliver all deeds, agreements, proxies, receipts, releases, and satisfactions.

10. To make gifts.

11. To create a trust for my benefit.

12. To make additions to an existing trust for my benefit.

13. To claim an elective share of the estate of a deceased spouse.

14. To disclaim any interest in property.

15. To renounce fiduciary positions.

16. To withdraw and receive the income or corpus out of a trust.

17. To authorize my admission to a medical, nursing, residential, or similar facility and to enter into agreements for my care.

18. To authorize medical and surgical procedures.

19. To sign and file tax returns, claims, elections, protests, consents, waivers, extensions, and closing agreements in any federal, state, or local tax proceedings.

20. To compromise any claims, and to engage in litigation on my behalf.

21. To delegate any or all of the foregoing powers to any person or persons whom either of my attorneys may select.

I hereby ratify and confirm all that my said attorneys shall do or cause to be done by virtue of these presents. The act of either of my attorneys shall be valid and binding without the necessity of the joinder of my other attorney and without liability on the part of the nonacting attorney. I specifically direct that my attorneys shall not be subject to any liability by reason of the decisions, acts, or failures to act of either of them, all of which shall be conclusive and binding upon me, my estate and my heirs. Furthermore, I agree to indemnify my attorneys and hold them harmless from all claims which may be made against them as a result of their serving as my attorneys, and I agree to reimburse them in the amount of any damages, costs and expenses which may be incurred as a result of such claim.

This power of attorney shall not be affected by my subsequent disability or incapacity.

The following are specimens of the signatures of

_____

_____

In witness whereof, and intending to be legally bound I have hereunto set my hand and seal this _____ day of _____, 19_____.

Signed, sealed and delivered
in the presence of

_____

INDEX

A

Abuse. *See* Child abuse; Spousal abuse
Acquiescing, in marriage, 69–72
Adoption
  and delayed development, 104–7
  father's opposition to, 108
  legal issues in, 89
  and motherhood, 96
  and need for will, 296
  rights of child in, 89
Age discrimination, 232
  and retirement, 299–301
Alternative dispute resolution
  in child custody, 138–39
  in divorce, 136–37
  legal fees in, 141
Animal rights, as hidden agenda, 250
Antenuptial agreement, 169, 171–72
Appellate rights, in divorce settlement, 145
Appraisal, of property, 263
Arbitration, in divorce settlement, 136–37
Arranged marriages, 83–84
Assets

accounting for, in divorce settlement, 142–43
distribution of, in divorce settlement, 143
need for knowledge of marital, 305–6
Austen, Jane, 65
Auto accident, and need for power of attorney, 280–82
Autumn years
  blessings of, 312–13
  planning for, 314–15

B

Baker, Norma Jeane, 55
Balance sheet, application of, to relationship, 49–53
Bargaining, in divorce settlement, 144–45
Beauvoir, Simone de, 65–66
Bergoff, Pearl, 56
Birth of child, and need for will, 296

C

Cardozo, Benjamin N., 23
Career, effect of motherhood on, 93

Carnegie, Hattie, 55
Child(ren)
  abandonment of, 94, 95
  absence of, 98–100
  effect of, on relationships,
    35–38
  legal rights of father over, 94
  parent responsibilities for,
    94–95
  protecting, 277
  reasons for wanting, 103–7
  and remarriage, 158–59
  rights of, 95, 100–3
Child abuse, 95, 102–3
  trauma in, 189–90
Child advocate, 110
Child custody, 115, 117–18
  alternative dispute resolution
    in, 138–39
  and child abuse cases, 190
  court fights over, 131–33
  and divorce, 113–14, 143–44
  impact of lifestyle on, 79–80
  rearing of, in lesbian
    relationships, 89–90
  shared, 132
Child labor, 95
Child support, 37, 114
Clinton, Bill, 66
Clinton, Hillary Rodham, 66
  and use of maiden name, 59
Communitarian values, hidden
  agenda implied by,
  246–47, 254–57
Conciliation, in divorce
  settlement, 137
Condominiums, 261
Cooper, Douglas, 278
Cooperatives, 261
Couple-pape, 8–9
Court appearance
  balance sheet in, 200–2
  child abuse cases in, 189–90
  consequences of, 179
  of crime victim, 191–92

desires of plaintiffs in, 180–81
facts not in dispute in, 188–89
financial compensation in, 180
judge's duties at, 179–80
law on your side at, 182–84
planning for, 186–202
prosecuting rape case in,
  192–96
reputation at stake in, 184–85
uniqueness of cases in, 181–82
violence against women in,
  196–200
withstanding questions about
  past in, 185–88
Crime victim, court appearance
  by, 191–92
Cronkite, Walter, 300
Cruzen, Carol, 282

D

Daily life, impact of, on
  relationships, 32–35
Date rape, 198–99
Dickinson, Emily, 322
Disaster anticipation
  in divorce, 125–26, 128, 133
  in employment, 213, 214, 232
  in marriage, 76
  and motherhood, 91
  in relationships, 23, 32, 42,
    45, 49
  in remarriage, 174
  in spousal abuse, 198, 199
  in wills, 276, 292, 294
Dispute resolution. See Alternate
  dispute resolution;
  Arbitration; Conciliation;
  Mediation
Divorce, 112–35
  acting on best judgment in,
    125–26, 128
  balance sheet in, 134–35
  being correct in, 129–30

blame in, 116
and child custody, 113–14,
    115, 117–18, 131–33
and child support, 114
and cost of freedom, 121–23
disaster anticipation in, 125,
    128, 133
financial arrangements on,
    113, 128
grounds for, 113
half-a-loaf in, 130–34
"impact of, on name, 58–59
lifestyle following, 117
and need for will, 296
no-fault grounds for, 115
opportunities in, 118–21
questions in, 115–18
self-protection in, 125, 128,
    133
stigma in, 115
women's rights in, 112
worth of saving marriage in,
    123–28
Divorce settlement, 136–56
accounting for assets in,
    142–43
appellate rights in, 145
arbitration in, 136–37
balance sheet in, 155–56
bargaining in, 144–45
conciliation in, 137
controlling case in, 151–54
custody and visitation in,
    143–44
disaster anticipation in,
    147–48
distribution of assets in, 143
gender bias problem in,
    141–42
health care in, 144
issues to be decided in, 143
length of time in, 139–40
mediation in, 137, 145
need for lawyer in, 137
personal participation or

reliance on counsel in,
    140–41
private or public adjudicator
    in, 139
self-protection in, 148–51
support in, 144
Domicile, determining state of,
    308–10

E

Education, right of child to,
    100–3
Employee, rights of, 212–13,
    215–17, 224–25
Employee at will doctrine,
    230–31
Employment, 205–23
balance sheet in, 222–23
career track in, 215–17
disaster anticipation in, 213,
    214
employee versus independent
    contractor, 210–11
planning for future, 213–15
rights of employees in,
    212–13, 215–17
self-protection in, 213, 214
and sexual harassment,
    217–22
steady versus free-lance work,
    212–15
work as, not a hobby, 211–12
Employment change, 224–42
acting on best judgment in,
    232
balance sheet in, 242
disaster anticipation in, 232
and employee rights, 224–25
importance of job benefits,
    233–34
and job satisfaction, 226–28,
    231–33
benefits, 229

Employment change (*cont.*)
  compensation, 228–29
  opportunities for
    advancement, 229
  pleasure in the work, 226,
    227
  pleasure in the workplace,
    227–28
  and safety catastrophes, 225
  self-fulfillment in, 234–42
  self-protection in, 235
Employment discrimination
  compensation for, 208–10
  and retirement, 299–301
  self-protection in, 207
  velvet glove treatment in, 207
Estate taxes, saving, 308–10
Eyre, Jane, 65

F

Facts, ignorance of, as no
    excuse, 38–42
Family problems, and name
    change, 60–61
Family values, as hidden agenda,
    245–46, 252–54
Father
  legal rights of, 94
  opposition of natural, to
    adoption, 108
  parental rights of, 108
Financial arrangements, 25–26
  in divorce, 128
  in marriage, 76
  and motherhood, 92
  in relationships, 32, 42, 45, 49
  in remarriage, 174
  in spousal abuse, 200
  in wills, 292, 295
Financial problems, and name
    change, 59–60
Foster mothers, 109–11

Foster parents, and motherhood,
    97–98
Freelance work, steady
    employment versus,
    212–15
Freud, Sigmund, 189

G

Gender bias problem, in divorce
    settlement, 141–42
Gender relations, 26
  in relationships, 32, 42
Grounds, for divorce, 113
Guardian, appointment of,
    277–78, 281, 286–88

H

Health care, in divorce
    settlement, 144
Hidden agendas
  animal rights in, 250
  communitarian values in,
    246–47, 254–57
  family values in, 245–46,
    252–54
  law and order in, 244–45
  pornography in, 247–48
  pro-life in, 249, 250–52
Hill, Anita, 136, 184
Holmes, Oliver Wendell, Jr., 322
Home purchase, 259–72
  asking about restrictive
    covenants in, 263,
    265–66
  and changes in home market,
    260
  checking zoning laws in, 262,
    264–65
  checklist in, 262–63
  getting mortgage in, 268–69
  making wise, 271–72
  need for lawyer in, 263, 270

rights of women in, 259–60, 261
types of home ownership, 260–61
by unmarried couple, 266–68
watching out for termites in, 269–70
Housing inspections, 262, 269–70

I

Illness
    diagnosis of serious, and need for will, 284–86, 296
    and impending death, 284–86
    and right to explanation of treatment, 310
Independent contractor, versus employee, 210–11
In vitro fertilizations, 100

J

Job satisfaction chart, 226–28
Joint tenancy, 44–45
Jong, Erica, 66
Judgment, acting on best, 24
    in divorce, 125–26, 128
    in employment change, 232
    in marriage, 76
    in motherhood, 91
    in relationships, 32, 42, 45, 49
    in remarriage, 174
    in spousal abuse, 198, 199–200
    in wills, 276, 292, 295

L

Lauder, Estee, 93
Law, ignorance of, 38–42
Law and order, hidden agenda implied by, 244–45

Lawyer
    choosing, 288–91
    consulting, in remarriage, 168–69
    need for, in divorce settlement, 137
    need for, in housing purchase, 263, 270
    need for, in will, 278
    in safeguarding legal papers, 280
Legal profession, women in, 178–79
Lesbian relationships, child rearing in, 89–90
Living will, 276, 277, 279, 282, 283
    defining events in obtaining, 279–80
    needs for, 291–93

M

Maiden name, use of, 59
Malpractice cases, and withstanding questions about past, 185
Marriages, 64–86
    absence of free lunch in, 74–76
    acquiescing in, 69–72
    acting on best judgment in, 68–69, 72–74, 76
    checklist prior to, 84–86
    disaster anticipation in, 68, 76
    financial arrangements in, 69, 76
    five commandments in, 68–69
    following bliss in, 77–78
    issues to be considered in, 67
    impact of loan on, 80–83
    knowing thyself in, 78–80
    and name change, 58–59
    and need for will, 295

Marriages (*cont.*)
  self-protection in, 68, 76
  velvet glove treatment in, 69,
    76
Marriage of convenience,
    problems with, 169–73
Mead, Margaret, 83, 206
Mediation
  in child custody cases, 138–39
  in divorce settlement, 137,
    145–48
Medical treatment
  responsibilities of parent in
    providing, 95
  right to explanation of, 310
Mobile homes, 260
Mobile parks, 261
Monroe, Marilyn, 55
Mortgage, getting, 268–69
Motherhood, 87–111
  and absence of children,
    98–100
  acting on best judgment in, 91
  and adoption, 89, 96, 104–7
  disaster anticipation in, 91
  effect of, on career, 93
  and father's parental rights,
    108
  financial arrangements in, 92
  and foster mothers, 109–11
  and foster parents, 97–98
  reasons for wanting children,
    103–7
  responsibilities for children,
    100–3
  self-protection in, 90–91
  and single mothers, 107–8
  and surrogacy, 96–97
  velvet glove treatment in, 92

N

Name
  advantages/disadvantages of,
    55–56
  deciding to change, 54–63
  ethnic significance of, 55
  impact of divorce on, 58–59
  inappropriateness of, 57
  legal, 54–55
  subconscious effects of, 56–57
Name change
  and family problems, 60–61
  and financial problems, 59–60
  issues to be considered in,
    62–63
  on marriage, 58–59
  and occupation, 55, 58
  and professional problems, 62
  triggering events for, 56
National Organization of
    Women's Legal Defense
    Fund (NOW), 138
Negligence, and withstanding
    questions about past, 185
Never marrieds, 29
Not Without My Daughter, 256
Nursing home
  choice of, 311–12
  forced admission to, 290–91,
    307–8

O

Occupation, and name change,
    55, 58
O'Connor, Sandra Day, 93
Old age, preparing for, 298–315
Organizations, 243–58
  hidden agendas in, 243–50
    animal rights, 250
    communitarian values,
      246–47, 254–57
    family values, 245–46,
      252–54
    law and order, 244–45
    pornography, 247–48
    pro-life, 249, 250–52

P

Pamela (Fielding), 65
Parents. *See also* Father;
    Motherhood
  responsibilities for child,
    94–95
Pornography, hidden agenda
    implied by, 247–48
Power of attorney, 277, 278–79,
    282, 283, 306–8
  defining events in obtaining,
    279–80
  form for, 330–32
Prenuptial agreement, 50, 301
  advantages of, 161
  disadvantages of, 161–62
Professional problems, and name
    change, 62
Pro-life, as hidden agenda, 249,
    250–52
Promises, enforcement of, 306–8
Property
  need for will in protecting,
    276
  purchase of, as legal
    transaction, 42–46
  retaining control of, 302–4
Protection orders, 124

Q

Quinlan, Karen, 282

R

Rape, date, 198–99
Rape case, prosecuting, 192–96
"Reasonable man" standard,
    186–87
"Reasonable person" test, 6
Reasonable women test, in

sexual harassment cases,
    178
Relationship, 29–53
  acting on best judgment in,
    45, 49
  balance sheet in, 49–53
  disaster anticipation in, 32,
    42, 45, 49
  effect of children on, 35–38
  entering into, and need for
    will, 297
  financial arrangements in, 32,
    42, 45, 49
  five commandments in
    protecting, 46–49
  gender relations in, 32, 42
  illusions in, 31
  impact of daily life on, 32–35
  legal standing of, 29–30
  questions on, 30
  reasons for entering into, 30
  self-protection in, 32, 42, 45,
    48
  velvet glove treatment in, 32,
    42, 45, 49
Remarriage, 157–76
  acting on best judgment in,
    174
  balance sheet in, 175–76
  children in, 158–59
  consulting lawyers in, 168–69
  convenience in, 169–73
  demands in, 159
  disaster anticipation in, 174
  financial arrangements in, 174
  and need for will, 297
  prenuptial agreements in,
    161–62
  protection of assets in, 305–6
  reasons for, 160–61
  role of stepfather in, 165–68
  role of stepmother in, 163–65
  saying yes in, 168
  self-protection in, 174
  statistics in, 160

Remarriage (*cont.*)
  success in, 159
  unenforceable promise in, 173
  velvet glove treatment in, 174
Reputation, protection of, in
      court appearance, 184–85
Restrictive covenants, 263,
      265–66
Retirement, 299–301
  mandatory, 300
Roosevelt, Eleanor, 313
Roosevelt, Franklin Delano, 313
Rousseau, Jean Jacques, 94

S

Sanger, Margaret, 248
Sartre, Jean Paul, 66
Scarlet Letter, 64–65
Schroeder, Patricia, 93
Self-employment, 236–42. *See
      also* Freelance work;
      Independent contractor
Self-protection, 22–23
  in divorce, 125, 128, 133
  in divorce settlement, 148–51
  in employment, 207, 213, 214
  in marriage, 76
  in motherhood, 90–91
  in relationships, 32, 42, 45, 48
  in remarriage, 174
  in spousal abuse, 198, 199
  in wills, 276, 292, 294
Semiotics, 243–44
Separation, and need for will,
      296
Sexual discrimination, litigation
      in, 182–84
Sexual harassment, 217–22
  reasonable women test in cases
      involving, 178
Siebert, Muriel, 185
Sills, Beverly, 93
Single mothers, 107–8

Smith, William Kennedy, 192
Spousal abuse, 123–26, 196–200
  acting on best judgment in,
      198, 199–200
  disaster anticipation in, 198,
      199
  financial arrangements in, 200
  self-protection in, 198, 199
Stepfather, role of, 165–68
Stepmother, role of, 163–65
Support, in divorce settlement,
      144
Surrogacy, and motherhood,
      96–97
Survey, 262

T

Tax savings, 308–10
Termites, watching out for,
      269–70
Testimony, of wife, 41
Title, checking, 262
Title insurance, 262
Trillin, Calvin, 58–59

U

Unmarried couple, purchase of
      house by, 266–68

V

Velvet glove treatment, 24
  in employment discrimination,
      207
  in marriage, 76
  in motherhood, 92
  in relationships, 32, 42, 45, 49
  in remarriage, 174
  in wills, 292, 295

Virtue Rewarded (Fielding), 65
Visitation, in divorce settlement, 143–44

W

Widow, legal protection of, 301–2
Wife, testimony of, 41
Wills, 275–97
    acting on best judgment in, 276, 292, 295
    and appointment of guardian, 277–78, 281, 286–88
    balance sheet in, 295–97
    choosing lawyer for writing, 288–91
    comfort of wise precautions, 293–94
    on deathbed, 282–84
    defining events in obtaining, 279–80
    disaster anticipation in, 276, 292, 294
    financial arrangements in, 292, 295

and impending death, 284–86
    in protecting children, 277
    self-protection in, 276, 292, 294
    velvet glove treatment in, 292, 295
Women. *See also* Spousal abuse
    legal needs of, 3–13, 14–20
    rights of, in divorce, 112
    rights of, in home purchase, 259–60, 261
    violence against, 196–200
Women's support group, in obtaining divorce settlement, 137–38

Y

Yalow, Rosalyn, 93
Yin and yang, 9

Z

Zoning laws, checking, 262, 264–65